Neurodiversity Coaching

Neurodiversity Coaching demystifies the themes and assumptions affecting neurodivergent coachee experiences at work, whilst at the same time exploring the necessary safeguards required for working with this vulnerable group.

The book supports existing coaching practitioners, managers and community leaders to understand the essentials of neurodivergence, a term that encompasses ADHD, autism, dyslexia, dyspraxia and Tourette's syndrome, and how these diagnoses require specific coaching approaches to support individuals to thrive at work. This book is practically focused on the "how", sharing coaching exercises and activities that have been evaluated and researched by authors with extensive experience in the field. Grounded in coaching psychology theory, those with existing knowledge will be able to transfer their skill set to the neurodiversity context and those who are considering learning more about coaching can be signposted to essential knowledge and skills.

Neurodiversity Coaching will be suitable for independent coaching practitioners and internal organisational coaches and managers seeking a coaching approach.

Nancy Doyle is a registered occupational psychologist and coaching psychologist who has practised in the disability support and social justice space for over 20 years. Nancy founded the non-profit company Genius Within, which is a majority neurodivergent/disabled staffed and led company providing support for adults and businesses on neuroinclusion in society and work. Nancy is a Visiting Professor at Birkbeck, University of London.

Almuth McDowall is Professor of Organisational Psychology at Birkbeck, University of London, where she co-directs the Centre for Neurodiversity Research at Work with Nancy. She is a registered practitioner psychologist (occupational) and undertakes consultancy for the public, private and third sector. She is committed to helping businesses make their people happy.

Coaching Psychology
Series Editor: Stephen Palmer

Coaching psychology is a distinct branch of academic and applied psychology that focuses on enhancement of performance, development and wellbeing in the broader population. Written by leading experts, the **Coaching Psychology** series will highlight innovations in the field, linking theory, research and practice. These books will interest professionals from psychology, coaching, mentoring, business, health, human resources and management as well as those interested in the psychology underpinning their coaching and mentoring practice.

Titles in the series:

The Art of Dialogue in Coaching: Towards Transformative Change
Reinhard Stelter

Constructivist Coaching: A Practical Guide to Unlocking Potential Alternative Futures
Kim Bradley-Cole and Pam Denicolo

Constructivist Approaches in Coaching Psychology
Jelena Pavlović

Introduction to Coaching Psychology
Siobhain O'Riordan and Stephen Palmer

Coaching Psychology for Mental Health: Borderline Personality Disorder and Personal Psychological Recovery
Martin O'Connor and Hugh O'Donovan

For more information about this series, please visit: https://www.routledge.com/ Coaching-Psychology/book-series/COACHPSYCH

Neurodiversity Coaching

A psychological approach to
supporting neurodivergent talent
and career potential

Nancy Doyle and Almuth McDowall

Routledge
Taylor & Francis Group
LONDON AND NEW YORK

Designed cover image: © Frank Duffy

First published 2024
by Routledge
4 Park Square, Milton Park, Abingdon, Oxon OX14 4RN

and by Routledge
605 Third Avenue, New York, NY 10158

Routledge is an imprint of the Taylor & Francis Group, an informa business

© 2024 Nancy Doyle and Almuth McDowall

The right of Nancy Doyle and Almuth McDowall to be identified as the authors of this work, has been asserted in accordance with sections 77 and 78 of the Copyright, Designs and Patents Act 1988.

This book is printed in sans serif, 12 point font, with extra line spacing, with the first line of each new paragraph indented. This is to improve ease of reading for dyslexic people, who are a large contingent in the neurodivergent community. See https://dl.acm.org/doi/10.1145/2513383.2513447 for more details.

British Library Cataloguing-in-Publication Data
A catalogue record for this book is available from the British Library

Library of Congress Cataloging-in-Publication Data
A catalog record has been requested for this book

ISBN: 978-1-032-43653-1 (hbk)
ISBN: 978-1-032-43652-4 (pbk)
ISBN: 978-1-003-36827-4 (ebk)

DOI: 10.4324/9781003368274

Typeset in Calibri
by Apex CoVantage, LLC

To
Martin Sebastian Brannahl (AMD)
Kathleen Doyle and Janette Harries (ND)

Contents

Acknowledgements

The authors are indebted to Marcia Brissett-Bailey, Jo Price, Lyric Rivera, Whitney Iles and Marianne Cole for their help with proofing, as well as Frank Duffy (frankduffy.co.uk) for the cover illustration.

Section A

Setting the scene

Chapter 1

Our approach to writing this book

Almuth McDowall and Nancy Doyle

Introduction

Our introductory chapter to *Neurodiversity Coaching* documents our motivation for writing the book and our passion for the topic. We will discuss how we, as authors, bring complementary experience and expertise from work roles as academics, practitioners and leaders with lived experience; we draw on these perspectives to varying degrees across our chapters. We outline our position as pragmatic scientists paired with a commitment to evidence-based management: we do not think that it is healthy or justified to implement activities in organisations if we don't know that they work! Our intended readership is workplace coaches, neurodiversity advocates interested in coaching and line managers who want to upskill and learn how to support their neurodivergent employees. Coaching is regularly given as a reasonable disability adjustment activity; we will introduce how this context can change the parameters of workplace coaching. We outline how different types of information are integrated across the book, including case studies and vignettes. We conclude with an outline of the subsequent chapter sequence and recommendations for how to read these chapters in order.

Our motivation for writing this book

Neurodiversity is a topic that invites reaction ranging from strongly positive to strongly negative, but rarely indifferent or 'meh'. Advocacy has mushroomed and so has lived-experience literature with a whole range of books, blogs, forums and so on. Organisations are joining

DOI: 10.4324/9781003368274-2

the bandwagon with specific positive action programmes, training and in-house champions. More and more celebrities are 'coming out' as neurodivergent. At the same time, we are starting to debunk myths and establish a cohesive narrative of neurodiversity. When we did our own undergraduate degrees in psychology over two decades ago, it was purportedly up for discussion whether attention deficit hyperactivity disorder (ADHD) even existed. Now we know for sure ADHD is not made up, where 'boys will simply be boys'. At the university where Almuth studied for her undergraduate degree, students were offered part-time placements as Applied Behavioural Analysis (ABA) tutors with children living locally. This is an approach using reward and restriction aimed to increase behaviours that are deemed 'good' and decrease behaviours that are deemed 'not helpful'. This continued until one of Almuth's classmates acted and challenged the department's management. Given that no positive academic evidence existed at the time (and even now is strongly contested), surely the university should have stopped offering such positions as they covertly gave the message that ABA was a positive thing? To their credit, management listened, stopped advertising the opportunities. Almuth's classmate was ahead of their time, and what they did chimes with our approach. We do not believe that difference needs 'fixing'. Difference should be celebrated and supported, in a way that allows the development of independence and potential. Further, we believe that support offered should be based on evidence and longitudinal studies of effectiveness. As we write this book, academic research is now aplenty but remains focused on a relatively limited view of neurodiversity. Studies focus on diagnostics and neuroscience. Yet all this emerging knowledge of the brain, genetics, changes in criteria and advances in measurement have not resulted in a commensurate growth of literature on 'what works', certainly not in the context of employment and careers.

Why the focus on neurodiversity coaching?

So why did we write this book focused on coaching in neurodiversity? We wrote this book because coaching is offered as a reasonable disability adjustment activity and integral part of learning and development in organisations. We want to ensure that neurodivergent coachees get access to high quality, evidence-informed, safe coaching practice. Coaching is well researched and has a strong evidence base. Meta-studies tell us that coaching works – people will learn more, perform better and be more well in themselves as a result (e.g. Theeboom et al., 2014; Graßmann et al., 2020). However, we also know that neurodivergent people think, feel and act differently. No behavioural intervention, including coaching, is going to make an ADHD-er work at their best in a linear and consistent fashion – there will always be sprints and rests. But what we can learn in coaching is how to honour our values at work, recognise who we are and how we do our best work. There are many common issues across the neurominorities: concentration, memory, organisation, wellbeing and self-care . . . the list goes on. Coaching is an ideal activity to address these through self-knowledge and working out the right scaffolds for our neurotype. Individual circumstances and issues vary, therefore a tailored approach such as coaching is likely to be effective.

Our background and approach

What is our background and our approach? We are both Occupational Psychologists, which means that we apply the science of the mind to careers and the workplace. Individual welfare and wellbeing are our priorities. We know how beneficial work can be for humans – most people do better when they have a job than when unemployed. However, the work has to be 'good work'; a role that suits us, is well resourced and in a healthy environment. Coaches and coachees need to know about the science of how to make this happen, including how to implement healthy job design, support and the importance of resources. We need to know about how to use coaching techniques like 'Clean Language' (Chapter 5) and how to give good feedback (Chapter 7). But there are typical topics in neurodiversity coaching which come up time after time. Knowing what these might be and ways to address them is essential. Boundaries are important. Coaching is not therapy, and we need to know when to refer on. We advocate a tailored approach to adjustments and strategies. Yet not every adjustment is reasonable. We need to balance the needs of individuals with the requirements of the job in hand, as we need thriving organisations in order for civil society to work. Coaches working in this field need to understand this delicate balance and help their coachees navigate the resources in their environment.

Our experience is layered, and situated in lived, professional and academic experience. For example, Nancy has led a company for years with a neurodiverse workforce and both authors have decades of line manager experience. We'd like to think that we bring good coaching and mentoring skills, but neither of us is a fan of or particularly good at the administrative sides of management. Yet we both have had to do this as a pick and mix is rare in real-life settings. We've both experienced coaching as coachees to support us with such issues and continue to work on our self-awareness. We've both researched the long-term effects of coaching with neurodivergent adults for over a decade. Thus, we weave insights from different perspectives into our book – the neurodivergent coachee, the coach, the employer and research-led insight into the 'active ingredients' of good coaching. We walk our own talk.

Our position as researchers and practitioners

We are critical realists (see Bhaskar, 2016). We believe there is an objective world out there (realist), but that currently it's still a neuronormative world (critical). But perceptions and attitudes are changing. We will know that the 'job is done' when no one needs to talk about neurodiversity – it has simply become an aspect in life which is there and acknowledged like any other difference. From a critical realist perspective, one can only offer a glimpse of reality through our subjective understanding and knowledge; we acknowledge our limited lens of considering neurodiversity through the Western, Anglo-European workplace.

Neurodiversity by definition needs a pluralistic perspective, and acknowledgement of any socio-political context. Furthering equality of opportunity is at the heart of what we do. People need to thrive at work, regardless of their background and demographic characteristics. Both of us, at various times, have been and are being challenged on who we are, and how we do things – including not conforming to female stereotypes about being deferent or compliant. Of course, we care deeply for our colleagues and coachees. But this does not equate to deference for us, we are also radically candid and direct. These qualities have been helpful when we have advocated for others outside work, but they have also attracted judgement and criticism. Time and time again, our experiences brought home that not everyone has the same chances in life and at work, and that there are many who are raised with fewer resources. Thus, we have made every effort to emphasise important topics of marginalisation (Ruggs et al., 2013), looking beyond our own perspectives as white women. Chapter 2 outlines how we need a wide, intersectional perspective to understand notions of exclusion and inclusion. Our starting point is unconditional positive regard, even when it requires compromise and humility. We care for human difference in all its technicolour, which is the essence of neurodiversity.

We have drawn on meta-studies in this book, which summarise evidence where relevant, because this remains the best way of aggregating knowledge. We also draw on distinct studies, including qualitative research and case studies, to illustrate processes and facilitate understanding because this remains the best way of understanding lived experience. We have integrated practitioner reports and policy documents, where this is warranted, in order to widen our perspectives. Throughout the book, we have included vignettes and case examples from our own experiences. These are fictional characters and not based on real people, but include example patches of conversations that match our lived experience as coaches and transforming journeys that are representative of our coachees.

Regarding our readership, we assume that most are experienced coaches who want to educate themselves on neurodiversity, neurodiversity advocates who want to know about coaching and, hopefully, also line managers. Line managers are first responders for managing neurodiversity at work and need our support in order to provide what is needed. Reading this book won't make you qualified at delivering skilled neurodiversity coaching – upskilling takes time, training and supervision. If you do not already have coach training, you will still need it. We regard this book as a toolkit to dip in and out of and come back to when you need it. Or, if like us, you like a good non-fiction book, read it from cover to cover and then read it again once you have applied some of the learning in practice.

This is how our book is structured:

Section A: Setting the scene
Chapter 1: Our approach to writing this book
Chapter 2: Introduction to neurodiversity
Chapter 3: Typical topics in neurodiversity coaching
Chapter 4: Harnessing neurodivergent potential in coaching
Section B: Coaching techniques and principles
Chapter 5: Clean Language interviewing
Chapter 6: Transactional analysis
Chapter 7: Positive communication in coaching
Chapter 8: The psychology of coaching
Section C: Context matters
Chapter 9: Good work
Chapter 10: Wellbeing and work–life balance
Chapter 11: Contracting
Chapter 12: Reflective practice

How to read this book

The chapters are arranged into three sections: about neurodiversity, coaching and the professional context of workplace coaching. You don't necessarily need to read the chapters in this order. That said, do engage with Chapter 2 first. This sets the scene and explains the key concepts and terminology of the neurodiversity paradigm. It is the most research-heavy chapter of the book, but we have tried to summarise what we have learned over the past decade to save you trawling through the literature! We've brought together this history of neurodiversity and touched on the medical, social and biopsychosocial models. Then you can either read on, or you could read the specific chapters on Clean Language, good work and so on first, before coming back to Chapters 3 and 4. Your choice! Chapter 11 is a 'must read' from a professional, safe practice point of view.

Neurodiversity coaching is hugely rewarding but requires specialist training. Our book is not the end, but the start. Coaching tools and techniques, such as those outlined in Chapters 5–8, demonstrate how to use models with your coachees, but this is not the same as modelling experience. Good coaches can apply models to chart a path with their coachees using handouts and techniques, but great coaches listen and fluently move between models depending on the context they are in and the remit that you hold. To be a great coach, we have found that you need to practise long enough to hold a multitude of approaches in your long-term memory and know when there is a match to the coachee's experience. You also need to know when to just listen. Some of your coachees will need radical acceptance. Some will need to be respectfully and articulately challenged. Learning the balance between these stances is delicate; it requires reflection on your own practice to identify where you went wrong or right, where you missed opportunities and where you delivered. When Almuth did some coaching training early on in her career her trainer said "there is nothing soft about coaching. It is hard graft". We concur. It is possible that you will come across topics in this book that you find thought provoking, don't agree with, or which you find distressing. We see it as part of our job to portray the reality of coaching with people who have been marginalised, and to challenge you to rise to the level required for safe, ethical practice. We also hope you will be inspired and enthusiastic to adopt some of our ideas into your coaching.

Language and framing

We prefer identity-first language, so for example saying autistic people rather than person first (i.e. people with autism) because this is what most people with lived experience whom we have spoken to also prefer (Botha et al., 2023). In general, we use the original language that authors before us have used; so, for example, some have said 'schema' and others have said 'scripts' when they refer to the mental images and thought patterns we hold in our heads. We refer to coachees instead of clients, to highlight that the person you are working with is not always paying the bill. You will find a glossary in the appendix. We have endeavoured to use inclusive words where possible. That said, some of the studies we are drawing on did not when the authors wrote their papers. This is an evolving field, and we invite you to read papers regardless, as a product of their time and circumstance. That's the reality of working in a neurodiversity context – not all topics and issues will be comfortable, and expectations and norms continue to change. Our last chapter offers frameworks and guidance for ensuring your practice is safe for yourself and others and professional standards are adhered to. We are firm believers that coaching is one of the most powerful activities for personal change and growth, for the coach as well as the coachee.

Our inspiration: coaching stories

Both Almuth and Nancy are driven by their love of stories that create connection and keep us in touch with our humanity. We are both devotees of literature, music, dance and theatre. We find our coachee journeys poetic and poignant; neurodivergent coachees are so creative in their descriptions. As an opener to this book, we'd like to share one of Nancy's coaching stories from her work with neurodivergent people. In the story, Nancy uses Clean Language (Chapter 5) to facilitate her coachee towards their own resolution. The story also draws attention to self-organisation as a core topic in neurodivergent coaching conversations. It can be vital to address relevant topics first, to facilitate behaviour change and growth.

Sometimes the history inserts itself into the symbolism, via our subconscious wisdom. Nancy's coachee, Mo, was looking for an organisational strategy. Mo was a trainee counselling psychologist and needed to see their different clients in a private office that they rented alongside a team of other counsellors. They were convinced that they were disorganised and 'useless' when it came to being organised. In particular, they were concerned about arranging their office space, which threw Nancy a bit, because it looked the best organised office space she had ever seen! There was a wall with storage drawers that were neatly labelled with resources in different categories and a locked cupboard for containing client records. Mo reported that looks were deceiving! In practice, they continually lost resources: for example, diagrams of relationship modules and other visual prompts to help their clients think. They ended up rifling through the drawers and other client records during sessions to find the right resources for the client in front of them. This wasted time during and after sessions as Mo struggled to reorganise. Nancy asked permission to work with Mo around the idea of organisation using clean questions (see Chapter 5 – so, very direct and non-leading questions) to understand the process of being organised in more depth. They agreed.

Nancy: And when you are organised at your best, it's like what?
Mo: Well, I suppose it's a bit 'left/right/left/right' isn't it? [Mo mimics a marching movement, hands going up and down. There is a frown on their face.]
Nancy: And what kind of 'left/right/left/right' is that?
Mo: Well, you can't stick your head over the parapet, can you? You have to keep your head down and focus on one thing at a time.

Nancy was somewhat surprised by these answers. She had invited Mo to think of a positive metaphor, but these answers did not seem positive at all! Mo also seemed surprised. Nancy decided to ask a question to direct Mo to what they did want, rather than what appeared to be the problem.

Nancy: And when you have to keep your head down, what would you like to have happen?
Mo: I don't know! I can't see a way forward.

Mo had circled back to a problem again. Nancy asked a question that drew the two problem statements together.

Nancy: And when you can't see a way forward, and there's left/right/left/right, where could left/right/left/right come from?
Mo: Wow. Do you suppose that my dad being in the Army is relevant here? [laughs]
Nancy: [laughs] let's find out! And is there a relationship between your dad being in the army and being organised?

Er, yes! It transpired that Mo had spent their childhood in an army household, where the most important value was the efficient use of resources ('waste not want not!') and Mo had been eager to please but completely unsuited to this task. They had tried desperately to please their father, but were unable to comply, because their neurodivergent brain always needed to see the bigger picture. With the visual prompt resources, they had several laminated A4-sized diagrams, which they would get out to use when in sessions. The resource cards were laminated so that they could be used over and over again with different clients, using dry wipe markers. This did not suit Mo and they would absent-mindedly place the resource cards in the client's folder at the end of the session. The next time they needed the resource they would have to hunt for it, trying to remember which client had used it last!

The solution was for Mo to print lots of copies of the resource, rather than have one that was laminated. They could then stick to their intuitive pattern of placing the completed diagram in the folder of the client who had used it. This was a lot less trouble, even though it used more paper. There was an additional benefit – before the client arrived, Mo could open their folder and lay out all the diagrams they had worked through together, which enabled Mo to instantly see the 'bigger picture' of where that client was at. This strategy totally played to Mo's thinking style, but they had been blocked by running their father's script of 'waste not want not'. To print several copies of a resource that would be reused would have been seen as a colossal waste of paper by their father.

Nancy's coaching with Mo involved careful reflection of what they were already doing, rather than trying to change Mo, or making suggestions. Clean questions allowed Mo to understand the logic of their process, without judgement, uncovering a values clash and an internal script that Mo had been running from childhood that was not useful for Mo as an adult. Understanding this meant that Mo stopped trying to force themselves to adhere to a mismatched ideal and started playing to their strengths. By releasing themselves from their father's imperative, they were able to develop their own, intuitive process that matched their natural thinking style. Notice how Nancy says very little about the content of Mo's explanations, only signposting them towards sections of it. She is holding the pattern of the whole story, without adding her opinions or ideas. This technique is the focus of Chapter 5 on Clean Language coaching.

We hope Mo's story, and other stories later in the book, will inspire you to consider how transformational coaching can be for neurodivergent people. It is helpful in bringing out one's authentic self and becoming more aligned with one's thinking style. Like Mo, many neurodivergent people struggle because they are trying to conform to expectations. Yet, through coaching, we can release ourselves from the need to conform, to do what others seem to find easy, and instead find our own path. What a wonderful outcome!

Conclusion

To conclude, we note the pragmatic need to take an evidence-based approach to coaching in the neurodiversity context. We draw on good science from psychology and other areas as well as practice-focused literature to provide you with a sound overview. We also hope that you will find the stories and examples woven into the book inspiring. We see this book as a resource and toolkit to support your practice and expect that not everyone will agree with our views and experiences. That's okay we can agree to differ. Sometimes we learn more about what's important to us by finding someone who thinks the opposite! This is still a positive outcome for self-development, and we hope that you continue to challenge yourself and reflect on triggers that may arise or practice points from which you can learn. You can take yourself on your own coaching journey whilst reading by following our reflective practice questions at the end of each chapter. We invite you to reflect on your expectations of reading this book and then report back to yourself at the end.

Reflective questions

- What are your hopes and expectations for reading this book?
- Which of the chapters listed above appears of most interest to you, and why?

- What is your own experience of neurodiversity to date, in coaching and life? Do you have lived experience? How might any experiences influence your approach to coaching?

References

Bhaskar, R. (2016). *Enlightened common sense: The philosophy of critical realism*. Routledge.

Botha, M., Hanlon, J., & Williams, G. L. (2023). Does language matter? Identity-first versus person-first language use in autism research: A response to Vivanti. *Journal of Autism and Developmental Disorders, 53*(2), 870–878. https://doi.org/10.1007/s10803-020-04858-w

Graßmann, C., Schölmerich, F., & Schermuly, C. C. (2020). The relationship between working alliance and client outcomes in coaching: A meta-analysis. *Human Relations, 73*(1), 35–58. https://doi.org/10.1177/0018726718819725

Ruggs, E. N., Hebl, M. R., Law, C., Cox, C. B., Roehling, M. V., & Wiener, R. L. (2013). Gone fishing: I–O psychologists' missed opportunities to understand marginalized employees' experiences with discrimination. *Industrial and Organizational Psychology, 6*(1), 39–60. https://doi.org/10.1111/iops.12007

Theeboom, T., Beersma, B., & van Vianen, A. E. (2014). Does coaching work? A meta-analysis on the effects of coaching on individual level outcomes in an organizational context. *The Journal of Positive Psychology, 9*(1), 1–18. https://doi.org/10.1080/17439760.2013.837499

Chapter 2

Introduction to neurodiversity

Nancy Doyle and Almuth McDowall

Introduction

This chapter charts the evolution of the neurodiversity paradigm and neurodevelopmental differences as a brief history through time. We then turn to diagnostic criteria and outline how different conditions such as autism, dyslexia and others have been diagnosed, what people's experiences have been and how this might impact on work and life experiences. The question whether neurodivergence is a superpower or disability provides room for reflection. In the next section we discuss the notions of stigma, exclusion and intersectionality to highlight the experience of marginalised groups. As this chapter is somewhat research- and content-heavy we encourage our readers to skip forward and flick back if that works better for you. Despite the complex medical, psychological and sociological language, the practicalities of coaching neurodivergent people are grounded in solid coaching psychology, which should provide a sense of relief for all our readers. The chapter draws out five implications for coaching. Finally, we invite you to reflect on your positioning and level of privilege to contextualise your approach to coaching.

The neurodiversity paradigm

The term neurodiversity was first academically conceptualised by the Australian sociologist Judy Singer, who mentioned this term in her thesis (Singer, 1998), and identified as being in the middle of three generations of females who were on what was then known as the Autistic Spectrum. Singer was in regular conversation with autistic people across the globe, using emerging internet chat

DOI: 10.4324/9781003368274-3

groups and an Autistic Self-Advocacy Movement (Walker, 2012) was beginning to challenge the old Psycho-Medical Deficit model. Their active narrative evolved to include psycho-medically labelled groups including ADHD and the four 'Dys' (dyscalculia, dyslexia, dysgraphia, dyspraxia), which were joining up to the concept of a Neurodiversity Movement; some of this history is captured by Nick Walker in her book *Neuroqueer Heresies* (Walker, 2021). Many within this movement wished to co-opt the advances of more established inclusion activity, for example aligned minoritised groups such as transgender, gay, lesbian, bisexual and queer people, intersectional feminism, ethnic and race minorities (or indeed global majorities under-represented in global culture), and use these lessons to improve social justice for neurominorities. Essentially, the premise is that unusual, minority neurotypes might be disabling but are also a regular feature of the rich tapestry of human cognition. Thus attention is given to strengths as well as struggles – a neutral framework in which great things are possible but equally so are significant challenges. Neurodiversity is a term that reflects our whole species, just as biodiversity reflects the planet. Minority neurotypes that we typically associate with the term include: ADHD, autism, the Dys and tic disorders such as Tourette's syndrome; these are referred to as neurominorities (Walker, 2021; Chapman, 2020; Singer, 1999). Logically, we might also include learning/intellectual/developmental disabilities, acquired health conditions that affect brain function, such as multiple sclerosis, and mental health conditions such as bipolar or anxiety disorder. Activist Kassiane Asasumasu termed those who are not part of the neurotypical majority 'neurodivergent' (Asasumasu, 2022).

Understanding neurodevelopmental differences

The next sections outline models for neurodevelopmental differences and their biological origin.

The medical model

Evidence of the existence of learning disabilities, ADHD and autism date back hundreds of years. ADHD is first referenced as early as

1775 by the German physician Melchior Weikard (Lange et al., 2010). The first mention of dyslexia was in the late 1800s (Berlin, 1884). The term 'autism' was first used by Dr Bleuler in the early twentieth century (Bleuler, 1912) who described autism as a childhood schizophrenia. This idea was developed by Dr Ssucharewa (Ssucharewa, 1927) into a description eerily similar to the present-day diagnostic criteria, as listed in the Diagnostic Statistical Manual version five (DSM-V; American Psychiatric Association, 2013). Early texts aim at listing 'symptoms' of deficiencies, quantifying the extent of the difference and detailing treatment or intervention to make people 'normal'. This is known as the 'medical model' of disability.

The biological reality

ADHD, autism, dyslexia and dyspraxia have undisputed genetic origins (Koi, 2021). Indeed, the biological certainty of neurodiversity is a strong argument for its essential role in the rich tapestry of our species. Why would we consistently replicate neurodiverse genes if they weren't helpful to human cooperative functioning? Modern neuroscience has identified clear patterns of cognitive differences. These include less electrical activity in language centres, visual centres, memory centres and/or in the pre-frontal cortex where our 'executive functions' reside (Hofmann et al., 2012). Executive functions are where we plan, process, filter and hold our working memory (Baddeley, 2007). Working memory is the ability to hold pieces of information in our minds long enough to work with them – for example repeating a phone number whilst rummaging for a pen. Remember this, it will be useful later! Research has found differences in the strength of neural interconnectivity and sensory processing and enhanced senses for some neurominorities (Siugzdaite et al., 2020; Thye et al., 2018). There are also significant differences in some neurotransmitters – more or less, different thresholds (see ADHD section below). All these neurological functions control how well we can focus our attention and experience, and handle strong emotions, read and write, plan more than a few steps in advance, execute dexterity and balance, filter our thoughts/communication. Neurodiversity affirmative practitioners challenge that such differences are pathological as different neurological functions do automatically equal an impairment. This is where the biological reality deviates from the medical model.

The evolutionary argument

This categorisation and treatment of neurominorities developed during the socio-historical context of the industrial revolution when family farming or trades were usurped by factory lines and mainstream education was replacing informal apprenticeship learning. Anyone who wasn't able to read, write, do maths, operate machinery, sit still for hours, concentrate in a loud and busy environment had to be 'atypical'. Yet prior to industrialisation, specialists found roles as an apprentice to the local barber, silversmith, farrier; families passed down farming along genetic lines, knowledge was transferred via story and song rather than books, a time when the world was quieter, slower and movement was an essential part of everyday life.

Interestingly, prior to the rise of the medical model, people with unusual neurotypes, including learning/intellectual disabilities and autism, were welcomed in the Tudor courts, to speak truth to kings and queens, so that powerful people were not overly influenced by fawning courtiers (Jarrett, 2012). Our view of disability and in general what is 'normal' is intrinsically linked with our day-to-day current frame of reference; this is an essential thing on which to reflect when we consider neurodiversity.

To go back even further, humans lived in small tribes of approximately 150 when having a small specialist minority was advantageous. Approximately 5% are naturally more curious and hypervigilant (ADHD), another 2% excel at detailed investigation of specific tools (autism) and have super sensitive noses, ears, eyes and/or taste buds (most ND), a persistent group of 10% find building and moving things easier than their peers (dyslexia) and another group have highly developed language and empathy abilities (dyspraxia) Doyle (2020).

Using the evolutionary critique, many neurodivergent people ascribe to the 'social model' of disability (Charlton, 1998), which holds that our world, which is not accommodating of difference, makes us disabled. The prehistoric origins of neurodiversity are explored in Dr Taylor's Theory of Complementary Cognition (Taylor H. et al., 2021), which explains that distribution of ability equates to efficiency and survival advantages, different to the current context of having to fit in.

In summary, the evolutionary argument highlights that neurotypes are framed as helpful or unhelpful depending on what is required of humans at the time. Yet their variety is remarkably persistent in our gene pool, indicating some lasting long-term advantage. Having read some of our draft chapters, Singer (in personal communication) reminded us that nature is not always benign and that some suffering in the world comes with human existence; neurodiversity is not a panacea for inclusion, equality or opportunity. While the social model is essential as a frame to advocate for the rights of minoritised people, its purpose is not to negate neurominorities' lived experience.

A biopsychosocial model

Curiously, researchers at Cambridge University have found few correlations between which part of the brain is underactive and the label given to a person; diagnosis seems more predicated on behaviour and expectations than neurocognitive differences (Jones et al., 2021). Regarding the biology, there is no obvious way to justify diagnostic criteria as labels are more akin to symptoms than causes. However, the multiple research strands have a clear theme: there are biological differences with psychological and social impacts for neurodivergent people. Some of these impacts are disabling. People are more or less disabled dependent on the extent of their neurological difference, their history, their demographics and social context. This is called the 'biopsychosocial model' (Doyle, 2020), which holds that people may experience neurodivergence as simultaneously enabling and disabling. In practice, typical strengths and some, although not all, difficulties are similar across neurominorities. We see repeated strengths reported in creative and innovative thinking (McDowall et al., 2023), described in more detail in Chapter 4. We also see persistent difficulties in memory, attention, self-organisation, communication and managing wellbeing (Doyle & Bradley, 2022). We turn to such everyday performance difficulties in Chapter 3.

The advocacy perspective

Over the last three decades, advocacy for neurodiversity has continued to gain momentum, championed by charities, many of which are condition specific, interest groups and other advocacy networks. The internet is a great facilitator, and many communities use social media. Books from a lived-experience perspective are aplenty. We acknowledge the committed work done by so many and the strides made in awareness raising. But awareness is one thing, embedding good practice based on evidence, and truly opening hearts and minds another. We need awareness of the potentially unhelpful dynamics in the neurodiversity ecosystem, for example some groups seen as more deserving at any one time. For instance, we have witnessed many Autism at Work Programmes. But we have not witnessed ADHD at Work programmes on a similar scale. Dyslexia research was prolific in the 1990s but has ebbed away despite providing very little insight into the adult experience (Doyle & McDowall, 2021). There is 50 times more current research on autism than dyspraxia or Tourette's syndrome, despite similar population prevalence. So coachees might present with varied levels of validation and understanding, depending on their diagnoses, or lack of. We like this quote from Patricia Hill Collins, a Black Feminist writer: "Each group speaks from its own standpoint and shared its own partial, situated knowledge. But because each group perceives its own truth as partial, its knowledge is unfinished" (p. 46 in Yuval-Davis, 2012). Recognising that knowledge is never finite and inviting observation and enquiry with curiosity will be a good starting point in neurodiversity coaching. Engaging with the advocacy community online can be one way of connecting with the variety of lived experience and sometimes conflicting viewpoints. However, we also point to our notes of caution in the chapter on reflective practice (Chapter 12) about potential misinformation and the vagaries of algorithms. We encourage a stance of respectful curiosity to engage with coachees' lived experience.

Definitions and diagnostic criteria

It is important for coaches to have a high-level understanding of current diagnostic criteria to learn and understand about typical behaviour patterns – NOT to get involved in any level or talk about diagnosis.

ADHD: attention deficit hyperactivity disorder

ADHD is a neurodevelopmental health condition that is marked by impulsivity, hyperactivity and inattention. There is also a subtype called ADD without the signs of hyperactivity. It remains debated whether there is such a thing as adult onset ADHD, or whether diagnosis later in life happens because symptoms were masked at earlier ages or simply not assessed (e.g. Taylor L. E. et al., 2021). Theories of where ADHD comes from are multiple, but the most well-researched theory is that relating to a lower volume of the neurotransmitters dopamine and noradrenaline (aka norepinephrine; Engert & Pruessner, 2008). Dopamine is related to pleasure responses that let you know you have had enough and are satiated. If you don't have as much dopamine as others, you are likely to be constantly seeking the next boost – which can come from exercise, affection, smartphone notifications, finishing something, a new sensation, work or education success, food, alcohol/drugs. People with lower dopamine levels than the general population can appear driven and hyperactive but are looking for that sense of being satisfied so that they can rest. This is why stimulants work as medication – it gives them dopamine and then they can finally slow down. Noradrenaline is less well understood but has a positive effect on our executive functions as part of a stress response. There's a mid-range sweet spot that improves processing speed and working memory. Too little and we experience a type of brain fog, too much and we go into a flight/fight/freeze response. So the ADHDers, who start with too little, can often find that they hit the mid-range sweet spot just as everyone else is falling over. This is why they're so great in a crisis.

Diagnosis of ADHD, however, is still based on behavioural interviews and check lists, looking for symptoms of inattention, hyperactivity and impulsivity. Diagnosis requires evidence of these behaviours prior to the age of 12, and it must be seen in multiple contexts (e.g. home and school) and cause significant impact to at least one area of life – education, work, family or social integration (American Psychiatric Association, 2013). Critical in diagnosis is to differentiate ADHD as a developmental condition from a health condition that you might acquire which changes your behaviour (for example thyroid disease), or a trauma response. The background checking is essential. Prevalence of ADHD is estimated at around 5% worldwide (Doyle, 2020).

Autism

Autism is a neurological and developmental condition that affects how people think, interact, communicate, and behave. Diagnosis used to be split into autism and Asperger's syndrome, the former associated with having higher dependency needs and concurrent with learning (intellectual/developmental) disabilities,[1] the latter associated with the stereotype of the highly intelligent but socially compromised persona. About 33% of autistic people also have learning disabilities (Zeidan et al., 2022). Causal theories are numerous, to the extent that all may have some element of truth for some autists but not for others. We are unlikely to arrive at a single unifying theory, though many have tried (Wolff, 2004). Neurological presentation seems to frequently involve one or more of three patterns: firstly, heightened sensory sensitivity paired with reduced executive functions, giving the experience of being constantly overstimulated without the necessary thought space to understand what you are perceiving (Thye et al., 2018). It is in this context that the need for routine and predictability makes sense. Secondly, differences in the neurotransmitter GABA (Gamma-aminobutyric acid), which regulates anxiety in the amygdala, where we experience our flight/fight/freeze auto responses (Cellot & Cherubini, 2014). Lastly, the pattern of hyperconnectivity, as discussed in the section above. While heightened sensory perception might be evolutionarily advantageous for the person in charge of food tasting or listening for threats, it is frequently reported as pain for autists living in a noisy, smelly and chemical-filled world. These neurocognitive differences cause startle reflexes, shock and damage to the nervous system for many; they are not always neutral or benign.

Current diagnosis is dependent on there being marked difficulties in social interaction and communication, seen in multiple contexts, as well as evidence of repetitive behaviours, interests and routines, particularly those related to the senses and special interests (American Psychiatric Association, 2013). Psychiatry and psychology no longer differentiate between autism and Asperger's, arguing that these are both aspects of the same underlying cognition, however you may find coachees have a strong preference on how they self-identify, depending on the era they were diagnosed. Autism is estimated at around 1–2% worldwide – it could be higher when we include the cases that are missed by male/Anglocentric behavioural norms.

Dyscalculia, dysgraphia, dyslexia and dyspraxia

These used to be called 'specific learning difficulties' or 'specific learning disabilities' (SpLD) because they are all dependent on there being a level of competence in overall cognition compared to one or two specific domains of difficulty, rather than general difficulty. We note that this is often abbreviated to Learning Disabilities in the USA, but that term in the UK refers to more general, developmental or intellectual disabilities. Dyscalculia means difficulty with numbers. Dyslexia means difficulty with words. Dysgraphia means difficulty with writing. Dyspraxia means difficulty with movement. Other areas of cognition in which you are functioning well could be verbal or visual skills, long-term memory, abstract reasoning and more. Causal theories are numerous and indeed all are likely to have some merit. Dyslexia theories are related to our ability to process sound (if we are speaking an Indo-European language) or vision (if we are speaking an orthographic language like Chinese). In the UK and USA, phonological processing deficit theory is the most prevalent basis for diagnosis and support (Shaywitz, 1998). Some identify our ability to recognise shapes at speed as the problem or visual disturbances when processing text. Dyspraxia theories typically include a reduction in messages to the brain from the peripheral senses – literally fewer signals from our fingers and toes about where we are and what we need to do, leading to difficulties with balance and/or fine motor control (Gibbs et al., 2007). Additionally, there is some evidence of reduced communication between the left and right hemispheres of the brain, which is needed for coordination (ibid.). All four Dys come with evidence of reduced executive functioning (Swanson & Siegel, 2001). Dyslexia is estimated at around 10% worldwide, the other Dys between 2% and 8% (Doyle, 2020).

Other neurominorities?

Because the spectrum of human cognitive functioning is at the heart of neurodiversity there is good reason to extend the community to other minority neurotypes. If you have an unusual neurological profile, you should feel included. For this book, we are not going to deep dive into other neurominorities such as tic disorders (1% worldwide), learning disabilities (1% worldwide) or mental health conditions such as bipolar disorder (1–5% worldwide) Doyle (2020). This is because explaining the complexity between various conditions would then become the focus of our book, rather than coaching. We hope our readers have noticed the similarities and parallels between the neurominorities; namely, reduced executive function performance, differences in sensory processing and the management of information. Ticcers and those with intellectual or mental health diagnoses often share such traits. Executive functions are also impaired in people with multiple sclerosis, long Covid, chronic fatigue syndrome, people in menopause, undergoing cancer treatment and those recovering from brain injury. And, just like the four Dys, these disabilities have functions that are unaffected by their condition, such as their ability to remember long term, their ability to match colours, to listen well and so on. There are a lot of people with divergent and specialist brains as our current 'guesstimate' is that 15–20% of the population have conditions that are neurodevelopmentally acquired (Doyle, 2020) but this number could be potentially much higher when we cast a wider net.

Are neurodivergent people disabled?

Some coachees will want to align themselves to the 'superpower narrative', and work on their strengths. Others will come with experience of disablement and be seeking ways to address their barriers; they may find the superpower narrative insulting and a form of toxic positivity. For this reason, we tend to use the phrase 'talent'. Some may be experiencing a sense of 'learned helplessness' – that there is no point in trying because they always fail. It is really important for a coach to be neutral on this matter and avoid positioning any one side of this debate. An important step in neurodiversity coaching is to recognise coachees' narratives with unconditional positive regard and openness. A successful outcome for a coachee is self-awareness of when one is experiencing both sides of the coin, knowledge of where they are likely to succeed and where they are likely to need scaffolding, or even avoidance.

Let's give a simple answer to this direct question of talent or disability that is in line with both the biopsychosocial model and most legal statutes – it could be either or both and it is entirely context and task dependent. Take your ADHDers. Easily distracted or highly alert? ADHD is disabling when trying to concentrate in an open-plan classroom or office, but makes for talented soldiers, police, paramedics, firefighters, educators – people who need to remain on

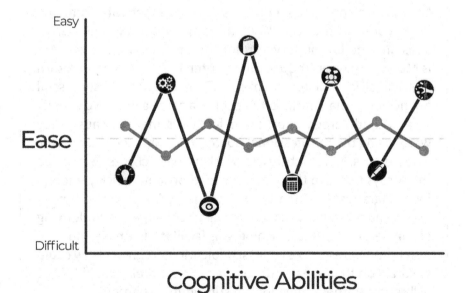

Figure 2.1 Cognitive abilities as summarised in a spiky profile.

constant watch for new information. Dyspraxics can be stumbling and struggling with equipment, or they can be persuasive articulators. This experience of strength and challenge in the same person, at different times and in different places is the defining criteria for neurodivergence. In fact, when psychologists diagnose, we are actively looking for a 'spiky profile' – a large difference between the peaks and troughs of a person's cognitive ability (Grant, 2009).

As depicted in Figure 2.1, a spiky profile charts individual's cognitive functioning as measured by a particular overall ability assessment, which has different subtests. A neurodivergent profile will have marked strengths, for example related to visuo-spatial recognition or verbal comprehension, and also difficulties, for example remembering things or accurate checking. A profile that is not neurodivergent would typically have scores on different tests in a similar range, indicated by a flatter line. We call a flatter profile neurotypical (see also our glossary for explanation of various terms), and statistically around 68% of humans will have a neurotypical profile (Weschler, 2008).

Nancy once conducted a diagnostic assessment with someone who scored in the top 3% of the population for their verbal skills and the bottom seventh for their processing speed – this is Mo, whom we introduced in Chapter 1. We're going to return to their story in later chapters. They had been a successful financier who had decided to become a counselling psychologist as a second career. They came for assessment because they were failing their professional doctorate. They aced their verbal assessments, when observed working with clients, but failed the essays because they couldn't read or write quickly enough for postgraduate standard. In this one person, we see both a talent and a disability. Coaching will not change the underlying cognitive profile. But coaching will facilitate learning and self-insight. What resources could scaffold Mo's progress? How could we draw on their 'peaks' to compensate for their 'troughs'? We will return to these questions in subsequent chapters.

Your coachees will have different experiences of diagnosis where the approach and level of positivity of the actual diagnostician makes a stark difference. The point in their lifespan in which this happened can also have a substantial impact. Early diagnosed people may have strong identities aligned with their neurotype. Late diagnosed people may be hanging onto the idea that their neurodivergence is some sort of personality flaw; for example, "oh I'm always really insensitive, I just don't think of others", or "I'm such a scatty person" or "I'm quite unlikeable, most people find me rude and abrasive". Unpicking these statements can be quite cathartic. "What lets you know you are rude? Can we work through an example? What were your intentions in the communication? What did you actually do or say? How was the interpretation compared to your intention?"

Neurodivergence often comes with co-occurring physical disabilities such as epilepsy which is a neurological condition marked by sudden and recurrent episodes of sensory disturbance, convulsions associated with abnormal brain activity (Lukmanji et al., 2019) and Ehlers–Danlos syndrome which causes hypermobility (e.g., Baeza-Velasco et al., 2018). While medical intervention is clearly beyond the realm of coaching, an appreciation of the potentially complex health challenges is necessary to ensure that for example goal setting and visioning exercises are realistic. Some coachees are on a journey to self-acceptance of their limitations and need to be kinder to themselves.

There's further nuance to the "am I disabled?" question. Some people avoid disability as a label because they do not feel they are 'deserving' of the protections of disability. Some neurodivergent people don't feel that they 'qualify' and indeed, they may not. Disability status in law is very particular – it concerns the extent to which one must struggle to conduct normal day-to-day activities rather than the label itself (United Nations Convention on the Rights of Persons with Disabilities, 2006). However, many neurodivergent people would qualify but feel anxious about taking up space or resources when others are 'more deserving'. Some people see disability as 'less than' and hold prejudices about disabled people.

This is called ableism (see e.g. Linton, 2017) which can be internalised. Avoidance of the disability identity can also come from holding other stigmatising characteristics related to gender, race, ethnicity, sexuality, transgender, social class, age or others, and simply not wanting to add to one's burden of exclusion. It's a complex question, your coachees will have their own, personal complex answers.

Stigma and exclusion

We have described above how coachees might align with either the talent or disability discourse. While we might relish the neurodiversity angle for thinking about a benign balance of skill and struggle, coaches need to understand the likelihood of experience of hurt, vulnerability and exclusion. The figures speak for themselves. The reality of work outcomes for neurominorities is statistically bleak. Around a third of long-term unemployed people are dyslexic (Jensen et al., 2000). Approximately 25% of incarcerated people meet the clinical criteria for ADHD (Young et al., 2018). Fewer than a quarter of autistic people have work (ONS, 2019). There is significant stigma experienced by neurominorities in education, resulting in parent blaming, as well as gaslighting children and young people into disbelieving their own experience of overwhelm and mental distress (Dalrymple, 2020). The rate of exclusion and suspension from schools for neurodivergent children is between twice and five times that of their neurotypical peers (ONS, 2022). Neurodivergent people become adults with a history of having felt chastised and blamed. Narratives of "must try harder", "so much potential but she lets herself down", "doesn't apply himself", "uncontrollable" become internalised. Practitioners estimate that an ADHD child has heard 20,000 more criticisms by the age of ten compared with their peers (Jellinek, 2010). When you are working with a neurodivergent coachee, you might be witnessing at best some low self-esteem and sense of failure and at worst some deep trauma from being forced to comply with painful activities because no one believed you were "so sensitive". There may be merit in exploring internalised narratives, but you will need to manage boundaries in order not to stray into counselling. We revisit this particular issue in more depth in Chapter 11, on contracting with your coachees.

Instances of prejudice against neurominorities remain, such as "oh, everyone's autistic these days" or "in my day kids were just clumsy and they grew out of it". There are also common microaggressions "everyone struggles with attention sometimes, don't they?" or "Oh I get so dyslexic when I take the minutes". Actually no, not everyone struggles with attention to the same degree and no, you do not suddenly get dyslexic when you take minutes. Such observations are akin to saying to a wheelchair user, "we all struggle to walk sometimes, don't we?" or to a Deaf person "in my day we all had to listen harder". Navigating persistent experiences of prejudice and microaggressions is tiring and exacerbated by being part of other minoritised groups.

Intersectionality

Any coach in the neurodiversity field needs to be aware of its deep roots of racism, misogyny, transsexism and homosexism.[2] These are present in the workplace, leading to greater marginalisation for those with additional protected identities (Doyle et al., 2022). We'll give you some examples of how different identities might affect your coachees, firstly looking at gender, then race and then a summary of other influencing factors.

Gender

Gender impacts are clear in diagnosis rates, which consistently favour boys for autism and ADHD at ratios between 2:1 and 12:1, depending on location and diagnostic criteria (Roman-Urrestarazu et al., 2021; Young et al., 2020). The disparities for dyslexia and dyspraxia are less marked, but nonetheless still favour boys (CDC, 2011). The origins of such disparities are contentious, with some arguing that genetically there are differences and others countering that because the diagnostic criteria is so weighted towards male presentation it is difficult to separate out a clear line of causation (Lai et al., 2015). Prof. Gina Rippon, author of *The Gendered Brain* (Rippon, 2019) argues that even the mere search for sex differences is evidence of sexism. She points out that there are so many other ways in which we could be supporting individuals! Devoting precious research time to this line of enquiry has no useful outcome other than priming professionals to see neurodivergence as a male phenomenon. In coaching, you are likely to see neurodivergent women who have not been diagnosed or have been diagnosed later in life. Those who are diagnosed are likely to have experienced higher levels of distress and challenge before they were referred for assessment. Many women are incorrectly diagnosed with mental health issues such as anxiety, depression, eating disorders and personality disorders before receiving an ND diagnosis (Mandy & Tchanturia, 2015; Young et al., 2020). Society is much harder on women who are messy and disorganised (e.g. ADHD) lacking in social niceties (autism) not good at handwriting or spelling (dyspraxia and dyslexia). Society is also more forgiving of women who are not good at maths (dyscalculia), which means they are less likely to receive help and might struggle throughout their life span. Female coachees may need to do some identity work and apply some retrospective compassion to their younger selves in order to address any self-chastisement; we return to the issue of building self-confidence in Chapter 9.

Race, ethnicity, nationality, religion

Any effects of race and ethnicity on neurodiversity experience are nuanced but broadly can be grouped as: (a) the effects of under diagnosis and (b) the additional stigma experienced in some communities. Those who are not of the dominant (white, Western) culture are under diagnosed (Ellenberg et al., 2019; Roman-Urrestarazu et al., 2021). This is due to interacting influences including lack of resources and white-typed diagnostic criteria. Appropriate eye contact varies between cultures, for example Caribbean cultures place a high value on averting your eyes from someone in authority (Levine et al., 2006). This will affect autism diagnosis where level of eye contact is a critical 'tell' when white assessors are not sure how to interpret behaviour. Just as with gender, the effects of culture on our childhood behaviour and development of skill are marked. There are twice as many Japanese autists, for example, as ADHDers, a flip from the Anglosphere where there are more ADHDers than autists (Miyasaka et al., 2018). This is thought to reflect Japanese culture, which prides itself on conformity, humility and compliance.

Interestingly, Chinese dyslexics and European dyslexics look completely different under neuroimaging, the Chinese experiencing less activity in their visual centres than neurotypicals, the Europeans in their sound-processing centres (Opitz et al., 2014). This is because our languages are so different that they rely on different neurological functions. Some communities experience neurodivergence as more stigmatising than others (for example, Roma and travellers, Asian and African communities). This is in part related to the additional stigma already experienced for people of colour or ethnic minority and a desire to avoid further discrimination. There is an influence of religion across all nationalities, races and ethnicities; some considering neurodivergence a punishment, or spiritual failure. This leads to sometimes devastating trauma and ostracism for neurodivergent people and their families.

In short, if you are coaching a neurodivergent person from a different racial, ethnic, national or religious background to your own, it is worth considering that their contextualised experience of neurodiversity might be very different to yours. This is particularly an issue if you are white and they are Black, Brown, Indigenous, Jewish, Roma or Asian. In white neurodiversity advocacy, for example, 'masking' one's differences is considered something to be avoided. There are many advocates extolling the virtues of 'unmasking one's authentic neurodivergent self' and feeling free to 'stim' in public (repeated movements like hand flapping that stimulate and soothe the nervous system). However, in Black communities living in Europe or North America, masking could literally be a survival strategy when interacting with police officers. Stimming in public could be viewed as aggression or lack of responsiveness to an authority figure and advocates in Black and Brown autistic communities frequently observe that 'de-masking' is privilege. It is important to remain curious about your coachee's experiences and set aside your own assumptions.

Other intersections

Very little is known about the intersection of neurodivergence and sexuality and gender identity, except that the prevalence rates are significantly increased in the LGBTQ+ community (Pecora et al.,

2020). We do not know why, but we can surmise that coachees of this background will be experiencing compound adverse impact, such as the cognitive burden of additional masking. Socio-economic status has an impact on diagnosis access and the provision of scaffold and supports in youth, which in turn influences reduced self-esteem in adulthood. Age is also of interest because of the changing popularity of neurodiversity and associated stigma. Boomers and Generation X were more likely to be diagnosed with dyslexia, Millennials with ADHD, Generation Z with autism because of the popularity and access to professionals in the era of their schooling. Younger generations in general are less likely to be ashamed of their diagnosis due to increased general awareness and social media influencers. In general, it is a complex picture for intersecting identities and our experience guides us to proceed with humility, without assuming that you know someone's experience and approach to their diagnosis or lack of one. People may surprise you!

A second reminder about language and terminology

Having read through all of the above, we hope that you appreciate the many nuances of different language and terminology currently in use. For a population who have potentially been marginalised, the right to self-identify becomes an act of empowerment. Using language that neurodivergent people don't like can result in a strong or blunt response. The best way to handle this is by pre-empting the issue. Ask a coachee what they prefer when first meeting them. If any strong reactions happen, issue a quick acknowledgement and where necessary an apology, and from now on use their preferred language. This is the same logic as we should apply for saying people's names. Names are core to our identity and saying them right is a way of demonstrating respect (Dali et al., 2022). Best practice is to not assume that you know how to pronounce, if in doubt double check, and be open to being corrected. Almuth has had a lifetime of being called all sorts of variations: "Allouth", "Helmuth" (historically a male name), "Almaz", "All-mouth" and so on. It's only been over the last few years that people have taken care to check pronunciation. Almuth's reply is: "my (dyslexic) nephew spells it Almoud. Read this out, and that's how you say it".

The same logic of checking and openness to correction applies to neurodiversity. Nuanced preferences are individual and in flux, just as is true for all diversity and inclusion movements. For example, a woman can identify as gay, lesbian or queer. She will have her own reasons for doing so, we can respectfully defer to her preferred terms without debate. Equally a person may identify as aspie, autistic, dyspraxic, neurodivergent, neurodifferent, neurodistinct, neurofabulous or neurodiverse. It is your professional responsibility to educate yourself in the language of inclusion because this signposts how you respect, which equally applies to coaches with lived experience. If you have a coachee who doesn't like the same terms as you, it is not your job to 'correct' them. Our glossary in the appendix gives you an overview of the terms in use at the time of writing, but bear in mind that it is important to stay engaged in how the language evolves.

What does all this mean for coaching?

Firstly, it simply means this: if you are finding neurodiversity ambiguous and confusing, that it is because it **is** ambiguous and confusing. The science is not clear as it is rooted in biased assumptions and we're only just starting to ask the right questions. Newer research is still weighted towards identification of issues in children, rather than support through the lifespan. There's no clear roadmap, no secret ultimate defining test or characteristic as it remains hard to name, define and categorise. Coachees are likely to have symptoms of more than one condition, may have been misdiagnosed and their lived experience of pathologisation versus celebration of difference will have framed their experience. They may be seeking your help in integrating the various identities in relation to their work and career goals, which is what coaching is for.

Secondly, you do not need to be a neuroscientist, psychiatrist or geneticist to help coachees work stuff out. Your role is to coach the individual on their pathway to identifying with specific strengths and challenges to live their best working life. Your background knowledge of neurominorities may help you frame and signpost some of the way, but you do not need to be an expert on neurotransmitters to help someone think about their goals, their resources and the steps in between, which means that your working knowledge of good coaching psychology is just as applicable. If you are not yet a trained coach, we recommend this step before you start working with coachees. Neurodiversity knowledge is not the same as coaching competence.

Thirdly, intersectionality matters. You need to explore your own biases and blind spots and acknowledge levels of privilege. For example, Nancy is herself a late diagnosed ADHDer who was diagnosed with eating disorders and major depression as a teen. She is a white woman, presenting as cisgendered and heterosexual, who grew up in a mixed working-class and middle-class family. Nancy displayed typically female styles of inattention and hyperactivity such as hair twiddling and daydreaming rather than jumping around and therefore was not noticed as an ADHDer in the 1980s. She was misdiagnosed and mistreated, including a stay in a psychiatric unit and a label of school phobia; she did not attend school for the last two years of secondary education. This is gender discrimination. However, as a white woman, with qualified teacher parents who could advocate for her, this truancy was considered mental distress rather than wilful misbehaviour. Nancy does not have lived experience of her ADHD being perceived by authorities as dangerous or threatening, as it might have been if she were Black or Brown, or from a less well-resourced family. She received support, albeit the wrong support, instead of criminalisation. Her parents were pitied rather than blamed. This is racial and class privilege. Nancy identifies as gender non-conforming as she was raised in the '80s; however, if she were younger, she may have identified as non-binary. This would have added a lot more attention to her behaviour in school and might have been used to explain away her attention differences. There is both privilege and restriction of self-expression in her age group experience.

Fourthly, language matters. Always check and double check and show respect by doing so. Becoming familiar with and being able to switch different terms in use according to your coachees' preferences is a strong signal of allyship to neurodivergent people. We are creating our own reality with the labels we use to describe ourselves.

Finally, you will need to navigate the sometimes fine, and occasionally blurred, line between coaching and advocacy. Yes, we have encouraged you to consider your own biases, assumptions and background. No, you must not stray outside your area of competence and/or practice beyond what you have been contracted for. We return to these important issues in our final chapters on reflective practice and the future of neurodiversity coaching.

Conclusion

In this chapter, we have outlined neurodiversity history, neurodiversity research evidence including nuance in and critique of diagnostic criteria, as well as the need for neurodiversity-affirming language and etiquette. This knowledge will support you to build rapport with our coachees. We've also outlined some specific ways in which neurominorities have been marginalised, including when they have additional demographic characteristics. You've completed the most research-heavy chapter, the rest will be more practice orientated, but now you have a summary of what we know from our extensive research and analysis of this field. We know it can feel confusing – Nancy spent the first two years of her PhD looking for the research that would help her make it all make sense. She never found it because it doesn't exist!

But don't lose confidence with the complexity of this field. Despite the debate on origins, medicalisation, radicalisation and gender disparities, there are a lot of common themes to work with. Neurominorities are humans with hopes, dreams, barriers, performance, emotions and values just like everyone else. Your experience as a coach, and the insights and techniques offered in this book, will combine to form a solid ground on which to base neurodiversity coaching, and engage in reflected nuanced practice. The opportunities are many, and the rewards of working with marginalised people rich. We encourage you to stay the course and enjoy witnessing the transformations of your neurodivergent coachees as they connect to their strengths, overcome their challenges and grow in confidence.

Reflective questions

- What thoughts, views, values and beliefs do you bring to the neurodiversity coaching conversation?
- To what extent does your experience chime, rhyme or clash with the positions we've outlined on disability?
- What have you already learned about working with vulnerable groups that you could apply here?
- What are you doing personally to work on your own experience of privilege and discrimination right now?
- Where in your life do you have resources that your neurodivergent coachees may not?
- Do any of the descriptions of discrimination, prejudice and stereotyping for gender, transgender, race or sexuality invoke reactions for you? If so, what are you noticing?
- What language do you use to describe yourself?

Notes

1 Note that 'learning disability' in the UK refers to intellectual or developmental disability; we use this definition. In the US, learning disability sometimes refers to dyslexia; this is not what we mean.
2 Note we do not use 'phobia' to describe people who are prejudiced.

References

American Psychiatric Association, DSM-5 Task Force. (2013). *Diagnostic and statistical manual of mental disorders: DSM-5™* (5th ed.). American Psychiatric Publishing. https://doi.org/10.1176/appi.books.97808904 25596

Asasumasu, K. (2022). *Neurodivergence.* Wiktionary.org. https://en.wiktio nary.org/wiki/neurodivergen

Baddeley, A. (2007). *Working memory, thought, and action.* Oxford University Press. https://doi.org/10.1093/acprof:oso/9780198528012.001.0001

Baeza-Velasco, C., Bourdon, C., Montalescot, L., de Cazotte, C., Pailhez, G., Bulbena, A., & Hamonet, C. (2018). Low- and high-anxious hypermobile Ehlers–Danlos syndrome patients: Comparison of psychosocial and health variables. *Rheumatology International, 38*(5), 871–878. https://doi.org/10.1007/s00296-018-4003-7

Berlin, R. (1884). Über Dyslexie [About dyslexia]. *Archiv Für Psychiatrie, 15,* 276–278.

Bleuler, E. (1912). Das autistische Denken. In *Jahrbuch Für Psychoanalytis che Und Psychopathologische Forschungen* 4 (pp. 1–39). Deuticke.

CDC. (2011). Percentage of children aged 5–17 years ever receiving a diagnosis of learning disability by race/ethnicity and family income group, United States, 2007–2009. *Morbidity and Mortality Weekly Report, 60*(25), 853.

Cellot, G., & Cherubini, E. (2014). GABAergic signaling as therapeutic target for autism spectrum disorders. *Frontiers in Pediatrics, 2*(70), 1–11. https://doi.org/10.3389/fped.2014.00070

Chapman, R. (2020). Defining neurodiversity for research and practice. In H. B. Rosqvist, N. Chown, & A. Stenning (Eds.), *Neurodiversity Studies: A New Critical Paradigm* (pp. 218–220). Routledge, Taylor & Francis. https://doi.org/10.4324/9780429322297-21

Charlton, J. (1998). *Nothing about us without us: Disability oppression and empowerment.* University of California Press. www.jstor.org/stable/10.1525/j.ctt1pnqn9

Dali, S., Atasuntseva, A., Shankar, M., Ayeroff, E., Holmes, M., Johnson, C., Terkaw, A. S., Beadle, B., Chang, J., Boyd, K. & Dunn, T. (2022). Say my name: Understanding the power of names, correct pronunciation, and personal narratives. *MedEdPORTAL, 18,* 11284. https://doi.org/10.15766/mep_2374-8265.11284

Dalrymple, E. (2020). A parent's perspective. In *Mental Health and Attendance at School* (pp. 162–179). The Royal College of Psychiatrists.

Doyle, N. (2020). Neurodiversity at work: A biopsychosocial model and the impact on working adults. *British Medical Bulletin, 135*(1), 108–125. https://doi.org/10.1093/bmb/ldaa021

Doyle, N., & Bradley, E. (2022). Disability coaching during a pandemic. *Journal of Work-Applied Management* (pp. 135–147). https://doi.org/10.1108/JWAM-07-2022-0042

Doyle, N., & McDowall, A. (2021). Diamond in the rough? An "empty review" of research into "neurodiversity" and a road map for developing the inclusion agenda. *Equality, Diversity and Inclusion, 41*(3), 352–382. https://doi.org/10.1108/EDI-06-2020-0172

Doyle, N., McDowall, A., & Waseem, U. (2022). Intersectional stigma for autistic people at work: A compound adverse impact effect on labor force participation and experiences of belonging. *Autism in Adulthood, 4*(4), 340–356. https://doi.org/10.1089/aut.2021.0082

Ellenberg, J., Paff, M., Harrison, A., & Long, K. (2019). Disparities based on race, ethnicity, and socio-economic status over the transition to adulthood among adolescents and young adults on the autism spectrum: A systematic review. *Current Psychiatry Reports, 21*(32), 1–16. https://doi.org/10.1007/s11920-019-1016-1

Engert, V., & Pruessner, J. (2008). Dopaminergic and noradrenergic contributions to functionality in ADHD: The role of methylphenidate. *Current Neuropharmacology, 6*(4), 322–328. https://doi.org/10.2174/157015908787386069

Gibbs, J., Appleton, J., & Appleton, R. (2007). Dyspraxia or developmental coordination disorder? Unravelling the enigma. *Archives of Disease in Childhood, 92*(6), 534–539. https://doi.org/10.1136/adc.2005.088054

Grant, D. (2009). The psychological assessment of neurodiversity. In D. Pollak (Ed.), *Neurodiversity in higher education* (pp. 33–62). Wiley-Blackwell. https://doi.org/10.1002/9780470742259

Hofmann, W., Schmeichel, B. J., & Baddeley, A. D. (2012). Executive functions and self-regulation. *Trends in Cognitive Sciences, 16*(3), 174–180. https://doi.org/10.1016/j.tics.2012.01.006

Jarrett, S. (2012). *Disability in time and place*. Historic England. https://historicengland.org.uk/content/docs/research/disability-in-time-and-place-pdf

Jellinek, M. S. (2010). Don't let ADHD crush children's self-esteem. *Pediratic News, 44*(2), 36. https://doi.org/10.1016/S0031-398X(10)70072-2

Jensen, J., Lindgren, M., Andersson, K., Ingvar, D. H., & Levander, S. (2000). Cognitive intervention in unemployed individuals with reading and writing disabilities. *Applied Neuropsychology, 7*(4), 223–236. https://doi.org/10.1207/S15324826AN0704_4

Jones, J. S., the CALM Team, & Astle, D. E. (2021). A transdiagnostic data-driven study of children's behaviour and the functional connectome. *Developmental Cognitive Neuroscience, 52*, 101027. https://doi.org/10.1016/j.dcn.2021.101027

Koi, P. (2021). Genetics on the neurodiversity spectrum: Genetic, phenotypic and endophenotypic continua in autism and ADHD. *Studies in History and Philosophy of Science, 89*, 52–62. https://doi.org/10.1016/j.shpsa.2021.07.006

Lai, M.-C., Lombardo, M. V., Auyeung, B., Chakrabarti, B., & Baron-Cohen, S. (2015). Sex/gender differences and autism: Setting the scene for future research. *Journal of the American Academy of Child & Adolescent Psychiatry, 54*(1), 11–24. https://doi.org/10.1016/j.jaac.2014.10.003

Lange, K. W., Reichl, S., Lange, K. M., Tucha, L., & Tucha, O. (2010). The history of attention deficit hyperactivity disorder. *ADHD Attention Deficit and Hyperactivity Disorders, 2,* 241–255. https://doi.org/10.1007/s12402-010-0045-8

Levine, T. R., Asada, K. J. K., & Park, H. S. (2006). The lying chicken and the gaze avoidant egg: Eye contact, deception, and causal order. *Southern Communication Journal, 71*(4) 401–411. https://doi.org/10.1080/10417940601000576

Linton, S. (2017). Reassigning meaning. In L. J. Davis(Ed.), *Beginning with disability* (pp. 20–27). Routledge.

Lukmanji, S., Manji, S. A., Kadhim, S., Sauro, K. M., Wirrell, E. C., Kwon, C. S., & Jetté, N. (2019). The co-occurrence of epilepsy and autism: A systematic review. *Epilepsy & Behavior, 98,* 238–248. https://doi.org/10.1016/j. yebeh.2019.07.037

Mandy, W., & Tchanturia, K. (2015). Do women with eating disorders who have social and flexibility difficulties really have autism? A case series. *Molecular Autism, 6*(6), 1–11. https://doi.org/10.1186/2040-2392-6-6

McDowall, A., Doyle, N., & Kiseleva, M. (2023). *Neurodiversity at work 2023: Demand, supply and gap analysis* . Neurodiversity in Business. www.researchgate.net/publication/369474902_Neurodiversity_at_Work_2023

Miyasaka, M., Kajimura, S., & Nomura, M. (2018). Biases in understanding attention deficit hyperactivity disorder and autism spectrum disorder in Japan. *Frontiers in Psychology, 9,* 1–13. https://doi.org/10.3389/fpsyg.2018.00244

ONS. (2019). Disability and employment, UK (pp. 1–19). Office of National Statistics. www.ons.gov.uk/peoplepopulationandcommunity/healthandsocialcare/disability/bulletins/disabilityandemploymentuk/2019

ONS. (2022). *Permanent and fixed term exclusions in England and Wales.* Office of National Statistics, UK. https://explore-education-statistics.service.gov.uk/find-statistics/permanent-and-fixed-period-exclusions-in-england

Opitz, B., Schneiders, J. A., Krick, C. M., & Mecklinger, A. (2014). Selective transfer of visual working memory training on Chinese character learning. *Neuropsychologia, 53*(1), 1–11. https://doi.org/10.1016/j.neuropsychologia.2013.10.017

Pecora, L. A., Hooley, M., Sperry, L., Mesibov, G. B., & Stokes, M. A. (2020). Sexuality and gender issues in individuals with autism spectrum disorder. *Child and Adolescent Psychiatric Clinics of North America, 29*(3), 543–556. https://doi.org/10.1016/j.chc.2020.02.007

Rippon, G. (2019). *Gendered brain: The new neuroscience that shatters the myth of the female brain.* Bodley Head.

Roman-Urrestarazu, A., Van Kessel, R., Allison, C., Matthews, F. E., Brayne, C., & Baron-Cohen, S. (2021). Association of race/ethnicity and social disadvantage with autism prevalence in 7 million school children in England. *JAMA Pediatrics*, *175*(6), 1–11. https://doi.org/10.1001/jamapediatrics.2021.0054

Shaywitz, S. A. (1998). Dyslexia. *New England Journal of Medicine*, *338*, 307–312. https://doi.org/10.1056/NEJM199801293380507

Singer, J. (1998). Odd people in: The birth of community amongst people on the 'autistic spectrum': A personal exploration of a new social movement based on neurological diversity. [Published/Unpublished undergraduate thesis]. University of Technology, Sydney. www.academia.edu/27033194/Odd_People_In_The_Birth_of_Community_amongst_people_on_the_Autistic_Spectrum_A_personal_exploration_based_on_neurological_diversity

Singer, J. (1999). "Why can't you be normal for once in your life?" From a problem with no name to the emergence of a new category of difference. In M. Corker & S. French (Eds.), *Disability discourse* (pp. 59–67). Open University Press.

Siugzdaite, R., Bathelt, J., Holmes, J., & Astle, D. E. (2020). Transdiagnostic brain mapping in developmental disorders. *Current Biology*, *30*(7), 1245–1257.e4. https://doi.org/10.1016/j.cub.2020.01.078

Ssucharewa, D. G. E. (1927). Die schizoiden Psychopathien im Kindesalter. *Monatsschrift für Psychiatrie und Neurologie*, *62*(3), 171–200.

Swanson, H. L., & Siegel, L. A. (2001). Learning disabilities as a working memory deficit. *Issues in Education*, *7*(1), 1–48. www.researchgate.net/publication/284802542_Learning_disabilities_as_a_working_memory_deficit

Taylor, H., Fernandes, B., & Wraight, S. (2021). The evolution of complementary cognition: Humans cooperatively adapt and evolve through a system of collective cognitive search. *Cambridge Archaeological Journal*, *32*(1), 61–77. https://doi.org/10.1017/s0959774321000329

Taylor, L. E., Kaplan-Kahn, E. A., Lighthall, R. A., & Antshel, K. M. (2021). Adult-onset ADHD: A critical analysis and alternative explanations. *Child Psychiatry & Human Development*, *53*, 635–653. https://doi.org/10.1007/s10578-021-01159-w

Thye, M. D., Bednarz, H. M., Herringshaw, A. J., Sartin, E. B., & Kana, R. K. (2018). The impact of atypical sensory processing on social impairments in autism spectrum disorder. *Developmental Cognitive Neuroscience*, *29*, 151–167. https://doi.org/10.1016/j.dcn.2017.04.010

United Nations Convention on the Rights of Persons with Disabilities, 1 (2006). www.un.org/development/desa/disabilities/convention-on-the-rights-of-persons-with-disabilities/convention-on-the-rights-of-persons-with-disabilities-2.html

Walker, N. (2012). Throw away the master's tools: Liberating ourselves from the pathology paradigm. In J. Bascombe (Ed.), *Loud hands: Autistic people, speaking* (pp. 225–237). Autistic Self Advocacy Network.

Walker, N. (2021). *Neuroqueer heresies: Notes on the neurodiversity paradigm, autistic empowerment, and postnormal possibilities.* Autonomous Press.

Weschler, D. (2008). *Weschler Adult Intelligence Scale version IV.* Pearson.

Wolff, S. (2004). The history of autism. *European Child & Adolescent Psychiatry, 13*, 201–208. https://doi.org/10.1007/s00787-004-0363-5

Young, S., Adamo, N., Ásgeirsdóttir, B. B., Branney, P., Beckett, M., Colley, W., Cubbin, S., Deeley, Q., Farrag, E., Gudjonsson, G., Hill, P., Hollingdale, J., Kilic, O., Lloyd, T., Mason, P., Paliokosta, E., Perecherla, S., Sedgwick, J., Skirrow, C., & Woodhouse, E. (2020). Females with ADHD: An expert consensus statement taking a lifespan approach providing guidance for the identification and treatment of attention-deficit/ hyperactivity disorder in girls and women. *BMC Psychiatry, 20*(1), 404. https://doi.org/10.1186/s12888-020-02707-9

Young, S., González, R. A., Fridman, M., Hodgkins, P., Kim, K., & Gudjonsson, G. H. (2018). The economic consequences of attention-deficit hyperactivity disorder in the Scottish prison system. *BMC Psychiatry, 18*(210). https://doi.org/10.1186/s12888-018-1792-x

Yuval-Davis, N. (2012). Dialogical epistemology: An intersectional resistance to the "oppression Olympics". *Gender and Society, 26*(1), 46–54.

Zeidan, J., Fombonne, E., Scorah, J., Ibrahim, A., Durkin, M. S., Saxena, S., Yusuf, A., Shih, A., & Elsabbagh, M. (2022). Global prevalence of autism: A systematic review update. *Autism Research, 15*(5) 778–790. https://doi.org/10.1002/aur.2696

Chapter 3

Typical topics in neurodiversity coaching

Nancy Doyle and Almuth McDowall

Introduction

In this chapter we outline the typical topics that come up when coaching neurodivergent people at work. Some may seem familiar to experienced coaches, but there will be an additional nuance to consider for the neurodivergent coachee. Coaching topics in general tend to be split into the following issues: cognitive, emotional, behavioural and social (Jones et al., 2016). For neurodivergent people these are all highly relevant areas for effecting positive change. Which topics arise in coaching has been the topic of our joint research since 2013, starting with dyslexia specifically but branching out to all neurominorities later (Doyle & Bradley, 2022; Doyle & McDowall, 2015, 2019; Lauder et al., 2022). We have found repeatedly that, in a workplace context, spiky profile neurotypes come up against consistent barriers. We are focusing in this chapter on challenges that need addressing in the cognitive, emotional and behavioural domains. In Chapter 4 we will turn to a more positive focus on strengths. Balance is needed in neurodiversity coaching – both sides of the coin are relevant.

In a disability support context, coaching is not aimed at changing the person, but equipping them with the tools to influence their environment. That said, from a humanistic perspective and for ongoing career advancement, a coachee may wish to seek more self-awareness and self-control over patterns of thought, emotion, behaviour and social interaction than they currently hold. Navigating this balance between changing the person versus their environment is tricky. On

DOI: 10.4324/9781003368274-4

the one hand it is simple to say "be client-led" and follow their interest. On the other, if the individual is the subject of bullying and ostracism for acts that are outside their control, accompanying them down a path where they seek to deny themselves or 'mask' their experiences can set them up for later burnout (Wissell et al., 2022). Remember that masking is particularly complex for people with additional marginalisation by gender, race, sexuality or transgender, for example. You might need a step-wise and gentle approach to unpick issues and double check your understanding to illuminate context and impact for your individual coachee. The coaching topics also depend on what you have been contracted to undertake. Your role in coaching may be to help them to more effectively self-advocate for their rights at work, it might be to help them work through a difficulty they are having with their peers, or it might be to help them stay clear of ableist, neuronormative, racist, sexist, transsexist or homosexist structures in their work context. This will depend on potentially complex issues. Your role might also be to help them develop the confidence to leave their job, or to gain the confidence to apply for a promotion that they thought out of reach. Where and how best to focus coaching, balancing what you have been contracted to do and can reasonably deliver with the needs and wants of your coachee, takes experience. Supervision and anonymous case review sessions with your peers are invaluable as you develop this skill. As we work through the different topic domains, bear this nuance in mind.

Cognitive topics

Cognitive topics are to do with thinking, patterns of thought, memory and processing. Since many neurominorities are defined and diagnosed by such cognitive differences, it is no surprise that this is the most prevalent topic. The majority of neurodivergent coachees seek help with memory, attention and concentration, as well as dependent tasks such as time management, organising, planning and prioritising. These topics fundamentally rely on 'executive functioning', the part of the brain that includes 'working memory', which broadly means how much data we can 'hold' in mind at any one time before things start dropping off (Baddeley, 2007; Bailey, 2007). Executive functions determine our ability to filter our attention, to filter our thoughts and behaviour and think through several consequences/steps at once, which is necessary for planning and managing time.

There is significant evidence that these abilities are compromised for neurodivergent people of all types, as outlined in Chapter 2. Coachees are likely to have varied levels of ability, for example low underlying processing speed capacity, but may have developed strong scaffolding techniques with support from childhood. They could have reasonable capacity but no strategies, or anywhere between. Generally, by the time coachees get to coaching, they have exhausted their resources. It may be that their strategies take emotional and mental reserves, or additional time, and that they can no longer invest this – perhaps a life event has taken up more than usual, such as a sick relative, a divorce, a house move or a new child. It might be that a new manager, a new location, some new software or a sideways move/promotion has destabilised their rhythm. It is not unusual to hear that coachees have coped for years by taking work home, by coming into work earlier/staying later than colleagues. Tiredness, illness and change further compromises the executive functions, which means that life events can easily tip a neurodivergent person from 'coping' to 'struggling'. Working with cognitive topics for neurodivergent people is a triage process, where you start with the simple fixes before tackling more complex issues.

Degrees of distraction

The path of least resistance, and therefore step one on our triage, is making changes to environment and time. When and where do they think most clearly? You can ask for examples of when they worked at their best and work backwards to look for common themes in environment and context. Nancy, for example, works best when she is on the move. A train journey is brilliant for her concentration. Almuth, alternatively, relies on the large dual screens she has in her home office. This is where your coachee's industry and job role might be a factor – people working in busy, open plan offices, workshops, warehouses, wards, classrooms, shop floors may find that they have nowhere to hide and little flexibility! The level of background activity compromises your effectiveness at work when you have low working memory and high levels of alertness/sensory sensitivity. This can include noises, lighting levels, smells and temperature changes but also movement around you, which some people find disorientating. Perceiving stronger/larger amounts of sensory input compared to peers, paired with lower capacity for sorting information and making sense of it, are the fundamental differences that make it hard for neurodivergents to concentrate. This then leads to mistakes and low productivity. If this is true for your coachee, a first step triage process may be to help them think about opportunities to change where they work, the time of day and more. For example, if they can find a location in a corner, or with a wall to their back or side, they can reduce the 'degrees of distraction' from which activity arises. A corner is best, resulting in only 90 degrees of distraction, with a wall behind or to the side resulting in 180 degrees of distraction. If this is not possible, or insufficient, the next approach is to consider when they are doing which tasks. If they need to write reports, or client notes, or analyse data, it might be possible for them to move only for this task or use a quiet space. It might be possible for them to do some work remotely or to have flexible hours so that they have one or two hours in the morning/afternoon when the workspace is less busy. Remember that these ideas have to be coachee-led – you can't prescribe adjustments to environment and timing as a coach – but your coachee can ask their employer and you can help them articulate why any changes are important (see also Chapter 9 about healthy work).

Barriers to distraction

Once you have addressed any changes to environment and time, creating barriers to the distraction is next to discuss with your coachee – noise-cancelling headphones, noise-reduction ear buds, sunglasses and head wear. Notes on workstations indicating 'do not disturb' are useful, as are designated time periods where you don't have to answer the phone, for example, so that you can focus on a task in one hit. When you have minimal working memory, every distraction takes longer than peers to resettle. A moment's noise and a neurodivergent brain is asking: What was that? Oh nothing. Right, where was I? Which line? What was I doing? What's next? These micro distractions might not even register in the conscious mind, but they are devastating to accuracy and flow. Nancy cannot work without music to barrier odd noises that come and go. She always travels with ear buds. But the music has to be music she knows well, it can't trigger her dopamine responses by being too novel or interesting, it has to be background.

Remember Mo? They had the very spiky profile and were failing their professional doctorate? Well, Mo found it easiest to write up client notes sitting in a café, where there is lots of background bustle but none of it is related to them, so it doesn't distract them. If they were in an office and people were talking about things they were involved in, but with the same levels of noise, they would be completely distracted! Some people find the TV a great barrier, or talk radio, or pod casts. It's very personal. Even harsh office lighting can be barriered with a desk lamp to create a softer glow. You can barrier unwanted smells with a scented candle, temperature changes with a heater or a fan. Personalising the workspace isn't about fickle preferences, it serves very useful cognitive purposes. Simply understanding this can be liberating for coachees, who may be holding the thought that they are at fault for not trying hard enough or that they were 'being picky'. They may also have been told this by colleagues. Having the language to describe their experiences as cognitive and related to sensory sensitivity and/ or low capacity for managing interruptions can enable them to acquire the right adjustments. This alone can be empowering and life-changing for coachees.

Patterns of distraction

Finally, you can work with your coachee on their thought processes around cognitive skills like concentration, attention, memory and related tasks. For example, it is possible to improve your working memory capacity through increased self-awareness and practice of specific tasks in context (Bailey et al., 2014). This is called 'metacognition' – thinking about thinking (Flavell, 1979). You can become metacognitively aware of your attention and working memory patterns, for example, and change them. Working memory is not one thing – it is a combination of your sensory short-term memories (visual/spatial and verbal) as well as your attentional radar. To improve, you can either (a) visualise information, (b) verbalise information or (c) map out information using spatial anchors, for example tapping out a sequence on your head, shoulder, knee and toe. If you have a weakness in verbal processing, like many dyslexics, a visual strategy might work. If you have a weakness in spatial processing, like many dyspraxics, a verbal strategy might work. If your weakness is controlling your attentional radar, like many ADHDers, then a double strategy of verbal and spatial, or visual and spatial, might help hold your concentration. You can establish this by asking them how they concentrate at their best – what information do they find easier to retain, and how do they do it? They can practise and spend time between sessions figuring out what works best. Developing metacognition is an effective strategy for neurodivergent thinkers when it comes to working memory (Doyle et al., 2022; Stoeger & Ziegler, 2008) and it is certainly worth exploring when coaching.

Translating cognitive skills into context

Based on a metacognitive exploration it is possible to devise specific, targeted strategies for dependent tasks such as time management, organising etc. Again, and always, start by asking your coachee when they do this well. What's an example of a time they organised something really well, or had a week where their time management was more accurate? What were the conditions of this? Where were they? What were they doing? Which tools did they use? How does this compare to times when they have felt challenged? What are the patterns in the ideal scenario compared with the challenging scenarios. Pay attention to their environmental descriptions, the actual behaviours and sensory experiences, any skills, or tools they relied on, their values about what was happening and their sense of self-belief and wider purpose. Then help coachees transfer any learning to their work context.

Mo had specific difficulty when it came to prioritising their tasks. They frequently felt completely overwhelmed and didn't know where to start because they couldn't 'hold' all the items and stages in one go. They had tried writing lists, but they couldn't work out where to start. Nancy asked Mo if there was anything that they organised well, that they enjoyed organising. Mo responded that they were an excellent cook and loved to cook for large groups of friends when they came over. They became quite animated at this tale, relaying that they would always provide starters and nibbly bits to keep people going while they prepared a main meal. Nancy asked Mo how they did it. Mo explained that they would take all the possible ingredients out and place them all on the kitchen side. When they could see them all once, they would begin putting them in different groups and imagining the flavour combinations. Nancy and Mo then devised a planning and organising strategy that involved sticky notes rather than writing a list. Mo could lay out all the tasks in one place and then move them around until the order became clear. This worked much better for Mo and gave them a clear guide of what to do when they felt overwhelmed.

Another of Nancy's coachees, Audrey, worked as an administrator in a health care setting. Audrey was sure that she had no memory skills at all. She was struggling to learn to use assistive technology and remember instructions from her boss. She expressed that she couldn't think of a time when her memory had worked well. However, at the end of the session, she and Nancy were informally chatting about clothes and Audrey was telling her about a Christmas jumper she had seen recently that they would both like. Nancy asked some questions: "Where was it in the shop? Whereabouts?", "Oh at the back of the store". "Was it on a high hanger or a low one?", "Oh, a low one, to one side of the fitting room, near the tills". Nancy noticed that as Audrey was describing she was using her hands to indicate the directions. Audrey's memory worked very well, for spatial information. Audrey confirmed that this was true and that she rarely got lost if she had been somewhere once, and that if she used equipment once she could usually do it again. She remembered her pin numbers by mentally tapping them out on the phone. So, she DID have a memory, it was just based on where things were and how they moved, rather than verbal detail, colour or numbers. This led to Audrey asking her technology trainer to let her 'drive' the equipment rather than telling her or showing her, and when she received instructions, she would tap each one on her fingers. She could do up to four instructions at a time like this which was a great improvement on previous sessions where she could only handle two stages at a time before she forgot all the details.

Nancy worked with Wes from his time unemployed through to successfully sustaining employment. Wes worked in a large manufacturing environment; he struggled working out how long things would take. When talking to him about how he managed his tasks best, he quickly identified that he preferred to do one thing at a time. He became overwhelmed when trying to think about them all at once – Mo's strategy would have been awful for him. His boss wanted him to have a weekly meeting in which they prepared a list of all the tasks Wes had to do in the following week and reviewed all the tasks Wes had done in the week prior. Wes found preparing for this hard work, even when they compromised on a bullet point list, taking no more than one side of A4 as notes. Wes's manager helped him work through the list step by step to make sure the workload was feasible for the week. After a coaching session exploring Wes's preference for one thing at a time, he hit upon a fabulous idea. He transferred each of the tasks onto a filing card, in a stack. Each day at work, he took the top card and worked through that task until it was complete, and then took the next one from the stack. At the end of the week, he had the completed tasks in a stack to talk through, and they would write the next week's stack together. His manager agreed that if he gave Wes additional tasks, he would also review the stack and place it in the appropriate place for the week.

We hope from these examples you can see that cognitive topics can be addressed creatively through various strategies and exercises. It is important to hold back your own lived experience and make space for your coachee to explore their own preferences as you cannot assume what works for you works for others. Metacognition is the key here. Once a coachee understands their sensory processing patterns, their environmental/behavioural patterns of distraction, they will be able to unlock their own strategies going forward. It is a beautiful thing to watch! Your role is to ask questions and help structure their environment and process to their thinking style, not to change the way they think or advise them to do what you do. Indeed, even if you are a well-matched neurotype, by telling them what to do you are deviating from good coaching psychology practice, as the coachee's self-discovery is confidence building. You don't want them to feel dependent on you but empowered by you.

Emotional topics

Emotional topics are to do with managing unwanted or unpleasant feelings, communicating feelings and interrupting patterns of feeling, such as catastrophising, hostile attribution bias and rejection sensitive dysphoria (Sun et al., 2018). Neurodivergent people are more vulnerable to dysphoria, which is literally translated from the Greek as 'hard to bear', which may be part of the neurotype (as in Bipolar Disorder) or it may be the result of years of exclusion. Either way, in coaching you are going to come across people who have outcomes concerning feeling less stressed and overwhelmed, more confident and relaxed as well as needing strategies for handling strong emotions such as fear, anger and jealousy. Further to note, many autists experience 'alexythmia', which is the inability to name or recognise emotions, so describing how they feel is not easy (Kinnaird et al., 2019). "How do you feel about that?" is possibly not a question that will resonate during coaching. Let's start with addressing everyday stresses, negative spirals, overwhelms and self-care. Chapter 10 unpacks a lot more of the psychology of wellbeing coaching, but this chapter gets us started on the typical emotional issues that crop up in neurodiversity coaching.

Everyday stress

Stress isn't, in and of itself, necessarily a bad thing. In fact, occupational psychology research has shown that as stress goes up, so does performance until we hit a peak point, and then the reverse is true: this makes a major difference to how people cope (Anderson, 1976). The critical issue here is to establish where that point is for each individual, and to know when they are approaching that point. "We're all finding it stressful", announces a colleague to a neurodivergent person during a period of change. Yes, this may be true, but remember the cognitive differences. When a neurodivergent person is already undertaking additional cognitive tasks including those described above – translating verbal instructions into visuals, re-mapping meeting notes to their own coding system, using assistive technologies – they have already used up cognitive resources, which makes them more vulnerable. Therefore, you might find that your coachees are hitting burnout points quicker than they expect or quicker than their colleagues. This is not because they are 'sensitive', it is because they are experiencing more intensity in their senses. Conversely, some might work better in a stressful environment because of the noradrenaline 'sweet spot', but they may need to be reminded to take breaks so that they don't crash.

A buffer to stress is the extent of control and resources that an individual can levy, as demonstrated by the Job Demands/Resources Model (Demerouti et al., 2001; more on this in Chapters 9 and 10). This means, simply, that people can handle job demands better if they feel they have more control and ability to add resources. This is where coaching comes in. You can work with your coachee to identify the areas that they can control and work specifically on these. This could be about using their paid leave, where they sit, what time of day they choose to do their most difficult tasks, having an awkward conversation to clear up something that is troubling them. You can also help them find the words to request more resources or help them make an inventory of possible resources. Asking for help can take courage, and intersectional marginalisation might make this even more difficult. Some people feel that asking is failing and that they don't want to cause 'trouble' by asking for different things than their colleagues. They might be working over and above to prove their worth, to make up for the perceived 'trouble' they have already caused. These emotional nuances add to everyday stress. Understanding that their spiky profile has put them at a disadvantage might help them to reframe 'help' as 'fair'; if they are starting two steps behind, asking for a small bridge seems reasonable. As for cognitive diversity, our attempts to understanding WHY they might experience stress in a different way is important. Do not underestimate how much time neurodivergent people spend feeling guilty or ashamed of their needs – gaining self-knowledge and reflection on cognitive differences is a fantastic coaching outcome to help coachees gain agency.

Negative spirals

A short email, perhaps written while commuting to work, could be interpreted as blunt or rude, an innocent reminder to complete a task could be interpreted as a passive aggressive insult for not having done it already. This goes both ways. Damian Milton, an autistic sociologist called this the 'double empathy problem' (Milton, 2012). Many neurodivergent people have different communication styles: high levels of precision, which some find pedantic; a hyper-focus on goals, which some may find obsessive or rushed; a tendency to avoid writing, which some may find lacking in diligence. Milton proposes that the presumptive position of the neurotypical norm – that the neurodivergent person should adapt and change to fit in – is indicative of a lack of empathy on the part of the neurotypical, whereas neurodivergent people are often characterised as lacking in empathy as part of the pathology. These misunderstandings flip back and forth from neurotypical to the neurodivergent but also between the neurominorities. A dyspraxic who thinks an ADHD lack of attention to typos in emails is deliberately discourteous, an ADHDer who finds the autistic need to stick to a routine oppressive and inflexible, an autist who finds a dyslexic tangent in the middle of a meeting agenda disruptive.

Fear and anxiety are part of human experience as a cue about when we might be in trouble and need to fight or flee. However, in minority neurotypes such feelings can sometimes cause difficulties in correctly interpreting the behaviour and intention of colleagues, particularly where there's a history of being misunderstood and ostracised. Some neurodivergent people, and we stress heavily not all, have a fine trigger for flipping into defence mode. This can result in negative emotional spirals, interpreting their colleagues as negative. This is called 'hostile attribution bias'. For an overview, see Klein Tuente et al. (2019). Once a misinterpretation of intention spiral has started between colleagues, all behaviour and communication can be framed through a negative lens, which destroys working relationships and team spirit. It is really exceedingly difficult and the cause of much distress to neurodivergent people who, like all humans, by and large mean well and don't deliberately cause harm.

Hostile attribution bias is made worse by rejection sensitive dysphoria (Normansell & Wisco, 2017), which is an intense reaction to perceived rejection, in which even a small request to improve or change something is perceived as a threat, leading to intense emotions. Even minor perceived rejections or well meant corrections can lead to intense experience of pressure, when paired with existing feeling of shame and seeing oneself as inadequate. In coaching neurodivergent people, you will come across these experiences. You can gently try to reframe with your coachee — "what did you see or hear that let you know your boss was trying to make you look bad in front of the team? Could there have been a different motivation for asking you to share your figures?" Beware of jumping to conclusions — the boss is ALWAYS bad, the colleagues are ALL out to get them — there are rarely true villains in life and, while bullying and ostracism happens, so does hostile attribution bias. Your job isn't to define their experience, it is to help them understand patterns in their thought and experiences, and develop self-knowledge. If the situation is dire, whether that be due to their actual experience of discrimination or their misinterpretation of it, and if gentle reframing makes no difference over several sessions, it is clear that relationships have broken down. In this situation, a good coaching outcome is that the individual moves on. It is perfectly valid to coach towards an exit – if that exit is elegant, free of distress, and avoids burning bridges, it can be seen as a success.

Overwhelm/shutdown/meltdown

These are three different words for similar things – a welling up of sensory perception, emotion and fight/flight/freeze activation to the point where an individual is unable to communicate or can only communicate with aggression (Ryan, 2010). We use the term 'overwhelm' to refer to the experience of the individual rather than our judgement of their actions. Further, some neurominorities have suggested that the term 'meltdown' has become a pejorative word, associated with spoilt children rather than sensory/emotional crisis. Overwhelms are incredibly frightening for the individual experiencing them, but can also be destabilising for those witnessing them. They might include shouting, saying hurtful things to colleagues, abruptly leaving a room or remote meetings without warning. They can happen suddenly, when an individual has reached the end of their coping mechanisms for stressors that are both obvious and not obvious, work-related and personal. They represent a tipping point. Neurominorities experience a number of stressors that neurotypicals may not, such as sensory sensitivity, battling with assistive technology, inability to cognitively think through more than one or two consequences at once, intensity of neurotransmitters. Whilst the overwhelm event may look like an irrational overreaction from the outside, it will make sense from the inside, or be caused by biological processes which are not in the persons control.

If you have a coachee who experiences overwhelm at work, you also have a coachee who is potentially having relationship difficulties at work. Addressing them follows three main stages: prevent, mitigate and recover. Prevent is the most helpful, and it should be possible to minimise overwhelms at work by carefully unpicking what happens beforehand. Work systematically through sensory/environmental triggers, time of day triggers, type of event triggers (e.g. criticism or someone failing to deliver as promised), health and personal triggers etc. Although beware, Nancy once worked with someone who was triggered by the word trigger! Try to identify the point where the coachee still has control. Nancy's coachee, Wes, discovered during his coaching that before an overwhelm he would start tapping his foot, knee or hand. He learned to recognise this as a precursor and was then able to take steps to avoid the overwhelm point. By negotiating with his manager, he began taking a short walk outside as soon as this happened and coming back via the break room for a drink of water. This interrupted the escalating pattern long enough to avoid an overwhelm, and to give Wes enough resource to handle a conversation about various stressors that needed to be mitigated.

Once an overwhelm has started, it can be mitigated with strategies to support the individual. They may want to have a conversation in advance, with colleagues or their boss, about how to handle it. For example, if you see me put my hood up and look down, sitting motionless, please leave me alone for at least an hour, or until I come back to you. Would I be able to use the break room or the meeting room for half an hour to reduce my sensory input until I am calm again? Bring me some water or my headphones if you want to offer support. Knowing what to do can help colleagues feel less concerned about overwhelms. Recovering from overwhelms is tricky if your coachee is verbally expressive during the event. You may need to plan conversations with colleagues with your coachee. Did they say anything they regret, which isn't true? This needs to be communicated. Did they say anything that was true but in a hurtful style? Again, this needs to be communicated. While it can be excruciating to learn how to handle conversations like this, once mastered they can really build confidence and empathy. Understanding what caused the overwhelm and working with those colleagues to help avoid them in future is helpful. Many neurodivergent people live in fear of an overwhelm that they can't control. Knowing exactly how to handle it and recover without damage to relationships can reduce anxiety across the board. It is important, as a coach, not to assume that your coachee's colleagues are all neurotypical, or without their own protected characteristics, and therefore that they should simply cope with or accommodate an overwhelm – it may be more complex and need a balance of adjustments in both directions.

Using spoon theory as a metaphor in coaching

A useful metaphor is 'spoon theory', coined by a woman with chronic fatigue syndrome (Miserando, 2018). Miserando proposed that, in each day, you have a limited number of 'spoonfuls' of energy. These can be used just getting dressed or commuting to work. Once you are out of spoons, you simply cannot function until you have spent time 're-spooning'. Your coachees may find it useful to list which activities take spoons, and which activities give spoons. Being able to say "I am out of spoons" is also a useful short cut for communicating with colleagues when you simply have no more capacity, as is "how can I support you to re-spoon?" Similarly, some coachees may benefit from thinking about their 'social battery' – that is, the amount of energy they have for social events. Batteries drain and can be recharged. These sorts of shortcuts in language are immensely helpful for people who struggle to communicate their emotions.

Referring on

Sometimes the intensity of emotion and overwhelms become beyond the scope of coaching. It is wise and sensible to have a list of counselling, clinical or medical practitioners to whom you can refer people who do not find improvement through coaching. Don't get caught trying to resolve a lifetime of trauma-related emotional outbursts in a few workplace coaching sessions, it won't help you or your coachees. It's also important to note that trauma responses come in many shapes and sizes, they may involve withdrawal, anger, projection, transference, defensiveness, avoidance, pretence, masking, but also perfectionism, setting unrealistic standards and more. More on some of these dynamics in Chapters 6 and 9. The important thing to note is that stress responses have a huge spectrum and whilst some, such as procrastination and communication avoidance, are within the remit of coaching, repeated overwhelm events causing personal damage to others, or indeed you, are not. If you are not sure, take your concern to supervision.

Behavioural topics

There are behaviours our coachees can control that make the everyday experience of neurodiversity more manageable. Some of these have been outlined above, in response to cognitive and emotional difficulties. Others are more general and work to relieve pressure on everyday activities and promote wellbeing. These include strategies, self-care and work–life boundaries.

Strategies

Strategies can be a bit like 'life-hacking', which basically means finding short cuts in everyday behaviour to avoid forgetting things, doing boring admin or making more efficiencies. For neurodivergent people, these can reduce overwhelm, which is essential for feeling calm and in control of workload. Never underestimate the time and emotional/cognitive reserves expended by a neurodivergent person on admin! Filling in forms, remembering actions and dates, planning the transporting of equipment from A to B, losing things generally. Nancy recently gave 11 different professional talks in four days, in three different UK cities – Edinburgh, Birmingham and London. She found the talks easy, but she left her suitcase on a train and spent hours retrieving it, got held in airport security for one and a half hours because her prescription to prove necessity for liquid medication was on her phone, which had run out of battery because she hadn't planned far enough ahead. She was 20 minutes late for one of the talks (online from her hotel room) because she had the wrong time zone on her diary and had missed the email with the right one, sent by the client. This is typical for ADHD: most people would be intimidated by the talks – Nancy was intimidated by the travel and logistics. Neurotypicals consistently underestimate the severity of this, the anxiety it causes, because they think of it as the 'easy stuff'. If you are a neurotypical coach, please really take a moment to appreciate that disorganisation equals high anxiety. It limits us. Sometimes we avoid taking opportunities because we are worried about the logistics. Other times, we make plans, but arrive late and dishevelled. A useful coaching activity is to identify the most common logistical and administrative annoyances that your coachees experience and find behavioural 'hacks' for them.

Mo found that they were continually losing things. Nancy suggested they try the intuitive filing strategy – every time they lost something (a folder on their PC, their keys, their sunglasses, the kitchen scissors) they noted where they looked for it first and then made that the designated space. Using their 'first look' intuition to guide their organisation, rather than where they 'thought it should live', they gradually rearranged their whole house and office! This included having more than one of some things – for example a towel for the dog was needed in the car and the hallway – so two dog towels were needed. This small change reduced the cognitive load of having to remember where the towel was in either situation in which it was needed, which also greatly reduced anxiety.

Wes had to complete a short inventory form after each shift. He found that this was very demanding on his concentration in a busy space and he would make errors when completing it on the factory floor. Nancy worked with him to develop two strategies based on his experiences: first, he would walk outside, stand still and look at the sky for a count of 10 to 20 before starting, and second, he used a piece of brightly coloured card as a ruler on the page to take each line at a time and hide the lines below. The walk was an anchor to signal that he could keep his eyes and body still after a long shift handling moving equipment. The card stopped his eyes from skipping on before they had taken in the detail.

Audrey used to find that she would always remember things she had forgotten to do whilst she was busy doing other, unrelated things, such as walking her dog, cooking her dinner or driving down the road. She would immediately become stressed and anxious, worried that she would forget them again and let her team down. To 'life hack' this problem, Nancy suggested that she ask her friends and family what they do about this. One of her friends used a memory 'bucket' – a WhatsApp conversation between his work phone and his personal phone through which he would send himself messages to pick up when he was in a different headspace and had time to plan. Audrey found that this simple action enabled her to hold onto those random thoughts and send them where they could be dealt with, which also freed up her mind to relax and enjoy her personal time. She also realised that part of the problem was a lack of planning time and down time in her life more generally. When she saw a space in her diary, she would automatically try and fill it. Since it was the space that seemed to trigger the adding of appointments and plans, Nancy asked her what would happen if she filled the spaces with a note to plan and have downtime? She tried it, highlighting them in yellow with the abbreviation 'KF' – keep free! This behavioural change added much needed calm focus time to Audrey's weekly timetable, and she started to feel much more in control.

You can set your coachee a task of searching online for life hacks, talking to others, or investigating the supports via assistive technology. Many standard software programs now come with the ability to delay emails, set reminders, read back documents, record voices and more. This is a useful and productive way to reduce the cognitive demands on a neurodivergent coachee.

Self-care

We've mentioned above a tendency for neurodivergent, marginalised people, to sometimes overwork, due to a misplaced sense of 'compensating' for being difficult, annoying, rude etc. Hand-in-hand with this goes a tendency to put others' needs first and neglect self-care. However, self-care is essential for sensitive brains! As discussed in Chapter 2, it is NOT your job to give nutrition, exercise or medical advice unless you are qualified, and you have been contracted to do so. However, it is a viable coaching activity to reflect on self-care and enquire as to the habits that your coachee finds restorative. Simply asking the question and making space for reflection can spark change and recognition of unhealthy patterns. As with spoon theory, coachees need to know how to re-spoon, what they can do for themselves to add energy back into their resource pool. There is a lot more on this in our dedicated wellbeing chapter (Chapter 10) later in this book.

Conclusion

You might find yourself working with coachees whose jobs are at risk if they don't improve. This can be stressful and emotional for them and you. It is valid to support these coachees towards a change of job rather than compliance with an unsuitable one, if you and they agree this is the case. It is also valid to refer them to seek support from Human Resources or legal advice if you think there is a serious issue. However, a major learning from this chapter should be staying within the boundaries of what can reasonably change as the result of coaching. Despite one of Nancy's coachee's wishes, coaching is not a magic wand and you won't be able to 'fix' someone. If this is what you are thinking, stop now! Coaching helps us travel towards our best selves, our goals and ambitions. It brings clarity and efficiency; it doesn't change who we are. There are lots of creative ways to support the unique patterns of cognition, emotion and behaviour that we see in neurominorities, plenty of great life hacks and sometimes just the reflection time itself provides enough validation for the coachee to create change.

Reflective questions

Consider the following questions as reflection on this chapter and take some time to jot down your answers:

- How do you relate to the cognitive difficulties described in this chapter? For example, have you noticed difficulties and strengths in remembering things, or concentration? Which environments are most conducive for you? What do your observations mean for how you coach?
- How good are you at time management and planning? How do you do it? Do you have colleagues or friends that have different

strategies to you? Spend some time asking people how they use their diaries, if they have reminders, whiteboards, phone-based strategies etc. What insights have you gleaned to inform coaching?
- How do you handle unwanted and/or intense emotions in yourself and in your coachees?
- What is your self-care routine? What types of activity soothe you and re-spoon your energy levels? Do you know people who are very different from you? What do they do?
- What are your favourite life-hacks? Can you ask this question to three friends or colleagues and get a good list going that you can share with coachees?
- Have you ever felt the need to change yourself to fit it? What was/ is it like?

References

Anderson, C. R. (1976). Coping behaviors as intervening mechanisms in the inverted-U stress–performance relationship. *Journal of Applied Psychology, 61*(1), 30–34. https://doi.org/10.1037/0021-9010.61.1.30

Baddeley, A. (2007). *Working memory, thought, and action.* Oxford University Press.

Bailey, C. E. (2007). Cognitive accuracy and intelligent executive function in the brain and in business. *Annals of the New York Academy of Sciences, 1118*, 122–141. https://doi.org/10.1196/annals.1412.011

Bailey, H. R., Dunlosky, J., & Hertzog, C. (2014). Does strategy training reduce age-related deficits in working memory? *Gerontology, 60*(4), 346–356. https://doi.org/10.1159/000356699

Demerouti, E., Bakker, A. B., Nachreiner, F., & Schaufeli, W. B. (2001). The job demands–resources model of burnout. *Journal of Applied Psychology, 86*(3), 499–512. https://doi.org/10.1108/02683940710733115

Doyle, N., & Bradley, E. (2022). Disability coaching during a pandemic. *Journal of Work-Applied Management, 15*(1), 135–147. https://doi.org/10.1108/JWAM-07-2022-0042

Doyle, N., & McDowall, A. (2015). Is coaching an effective adjustment for dyslexic adults? *Coaching: An International Journal of Theory and Practice, 8*(2), 154–168. https://doi.org/10.1080/17521882.2015.1065894

Doyle, N., & McDowall, A. (2019). Context matters: A systematic review of coaching as a disability accommodation. *PLoS ONE, 14*(8), 1–30. https://doi.org/10.1371/journal.pone.0199408

Doyle, N. E., McDowall, A., Randall, R., & Knight, K. (2022). Does it work? Using a meta-impact score to examine global effects in quasi-experimental intervention studies. *PLoS ONE, 17*(3), 1–21. https://doi.org/10.1371/journal.pone.0265312

Flavell, J. H. (1979). Metacognition and cognitive monitoring: A new area of cognitive-developmental inquiry. *American Psychologist,* 34(10), 906–911.

Jones, R. J., Woods, S. A., & Guillaume, Y. R. F. (2016). The effectiveness of workplace coaching: A meta-analysis of learning and performance outcomes from coaching. *Journal of Occupational and Organizational Psychology, 89*(2), 249–277. https://doi.org/10.1111/joop.12119

Kinnaird, E., Stewart, C., & Tchanturia, K. (2019). Investigating alexithymia in autism: A systematic review and meta-analysis. *European Psychiatry, 55*, 80–89. https://doi.org/10.1016/j.eurpsy.2018.09.004

Klein Tuente, S., Bogaerts, S., & Veling, W. (2019). Hostile attribution bias and aggression in adults—A systematic review. *Aggression and Violent Behavior, 46*, 66–81. https://doi.org/10.1016/j.avb.2019.01.009

Lauder, K., McDowall, A., & Tenenbaum, H. R. (2022). A systematic review of interventions to support adults with ADHD at work—Implications from the paucity of context-specific research for theory and practice. *Frontiers in Psychology, 13*, 893469. https://doi.org/10.3389/fpsyg.2022.893469

Milton, D. (2012). On the ontological status of autism: The "double empathy problem." *Disability & Society, 27*(6), 883–887. https://doi.org/10.1080/09687599.2012.710008.

Miserando, C. (2018). The spoon theory. In L. J. Davis (Ed.), *Beginning with disability* (1st ed., p. 5). Routledge. https://doi.org/10.4324/9781315453217

Normansell, K. M., & Wisco, B. E. (2017). Negative interpretation bias as a mechanism of the relationship between rejection sensitivity and depressive symptoms. *Cognition and Emotion, 31*(5), 950–962. https://doi.org/10.1080/02699931.2016.1185395

Ryan, S. (2010). Meltdowns, surveillance and managing emotions: Going out with children with autism. *Healthplace, 16*(5), 868–875.

Stoeger, H., & Ziegler, A. (2008). Evaluation of a classroom based training to improve self-regulation in time management tasks during homework activities with fourth graders. *Metacognition and Learning, 3*(3), 207–230. https://doi.org/10.1007/s11409-008-9027-z

Sun, J., Zhuang, K., Li, H., Wei, D., Zhang, Q., & Qiu, J. (2018). Perceiving rejection by others: Relationship between rejection sensitivity and the spontaneous neuronal activity of the brain. *Social Neuroscience, 13*(4), 429–438. https://doi.org/10.1080/17470919.2017.1340335

Wissell, S., Karimi, L., Serry, T., Furlong, L., & Hudson, J. (2022). "You don't look dyslexic": Using the job demands—resource model of burnout to explore employment experiences of Australian adults with dyslexia. *International Journal of Environmental Research and Public Health*, *19*(17), 10719. https://doi.org/10.3390/ijerph191710719

Chapter 4

Harnessing neurodivergent potential in coaching

Almuth McDowall and Nancy Doyle

Introduction

Having outlined the historical trajectory of neurodiversity and typical topics in coaching, we now turn to how such challenges can be transformed into resources for growth to realise coachees' strengths, values, hopes and ambitions. We outline the greatest joys and challenges in neurodiversity coaching as reported by coaches to provide context. This sets the scene for outlining typical neurodivergent strengths and how to harness these. We introduce specific techniques for eliciting and focusing on strengths with coachees, such as applied cognitive task analysis (ACTA), challenge reframing and modelling mastery. Last but not least, we turn to neurodivergent careers and helping coachees to fulfil ambitions for promotion, advancement and leadership.

As all humans have worth, value and strengths we do not ascribe to the 'high functioning/low functioning' dichotomies as we concur with various neurodivergent authors that such terminology is pejorative and limited (Alvares et al., 2019; Gregg et al., 2007). Yet we recognise that there are various levels of need and that not all neurodivergent people want or are able to be entrepreneurs, superstars or inventors. We frame positive outcomes for coachees as 'best fit' – when people are living and working at their best, in a context that suits them with appropriate levels of social support and interaction. Coaching isn't about achieving a normative top result, it's about fulfilling personal potential. Let's look at what happens in neurodiversity coaching.

DOI: 10.4324/9781003368274-5

Nancy surveyed a group of 42 coaches who work for her social enterprise, Genius Within. They said that the five biggest challenges of working with neurodivergent coachees are:

- Coachees wandering off track/topic in sessions.
- Organising the logistics and timings of the actual sessions.
- Managing the boundaries between coaching and therapy.
- Balancing what is best for the coachee with what you have been contracted to deliver.
- Knowing that the stakes are high and that people may lose their job if coaching doesn't work.

It is interesting that issues to do with keeping track and organisation feature highly; this aligns with our previous observation that cognitive and organisation issues often need to be addressed first. Our professional experience taught us that a starting point is often some immediate relief of the cognitive and wellbeing issues before turning to strengths in detail and depth.

We often think of neurodiversity as a technicolour rainbow that offers many rewards and makes our lives brighter. Indeed, the coaches who Nancy surveyed said that the five greatest joys of working with neurodivergent coachees are:

- Affirming coachees authentic selves.
- The 'aha' moments when coachees realise they are unique and valuable.
- Appreciating human difference in all its beauty.
- Seeing coachees achieve effective self-organisation as a baseline for success.
- Witnessing flourishing and flow.

This list illustrates beautifully what neurodiversity coaching brings – the affirming 'aha' moments are like switching on the technicolour rainbow and feeling the glow. Of course, when coachees are concerned about their job, or anxious about organising the sessions themselves, an initial focus on ability and talent may not be possible or appropriate. However, once you have addressed these pressing issues, you can focus on building confidence and orientating your coachees to their talents.

Strengths associated with neurodivergence

In the following section, we outline strengths associated with different neurotypes that, as we outlined before, can have an evolutionary advantage (Armstrong, 2010). We have these caveats: (1) many people have more than one neurotype and/or are misdiagnosed so these observations are broad categories that can't be interpreted at the individual level; (2) science has devoted much attention to the challenges of neurodivergence so we might not have good evidence for the strengths because no one has yet asked the right questions and; (3) we find the language in some original studies hard to digest – that which talks about 'suffering' from conditions, for example. However our recent research (McDowall et al., 2023) found that both the employers and the employees that we surveyed held consistent opinions of neurodivergent strengths at work.

ADHD

ADHD is associated with creativity as ADHDers perform better than non-ADHDers on standardised creativity tests and in research conditions (White & Shah, 2006) have more creative output in real world measures, such as the Arts, Music, Dance, Architecture, Writing, Humour, Invention, Science, Theatre and Culinary Arts (White & Shah, 2011). This is thought to be a result of the two styles in which the ADHD brain works. Style 1 is with attention diffused and dispersed, picking up random information and signals from the environment; Style 2 is with attention hyperfocused on a single, interesting goal (Boot et al., 2020). These alternating styles are thought to be essential to creative acts, which we define as the process of coming up with new or unusual ideas.

Looking at psychological resources, Newark et al. (2016) compared ADHDers to a control group and, while they found lower self-esteem, self-efficacy, and evidence for some reduced resources, they also found some resources that were comparatively strong in this group. The logic follows that any treatment or coaching should focus on building and harnessing such resources, for example strengthening people's relationships and bonds with others in and outside work could enhance self-esteem and courage, which in turn then foster positive self-beliefs. Focusing on what works and 're-spooning' helps coachees break out of negative cycles of self-appraisal and learn positive strategies for dealing with any difficulties.

Given overly deficit-focused language about neurodiversity in health care, it is perhaps not surprising that a Dutch study demonstrates that ADHDers find neurodiversity-affirming coaching more helpful than publicly provided mental health care even if they have to self-fund (Schrevel et al., 2016). ADHDers found that being accepted as a unique person and the personal relationship with the coach made all the difference. The study participants said that their self-insight increased noticeably during coaching, and that they were better able to craft solutions rather than becoming stuck on problems.

Autism

Reported strengths of Autists focus on capabilities in finding patterns, attention to detail, as well as sensory sensitivity (Baron-Cohen et al., 2009). An affirming book by Happe & Frith (2010) provides a deep dive into diverse autism strengths and talents and documents how the natural tendency for the autistic mind to seek order, routine and systems links to talents for music, art, language, mechanics or maths. The sensory sensitivity can lead to talents in culinary arts, music, art, forensic science – anything that is dependent on a high level of sensory acuity. Creativity is also associated with autism because autists tend to notice things in more detail than non-autists and gain enhanced insight.

There is some empirical support for the strengths autistic people bring to work. These include cognitive abilities such as attention to detail and tolerance for repetitive tasks, and highly specific personal interests. But they might also be less flexible and hypersensitive (see

Bury et al., 2020, for a recent overview). Yet, we are lacking concrete research from a work context. This is because a simple distinction between strengths and challenges can be misleading. For example, an exceptional focus on detail might be advantageous in a job that requires such skills – such as someone working in a compliance or contract management context – but might necessitate support in certain circumstances, such as there is time pressure to get an output delivered or task finished. Coaching is an ideal forum for coachees to practise self-observational skills and put strategies into place. A good coaching strategy is to facilitate neurodivergent coachees who are very detail-focused to work backwards rather than forwards. For any relevant coaching activity, ask the coachee first what the goals and objectives are for a work task, and reference these clearly. Then make a timeline and work backwards. Detailed focus often leads us to underestimate how long activities take, and working backwards counteracts this tendency.

Dyslexia, dyscalculia, dyspraxia and dysgraphia

Dyslexia has been referenced for strengths in visual abilities and creativity and a few meta-studies have been published which try to unpick how this works, yet these have found it difficult to pinpoint. Erbeli et al. (2022) conducted a meta-analysis of 20 studies and did not find an overall difference between dyslexic and non-dyslexic people, but they highlighted two trends: (1) adult dyslexics score more highly on creativity and visual skill compared with adolescent dyslexics and; (2) there is considerable variability between dyslexic thinkers. Male dyslexics scored lower than females on average in these areas. They also noted it was very hard to get good data, given than many primary studies didn't screen for co-occurring differences. Rajabpour Azizi et al. (2021) found that dyslexics scored better on holistic, big picture visual reasoning rather than all visual talent, which would explain why there are confusing results. Majeed et al. (2021) in their meta-study also found no differences on various measures of creativity, other than by age – there were no differences for children, only for adults. The authors saw this as support for the 'early choice hypothesis' that dyslexic people are more likely to use and practise non-typical methods to process information from childhood. Well, we might want to turn this argument on its head. If all children were offered more opportunity to learn creatively, then everyone could benefit from creating and nurturing these strengths at an earlier age!

What learning can we transfer from these studies for practising neurodiversity coaching? We learn that dyslexic coachees may well have visual and creative talent, but that they grow into such talents rather than always being able to 'perform' for test purposes. Visual talent is not one entity; there are different types of visual thinking. For example, thinking that is aligned with movement and mentally rotating shapes, detailed perception of fixed images, and visual mapping, where we connect ideas and processes in diagrammatic style. Struggling with one of these does not mean struggling with all of these. Our job in coaching is to facilitate dyslexic coachees to work out what style of visual thinking and/or creativity suits them best and how they can work with it. We can note the remarkable resilience of dyslexic people, developing compensatory strengths and talents, having been schooled in a system that was not designed for them.

Even less is known about the strengths for dysgraphia, dyspraxia and dyscalculia, and what there is tends to be about relative strengths in people, i.e. the spikes and troughs on their spiky profile (Sewell, 2022). We typically find peaks for verbal reasoning (Grant, 2009) but these have not been explored in the scientific literature, and are certainly not context-specific at work. There are a lot of master's and doctoral research projects out there waiting for those who want to develop our knowledge of neurodivergent talent beyond ADHD and autism. The four Dys are relatively unexplored territory from a neurodiversity-affirming perspective.

Other neurominorities

Tourette's syndrome is associated with higher levels of creativity and humour (Sacks, 1992) and this is thought to be connected to increased dopamine levels (Dina et al., 2017), though there is very limited research to explore this further. A report by McKinsey highlighted that people with Down syndrome are more reliable and consistent at work, as well as direct communicators, which reduces conflict (Assis et al., 2014). Anxiety has been shown to be an essential part of the creative process in the arts, but also in science, technology, engineering and maths (Daker et al., 2020).

Neurodivergent strengths at work

Given the very limited evidence on neurodivergent strengths and challenges at work more broadly, either condition-specific or across conditions, we published a practitioner report based on the first ever survey of neurodiversity practice in the UK (McDowall et al., 2023), where we surveyed employees and employers. We presented employees with a list of likely strengths, which were drawn from research on specific conditions (more on this later) and on our own observations from coaching and working with neurodivergent groups. We asked workers which of the following strengths they had noticed in themselves, which we outline here, ordered in ascending sequence (numbers rounded to next decimal):

1. Creativity   81%
2. Hyperfocus   79%
3. Innovative thinking   76%
4. Detail processing   70%
5. Authenticity   65%
6. Visual reasoning   59%
7. Long-term memory   53%
8. Entrepreneurialism   48%
9. Verbal comprehension   44%
10. Cognitive control   38%
11. Visual-spatial skills 33%
12. Numeracy   22%
13. Short-term memory   13%

We had an overrepresentation of autistic people and ADHDers in our sample, so we issue a caution not to overinterpret, although we double checked that there was no statistically significant difference between conditions. Psychologists will have differing views whether such strengths are innate and develop naturally as would be predicted by the neurodiversity paradigm, or whether they are compensatory and develop as a result of resilience and practice. However, this is not a question for coaching, where we simply need to identify strengths and use these to build mastery.

In all, what we document here about strengths tells us that neurodivergent workers will be innovative thinkers who bring different approaches and new ways of doing things to work. The strengths also profile people who make better specialists than generalists. You will notice that working with others and relationship aspects didn't feature in the list we gave to people in our survey research. But we asked people to report additional strengths. Several of these related to collaborative working and leadership. The following strengths all featured:

- Empathy, emotional intelligence, sensitivity to others and compassion.
- Leadership and crisis management.
- Values-driven working style, honesty and authenticity.
- Dealing with complexity, strategic thinking and scenario planning.
- High levels of passion and enthusiasm.

Yet, our respondents also cautioned that having these strengths was one thing but being able to apply them at work was another. Opportunity to apply these depended on the extent to which they could be their authentic selves and feel valued. A few respondents provided beautifully articulated responses regarding dealing with complexity; one respondent likened this to a 'gestalt approach' (whole picture, more than sum of parts). They were particularly good at 'cognitive walk-throughs', which they used to imagine workflows in their head. These were like mind maps of the work they had to do, including any potential impasses or bottlenecks. This visualisation enabled them to spot potential problems much earlier than their co-workers. Hence, they were able to anticipate problems, which if unaddressed, then often turned out to be a problem for everyone involved in the work. Despite them noticing issues earlier than others in their team, they would stay silent for fear of being seen as a timewaster when others had not noticed.

Over time, they realised that their internal walk-throughs were correct as the details they spotted would often turn into a big issue, which hampered business continuity and success. They gradually developed the confidence to speak up earlier and share their insights. This is exactly the kind of issue that coaching can help with. Neurodivergent minds often bring such expert insights yet might find it difficult to verbalise and communicate these.

Wes was 100% sure that he did not have any strengths. He first started being coached by Nancy before starting work – he was unemployed. Wes reported that he wasn't good at anything, and that he had left school with no qualifications. He hadn't worked since then and had been in prison for petty theft. His dream was to have regular jobs like his brothers – one was a mechanic, one a brick layer and one an electrician – but he kept saying that they were cleverer than him, that he didn't have anything to offer. As Nancy built rapport, she got him talking about hanging out with his brothers as children. Wes confessed that he loved bikes – road bikes, off-road bikes, motorbikes – anything with two wheels! He told Nancy about a time, aged 11, when he had taken his own bicycle to pieces in the garage and rebuilt it – brake lines, gears and all – just to see how it worked. Now that is not easy and gave Nancy a clue as to where his strengths might lie – visual, spatial and mechanical reasoning.

Nancy profiled different areas of intelligence with a cognitive ability test to identify both his comparative strengths and weaknesses – his spiky profile. Nancy found that Wes had very low scores for processing speed, working memory and verbal reasoning. He was scoring below the 25th percentile for all of these, which is below average, which explained why he had struggled at school. However, as predicted, he had a huge spike for mechanical reasoning and solid average scores for other forms of visual perception. He'd always been good at fixing things, building Lego sets, flat-pack furniture – he wouldn't even read the instructions, he could just 'see' how to put it together.

Wes wasn't upset with the low scores as he knew that he struggled with certain things. But he had not expected to achieve a competent average score at all, and the above average score in mechanical reasoning was a real surprise. It pepped him right up and gave him a focus for his employment journey – he needed a practical job! Nancy coached Wes to research different roles that would blend his natural talent with his interests in bikes and moving parts. Together, they pored over job descriptions from the internet, and looked at the actual tasks involved, rather than the qualification or experience, which Wes had found intimidating. This was transformative for Wes's hope and enthusiasm for finding work. He started visiting job sites and the Job Centre to look for entry-level apprenticeships. Through cold-calling local businesses and asking for an opportunity to shadow for experience, Wes found a work trial in automotive manufacturing and the supervisor was so impressed with his skills that they kept him on and gave him a permanent job.

The first step was that spark of hope, the recognition of strengths and abilities. You might not be able to do it with cognitive-ability testing unless you are also a psychologist and appropriately qualified, but there are other ways to do strengths profiling. The stories that people tell and how you signpost transferrable skills is part of the coaching for many neurodivergent people. Because education is dominated by literacy and numeracy, people can underestimate how valuable mechanical skills, visual and abstract reasoning, verbal abilities, great long-term memory or the ability to stick to the same pattern can be in employment. Working backwards from jobs your coachees aspire to, in a context that fits, is a great way to focus on strengths and can be very healing for many coachees.

Identifying specific neurodivergent expertise/ strengths during coaching

Applied Cognitive Task Analysis. You might notice from Wes's story that the identification of strengths was the hardest part, and there are other approaches that can be used by non-psychologist coaches. Applied cognitive task analysis (ACTA; Militello & Hutton, 1998) is a helpful technique that you can use in coaching or group coaching to pinpoint specialist insight and expertise. While ACTA was originally designed for training purposes, there is no rule book that says it can't be used in coaching. It takes some training due to its structured and in-depth process. However, it is very relevant because it is designed to make necessary cognitive demands and skills for specialist and expert work explicit through a set of structured exercises and interviews. Neurodivergent coachees often respond well to structure.

The first step in ACTA is a task diagram. You ask the coachee to imagine their work as a diagram or flow chart (see Gore et al., 2018 for an overview with plenty of examples from a training context). A useful starting point is, "tell me about aspects of your work where you find that you know more than others do or notice things in a different way. Can you do a flow chart with me?" Usually, it works best if this diagram has three to six different aspects so that you have an overview without getting lost in detail.

You might need to gently guide some coachees towards a simpler structure – balance detailed insight with high level overview. The next step is to find out which of the sub-tasks is particularly demanding, and where neurodivergent specialist skills come in particularly handy. This is the part which coachees suspect other people find more challenging, or which would be difficult to explain to people who are new to this kind of job and task. Good questions to ask are (see Gore et al., 2018 for an overview):

- **Big picture**: the big picture for this task/your work, it's like what? What are the most important things you need to know and keep track of?

- **Past and future**: when you come to the middle of a situation and you know exactly how things happened to get there and what will happen next, it's like what?
- **Noticing**: when you are part of a situation and things just pop out at you, you're like what?
- **Improvising/opportunities**: what's an example of when you have improvised in this task/role? What's an example of when you have noticed how to do something better in this task/role?
- **Anomalies**: When you spot that something is different from usual or notice something was amiss, it's like what?

There are a range of other questions, too, such as 'tricks of the trade', whether coachees have come across 'working smarter hacks'. Refining the diagram takes some time; you need to stop and start and 'play back' quite often to ensure mutual understanding. Think of this as a wonderful opportunity to learn about the coachees' job in depth. Be prepared to redo and refine the task diagram, assuring the coachee that this is normal and help them bear with potential frustration if it is not so obvious at first how things are sequenced, or to put into words what coachees have held in their head for a long time. Time and time again, focus on what coachees are thinking rather than what the outputs are as this helps them develop their metacognition. Next, you can produce a cognitive demands table together; a summary of everything you have talked about. This will have different columns, the first one usually one for "job thinking challenges at work" and why these are challenging. Then a column for "things you've noticed instead of 'they', so it's personal in the column headings or similar". This will provide a wonderful overview for the coachee of what they do well and help them articulate to others how they think differently and the contributions they make. This is important for many job roles, but particularly for knowledge work where a lot of what we do is going on inside our heads and not readily observed by others. You can also add a practice session, where you role-model in coaching how the coachee could share with others these newly verbalised insights about their thinking strengths to support communication skills. The entire process takes about two to three hours, so you might want to break this up over two coaching sessions. We have done quite a few ACTA sessions. Even seasoned 'experts' tend to report at the end that it was not easy to put their thoughts into words and that they were tired by the end. This is normal!

Pim works in software development in an Autism at Work programme. They are valued by colleagues and their line manager for their attention to detail, as they code diligently and usually spot potential issues in coding (their own and others') before anyone else does. They go to the quiet space in the office, put their headphones on for hours, and then come out to share their learning and insight – often rather unaware of whether they have picked the right moment, or whether they are interrupting others. They have been referred to coaching because they 'hold up projects' and don't always deliver. Pim and the coach talked through how they do their coding and also their checking, using the ACTA framework. "Well, I can mentally zoom in and things pop out at me when I think – it's like a road that I am driving down and then suddenly streetlights come on and make the bit of the road that I need to see really bright". The coach then asked whether the end of the road was also illuminated. Pim said that no, it wasn't. Together, they worked out a strategy where Pim imagined the end of the road as a house that had the finished code in it – the house number was the agreed delivery date for Pim's coding. Pim then made themselves a mental map, where they noted their 'zoom in moments' when they happened but also looked at the house each time. This helped them focus and they learned to better self-regulate their time by working backwards from a deadline rather than working forward.

There is much to be gained from harnessing specialist neurodivergent strengths – for the individual, for the business and for society at large. However, there can be a barrier to harnessing these strengths when people don't realise that they are there, or when businesses are set up to promote generalist, rather than specialist talent. In our

2023 survey, we asked a group of employers about the strengths neurodivergent workers bring (McDowall et al., 2023). They also rated creativity and innovation highly and the other aspects with a broadly similar pattern (although they rated numeracy skills and short-term memory far higher). Employers also noted the "add-on benefit" that having ND workers makes the organisation more inclusive as they help it to better support neurodivergent challenges and needs internally and also with clients. The World Economic Forum (ibid.) has published a list of the top ten skills for 2015, which feature analytical thinking and innovation, active learning and learning strategies, complex problem-solving, critical thinking and analysis, and creativity, originality and initiative in the top five. Note how these skills map neatly onto the neurodivergent strengths the employees and employers reported in our study! Where you observe self-confidence and esteem is low in coachees, it can be empowering to share our list, and then help them say out loud how their unique strengths map to these and what else they have noticed.

Challenge reframe

A further way to identify strengths for neurominorities is by reframing challenges. Table 4.1 describes the contextual difficulties that many associate with the various neurotypes and how these can be co-opted as resources in the right context.

The examples in Table 4.1 show that there are many ways to reframe an alleged deficit. There are plenty of careers and opportunities for specialist minds and a lot of scope for creative thinkers to be both reliable workers and community-minded neighbours. One of the most important things we can do with our coachees is reframe success in context not by social comparison. By reframing success, your coachees might be more likely to harness the talents they have.

Yet many career pathways are geared towards 'corporate generalists' rather than specialists. Relevant 'competency' frameworks are based on personal attributes and behaviours that people have to be good at to perform well in a particular work context. Historically, the

Table 4.1 Reframing challenges as resources

Neurotype	Medical model challenge	Neurodiversity model reframe
ADHD	Easily distracted by small noises and movements in vicinity. Finds it hard to hold attention.	Highly alert and likely to spot detail for example in a classroom, operating theatre, emergency room, building site, or in roles such as pilot, driver, live presenter on TV or radio, actor, soldier, police, firefighter, dog walker. Able to mobilise internal resources and 'hyperfocus', good in times of pressure and crisis.
Autism	Inflexible routine, bound by rigid rules, narrow interests	Ability to follow process with high levels of compliance. Spots errors easily with meticulous attention to detail. Can hold attention well and develop insights. Brilliant for example in industries such as media, law, finance, technology, engineering, logistics and planning, editing, tattoo artists, laboratory work, compliance.
Dyslexia	Difficulties with writing and spelling, e.g. confuses the letters b and d because they look the same in a three-dimensional space	Able to mentally rotate images in mind, which can lead to strong mechanical skills, abstract reasoning, particularly relevant for example in industries such as construction, hairdressing and beauty, physiotherapy, surgery, stacking and warehousing, graphic design, product design, fashion.
Dyspraxia	Difficulties with planning and working out the order to do things	'Gestalt' processing – seeing the 'whole' rather than the order of parts. This is useful in all work where an overview is needed such as composing, writing, performing, caring and social work roles, management.
Tic disorders	Observational tics – saying things that might be embarrassing or rude	Builds rapport very quickly by getting to the point and catching people in the moment, which is useful in many roles such as teaching, police work, sales, photography, tailoring.
Anxiety	Rumination, second guessing and self-consciousness, procrastination	Deep thinking, considering multiple perspectives, making sure there is adequate planning and preparation. Useful for compliance roles, project management, strategy and budgeting, risk management and safeguarding, health and safety, writing and media.

focus has been on 'soft' behavioural elements (for example communication), and only recently acknowledged technical competencies (CIPD, 2021). Employer competency frameworks feature a range of dimensions that include core competencies (how you enact mission/values); common competencies (e.g. for management roles); technical competencies (expertise) and leadership competencies, as well as what might be needed for the future. You get the picture; you have to be good at very many things in order to get a job, hold it down and then get promoted and advance in your career. Modern careers are rarely linear, however, and ND careers even less so. Having your capability benchmarked against such general frameworks, when your skills are specialist, can lead to feelings of self-loathing, frustration, anxiety and insecurity.

Modelling mastery

In the previous chapter, we explained how Nancy's coachees, Mo, Audrey and Wes, were able to overcome specific workplace challenges by tapping into areas of strength. There can be a case to start with the strengths in coaching and work forward, rather than starting with the challenges and compensating. Many ND coachees have had a lifetime of developing their awareness of what they can't do – it's liberating to forget all that for a session or three. Nancy calls this 'modelling mastery' and it's rooted in Cognitive Social Learning Theory (Bandura, 1986). Bandura, a social psychologist, observed the process by which humans naturally acquire skills, which is a consistent process:

- Step one: knowledge transfer – the awareness that there is something we need to learn.
- Step two: role modelling – we observe that other people can perform the skill and identify our role models.
- Step three: vicarious learning – we learn by watching others do it well and badly and learning the principles of success.
- Step four: we develop mastery through practice, so rehearsal and repeated cycles of trying, getting some bits right, checking what others think or are doing, and then trying again.

Bandura called this process the development of 'self-efficacy', which means our belief in our capability to do something. People who have experienced mastery of a new skill are more likely to believe that they will succeed in other new skills. It is a virtuous circle of trying, finessing, succeeding and then trying the next level. It is also a self-fulfilling prophecy – the better you do, the more likely you are to do better next time. High self-efficacy levels predict good future performance (Stajkovic & Luthans, 1988). Self-efficacy is known to be weaker in neurodivergent people (Nalavany et al., 2017). However, self-efficacy is also very amendable to coaching as there is solid research showing that coaching improves self-efficacy (de Haan et al., 2016; Moen & Allgood, 2009) and even with specific groups of ND people. This was the topic of Nancy's PhD research (Doyle, 2018).

Self-efficacy can be enhanced through coaching by facilitating the coachee to develop their awareness of where they already have mastery. Do you remember in the previous chapter when Audrey couldn't remember a time when she had ever used her memory well? And then she and Nancy identified a context, out of work, where she had used her memory well? This is an example of connecting a coachee to their mastery experiences. We can then work out the details of how that mastery occurs; the context, the behaviour, the skills they are using, their values and beliefs and their identity of being good at something. Sometimes you have to start outside the work context to identify an issue that is good to talk about. Wes couldn't talk about his career goals at first and wouldn't say he had any hobbies. Nancy found his bike story by asking him a really neutral question, "how did you spend your time at the weekends and in the summer holidays when you were younger?" Only then, armed with his own story of bike dismantling and reconstructing, was he able to identify that as a strength.

Here are example questions to get you started, but bear in mind Audrey and Wes's stories, and that, with some coachees, you might need to take a more gradual and less direct approach:

- When you are working at your best, you're like what?
- What's your favourite part of your job?

- What do you find easy, even when other people find it hard?
- Which jobs always get left to you because you do them really well?
- Can you remember a time when you've felt really good about your work/strengths?

You might need to set a context and give examples from outside work to get started; for example, basic tasks, such as wrapping presents, making a lovely cup of tea, choosing the right outfit to wear, listening to a friend and helping solve their problems, gardening, making friends with dogs. These things are more innocuous than work-focused tasks for anxious people but they can easily be related back to work examples. Wrapping presents is fine motor control and visual spatial skills. Making a lovely cup of tea is a caring thing to do for many and requires patience and precision. Choosing the right outfit to wear involves social skills and visual spatial skills. Listening to friends and helping them with their problems involves verbal reasoning and choosing the right words. Gardening is a gestalt skill – you need to consider the bigger picture and imagine how things will grow in the future, what will be the overall feel of the garden? Making friends with dogs means you need to be aware of body language, you need self-control and to be responsive to and respectful of boundaries. You can help your coachee draw out distinct abilities and weave them into a new identity of someone who is competent and confident. Once mastery resources are conscious they can be mobilised to address challenges. Nancy asked Mo the last question – "can you remember a time when you've felt really good about your work?"

When Mo was first starting out as a therapist, they were struggling to get the right processes in place for their clients. They were working in a shared space, under a brand with other experienced therapists. They kept forgetting to get the paperwork in the right order. They were often seen running out to the car park at the end of the first session waving a consent form which they had forgotten to get the client to sign. They struggled with the booking system and would make mistakes, like accidentally cancelling sessions and having to ask their colleagues for help, or failing to save client notes properly and having to redo all the work.

Mo recalled, during coaching, that they had been feeling less and less confident and were even considering quitting their practice. Then one day, a colleague was caught in a traffic jam and rang to say they would be at least 30 minutes late, and could Mo please welcome their client and let them know what was happening. The client arrived and promptly burst into floods of tears at the news. She had been having counselling to help process the emotions of a late-term miscarriage, and had just discovered that she was accidentally pregnant again. Mo took the client into their office and worked with her to hold the space for her tears, anxiety and grief. With no preparation and no prior knowledge of this client, Mo was thrown into the deep end but handled it beautifully. When Mo's colleague arrived, the client was discussing how she had been offered treatment to support further pregnancies and acknowledging her family resources, coming up with ideas about how to grieve, whilst simultaneously experiencing joy and hope.

Mo's colleague had listened at the door and, when they were finished, relayed to Mo how they had heard Mo build rapport with acknowledgements and language that centred and validated the client in her experience. Mo's colleague said he was glad Mo had chosen to be a therapist and thanked them for holding space for his client. Mo recalled that story in coaching as they were reminded to consider what made them good at their job, why they went into the work, and what was really important to them about their professional identity. Mo knew that their talent for building rapport was more unique and relevant than being able to work out a software system. Focusing on what they did well gave them courage to do more.

Mo's example highlights how reassuring and transforming it can be when we focus on our strengths. In this case, Mo had taken the feedback from their colleague and used it to update their sense of mastery in their new role as a therapist. Mo's colleague gave clear and detailed feedback, rather than just saying "thanks, that was great". He explained what he had heard that was useful which allowed Mo to hear that they had done good work, rather than deflecting it as a platitude.

Sometimes we get our beliefs about our identity and worth from other people (being externally referenced) and sometimes they come from ourselves (internally referenced), and some coachees will ricochet between such beliefs. There is a middle ground and part of your role might be to help your coachee establish a resilient sense of worth that is flexible to feedback and growth without being too vulnerable to external reference. For Mo, remembering this critical moment in their career development was pivotal to recovering self-efficacy.

Life design and career stories

You might need to spend some time supporting coachees to spot 'good patterns' and how they bring specialist and unique skills and knowledge. A lovely framing for this is 'life design' and thinking of careers as 'small stories' (Savickas, 2012). For example, you could get coachees to write down simple and abbreviated stories of success on large sticky notes, framing these explicitly as anything goes – there is no right or wrong or good or bad. The next step is to weave these into a story; what patterns and themes can you discover together? Can you summarise the narrative and give it a name? This exercise is different from a 'plotline' which is often used in career coaching, where coachees are invited to chart a trajectory over time. This approach can be unhelpful and enforce negative experiences when coachees are already discouraged – particularly when there have been repeated experiences of job loss, lack of success, or a somewhat disjointed pattern with lots of stopping and starting. That said, when there has been a history of stopping and starting, and you find it hard to make sense of the experience without a timeline, you could invite the coachee to plot the career timeline before a session, then invite them to talk you through this. Listen, and note what you have observed. Then the next step could be to rewrite the story through the 'micro-narrative', then co- and re-construct the career narrative together. Some coachees might prefer to do this as a collage, taking images and phrases from old magazines, or by choosing six songs that represent their different career stages. They might want to take you on a walk or describe a journey. Be as creative as your neurodivergent coachees and remember that not everyone finds talking the best way to engage their metacognition and subconscious. Images, movement and music can be a powerful alternative.

Neurodivergent leadership

Our examples have so far tended towards entry level work and mid-career. This is deliberate on our part, because we recognise that many experienced coaches are already used to working with senior staff and highflyers – those are the people who are most likely to afford to pay for coaches. However, we emphasise that good coaching works for all career stages. Some of you might be working with neurodivergent coachees in an executive coaching context where people hold senior and advanced roles. One issue to flag upfront is that these coachees may have been referred or have self-referred without any reference to neurodiversity. Yet, you might notice during coaching that their behaviour and thought patterns differ and suspect they are undiagnosed. You do not need to get them a diagnosis to work with potentially neurodivergent traits. You can just take your coachees as you find them and support their strengths. Nancy's coaching experience and research suggests that the challenges will remain stubbornly consistent – administration, time management, prioritisation, emotional wellbeing, concentration. Nancy has worked with several people transitioning into medical leadership as senior doctors. She often finds that they have masked their difficulties during education and the lower rungs of the medical hierarchy, but as they advance into more senior roles their skills can no longer outweigh their challenges. Going back to the basics of cognitive, emotional and behavioural challenges as per the previous chapter will be helpful – never assume that someone isn't struggling with something that you might consider basic, even when they are a highflyer.

There is a dearth of research on neurodivergent leadership, which is suggested to be more prevalent in entrepreneurial than corporate roles (Logan, 2009). A conceptual paper (Roberson et al., 2021) argues that neurodivergence brings cognitive strengths that facilitate task-based leadership – i.e. leadership by doing rather than relational-focused leadership. Focusing on tasks can be a helpful anchor to signpost in coaching that leadership is about making a difference and acts of leadership, rather than being merely attached to roles or job descriptions. We argue that neurodivergent coachees bring more than highly proficient task execution to leadership roles as they often bring a strong values-led approach. Honesty and transparency are particularly important to neurodivergent leaders, and these are good qualities to be harnessed in contemporary workplaces, which say that they place high value on corporate social responsibility.

The career strengths that got your leadership coachees where they are might be taken for granted and need reinforcement. They may be experiencing imposter syndrome (Bravata et al., 2020) where they are worried about being found out as not capable of their role, because they are holding shame about any lack of skill in diary management, using Excel or completing forms in the HR software. For these coachees, this chapter on strengths is essential grounding. Work on any challenges without judgement as set out in Chapter 2, but return to successes as a defining characteristic of coachee career identity and leadership potential. It can be a useful anchor to hold that leadership should not be defined by role and power. It's about the strategic and, in the case of neurodivergent coachees, often specific contribution to organisational effectiveness. We can all enact leadership in unique and valuable ways. It can be very grounding to work with your coachees on identifying an anchor that helps them hold this thought. Almuth always thinks of a woman ballet director as her role model, who was one of the first to lead a major company, was much maligned at first for being too strict and who is now revered all over the world.

Conclusion

In previous chapters we have signposted that employment outcomes for neurodivergent workers signpost disproportionate exclusion; yet this chapter shows us how much there is to be gleaned from fostering neurodivergent talent. In Nancy's social enterprise, coachees present with a whole range of issues from obtaining and sustaining work to issues and roadblocks in progression and promotion. Within one year of completing coaching, around 20% of coachees report being promoted, which is a fantastic testament to their underlying ability and the opportunity created by resolving obstacles and focusing on ability. In conclusion, neurodiversity coaching provides a wonderful opportunity for coachees to notice and embrace their specific strengths. Coaches may need to augment their toolkit and, if one approach doesn't work and coachees 'get stuck', then try another. Reframing challenges as resources, modelling mastery, eliciting specific expertise through a series of cognitive interview processes and 'life design' through reordering of success stories are all useful techniques. Listen, wonder and let your coachees surprise you!

Reflective questions

- To what extent do you struggle/have you struggled to identify your strengths and talents? Do you know what you do well and can you articulate it to yourself? Write some down or sketch out a diagram of you working at your best.

- Sit with it for a moment. Note what it is like to absorb yourself in a sense of worth – what do you notice? What thoughts does it evoke for you? What has changed over the lifespan?
- What is your 'life design' and your career story? How would you summarise this for someone who has never met you? Would you draw it, map it, or play/listen to it as a preference to talking about it?
- Given what you learned in this chapter, what do you foresee as some of the challenges to get neurodivergent coachees to work with their strengths? How can you harness your own resources to tackle such challenges?
- How have you observed your coachees enacting leadership? What insights have you had?

References

Alvares, G. A., Bebbington, K., Cleary, D., Evans, K., Glasson, E. J., Maybery, M. T., Pillar, S., Uljarevi, M., Varcin, K., Wray, J., & Whitehouse, A. J. O. (2019). The misnomer of "high functioning autism": Intelligence is an imprecise predictor of functional abilities at diagnosis. *Autism*, 24(1), 221–232. https://doi.org/10.1177/1362361319852831

Armstrong, T. (2010). *The power of neurodiversity*. De Capo Press.

Assis, V., Frank, M., Bcheche, G., & Kuboiama, B. (2014). *The value that people with down syndrome can add to organizations* (p. 28). McKinsey. www.edsa.eu/wp-content/uploads/2017/12/Brasil-value-that-people-with-Down-syndrome-can-add-to-organizations_ENG.pdf

Bandura, A. (1986). *Social foundations of thought and action*. Prentice Hall.

Baron-Cohen, S., Ashwin, E., Ashwin, C., Tavassoli, T., & Chakrabarti, B. (2009). Talent in autism: Hyper-systemizing, hyper-attention to detail and sensory hypersensitivity. *Philosophical Transactions of the Royal Society: Biological Sciences, 364*(1522), 1377–1383. https://doi.org/10.1098/rstb.2008.0337

Boot, N., Nevicka, B., & Baas, M. (2020). Creativity in ADHD: Goal-directed motivation and domain specificity. *Journal of Attention Disorders, 24*(13), 1857–1866. https://doi.org/10.1177/1087054717727352

Bravata, D., Madhusudhan, D., Boroff, M., & Cokley, K. (2020). Commentary: Prevalence, predictors, and treatment of imposter syndrome: A systematic review. *Journal of Mental Health & Clinical Psychology, 4*(3), 12–16. https://doi.org/10.29245/2578-2959/2020/3.1207

Bury, S. M., Hedley, D., Uljarević, M., & Gal, E. (2020). The autism advantage at work: A critical and systematic review of current evidence. *Research in Developmental Disabilities, 105,* 103750. https://doi.org/10.1016/j.ridd.2020.103750

CIPD (2021). *Competence and competency frameworks.* Chartered Institute for Personnel and Development. www.cipd.co.uk/knowledge/fundamentals/people/performance/competency-factsheet#gref

Daker, R. J., Cortes, R. A., Lyons, I. M., & Green, A. E. (2020). Creativity anxiety: Evidence for anxiety that is specific to creative thinking, from STEM to the arts. *Journal of Experimental Psychology: General, 149*(1), 42–57. https://doi.org/10.1037/xge0000630

de Haan, E., Grant, A., Burger, Y., & Eriksson, P.-O. (2016). A large-scale study of executive and workplace coaching: The relative contributions of relationship, personality match, and self-efficacy. *Consulting Psychology Journal Practice and Research, 68*(3), 189–207. https://doi.org/10.1037/cpb0000058

Dina, C. Z., Porta, M., Saleh, C., & Servello, D. (2017). Creativity assessment in subjects with Tourette syndrome vs. patients with Parkinson's disease: A preliminary study. *Brain Sciences, 7*(7), 80. https://doi.org/10.3390/brainsci7070080

Doyle, N. (2018). *A critical realist analysis of coaching as a disability accommodation.* City University of London.

Erbeli, F., Peng, P., & Rice, M. (2022). No evidence of creative benefit accompanying dyslexia: A meta-analysis. *Journal of Learning Disabilities, 55*(3), 242–253. https://doi.org/10.1177/00222194211010350

Gore, J., Banks, A. P., & McDowall, A. (2018). Developing cognitive task analysis and the importance of socio-cognitive competence/insight for professional practice. *Cognition, Technology & Work, 20*(4), 555–563. https://doi.org/10.1007/s10111-018-0502-2

Grant, D. (2009). The psychological assessment of neurodiversity. In D. Pollak (Ed.), *Neurodiversity in higher education* (pp. 33–62). Wiley-Blackwell.

Gregg, N., Coleman, C., Lindstrom, J., & Lee, C. (2007). Who are most, average, or high-functioning adults? *Learning Disabilities Research and Practice, 22*(4), 264–274.

Happe, F., & Frith, U. (2010). Autism and Talent (First). Oxford University Press.

Logan, J. (2009). Dyslexic entrepreneurs: The incidence; their coping strategies and their business skills. *Dyslexia, 15*(4), 328–346.

Majeed, N. M., Hartanto, A., & Tan, J. J. X. (2021). Developmental dyslexia and creativity: A META-ANALYSIS. *Dyslexia, 27*(2), 187–203. https://doi.org/10.1002/dys.1677

McDowall, A., Doyle, N., & Kisleva, M. (2023*). Neurodiversity at Work 2023: Demand, Supply and Gap Analysis* (p. 60). Neurodiversity in Business.

Militello, L. G., & Hutton, R. J. B. (1998). Applied cognitive task analysis (ACTA): A practitioner's toolkit for understanding cognitive task demands. *Ergonomics, 41*(11), 1618–1641. https://doi.org/10.1080/001401398186108

Moen, F., & Allgood, E. (2009). Coaching and the effect on self-efficacy. *Organization Development Journal, 27*, 69–82. https://doi.org/10.1007/s11613-009-0158-0

Nalavany, B. A., Logan, J. M., & Carawan, L. W. (2017). The relationship between emotional experience with dyslexia and work self-efficacy among adults with dyslexia. *Dyslexia, 24*(1), 1–16. https://doi.org/10.1002/dys.1575

Newark, P. E., Elsässer, M., & Stieglitz, R.-D. (2016). Self-esteem, self-efficacy, and resources in adults with ADHD. *Journal of Attention Disorders, 20*(3), 279–290. https://doi.org/10.1177/1087054712459561

Rajabpour Azizi, Z., Akhavan Tafti, M., Mohsenpour, M. (2021). Dyslexia and the visual- spatial talents: A critical review of new difference-oriented research. *Quarterly Journal of Child Mental Health, 7*(4), 197–214. https://doi.org/10.52547/jcmh.7.4.13

Roberson, Q., Quigley, N. R., Vickers, K., & Bruck, I. (2021). Reconceptualizing leadership from a neurodiverse perspective. *Group & Organization Management, 46*(2), 399–423. https://doi.org/10.1177/1059601120987293

Sacks, O. (1992). Tourette's syndrome and creativity. *British Medical Journal, 305*, 1515–1516. www.ncbi.nlm.nih.gov/pmc/articles/PMC1884721/pdf/bmj00105-0007.pdf

Savickas, M. L. (2012). Life design: A paradigm for career intervention in the 21st century. *Journal of Counseling & Development, 90*(1), 13–19. https://doi.org/10.1111/j.1556-6676.2012.00002.x

Schrevel, S. J. C., Dedding, C., & Broerse, J. E. W. (2016). Why do adults with ADHD choose strength-based coaching over public mental health care? A qualitative case study from the Netherlands. *SAGE Open, 6*(3), 215824401666249. https://doi.org/10.1177/2158244016662498

Sewell, A. (2022). Understanding and supporting learners with specific learning difficulties from a neurodiversity perspective: A narrative synthesis. *British Journal of Special Education, 49*(4), 539–560. https://doi.org/10.1111/1467-8578.12422

Stajkovic, A. D., & Luthans, F. (1988). Self-efficacy and work-related performance: A meta-analysis. *Psychological Bulletin, 124*(2), 240–261.

White, H. A., & Shah, P. (2006). Uninhibited imaginations: Creativity in adults with attention-deficit/hyperactivity disorder. *Personality and Individual Differences, 40*(6), 1121–1131. https://doi.org/10.1016/j.paid.2005.11.007

White, H. A., & Shah, P. (2011). Creative style and achievement in adults with attention-deficit/hyperactivity disorder. *Personality and Individual Differences, 50*(5), 673–677. https://doi.org/10.1016/j.paid.2010.12.015

Section B

Coaching techniques and principles

Chapter 5

Clean Language interviewing

Nancy Doyle and Almuth McDowall

Introduction

We outline the relevance of Clean Language (CL) for working with neurodivergent coachees – an approach used in therapy, research interviewing, coaching and group facilitation. This technique is incredibly powerful and well-designed for neurodivergent people because it makes few assumptions and takes a non-judgemental stance. CL transforms how 'heard' a coachee feels and is a direct route to developing metacognition and self-awareness. We describe the basic language and questioning models used in coaching are described, including tips and modifications for use with neurodivergent coachees and coachee stories to illustrate what happens in practice. Lastly, we outline a description of using everyday CL in group coaching exercises and pointers to inform coaches' reflective practice.

CL is a technique for enquiring about a coachee's experience, for developing their metacognition in a way that avoids contaminating their thoughts with those of the coach. The language itself is a series of questions and prompts that assume as little as possible about the answers to those questions, so that the coachee can stay in their own conceptual landscape, without having to decode the question before answering. It involves repeating back to the coachee their exact words and asking for more detail around those words. Sounds simple, right? Keep your inferences and interpretations to yourself? Actually, this is very hard. In learning CL you become acutely aware of each word, and how simple questions like "how do you feel about

DOI: 10.4324/9781003368274-7

that?" are leading, potentially disruptive and unhelpful. Learning CL is a one-way street – once you have taken the training, there's no going back! It is a profound form of communication, which can be transformational for coaches and their coachees. We are NOT going to teach you Clean Language in one chapter. Indeed, there are several comprehensive books on the subject, written by expert coaching trainers, therapists, organisational consultants and more (Dunbar, 2017; Lawley & Tompkins, 2000; Sullivan & Rees, 2008; Walker, 2014; Way, 2013). We recommend further reading and/ or training with some of these practitioners to try it out. Learning CL from reading is a bit like trying to learn karate from reading – you kind of have to do it to absorb the genius of the approach. We are going to draw out why and how it is particularly useful for neurominorities, and indeed anyone who has been taught to doubt themselves.

Clean Language is a humanistic approach to coaching, which holds that your coachees are whole people, who are not broken and therefore do not need fixing. In CL, there are no templates like ACTA to apply to the coachee's experience. It is totally free-form for the coachee's outcomes and insights to emerge in whatever shape, language, sensory modality, gesture, non-sequitur, location is most relevant. The template in CL is instead a template or restriction upon the coach, who must not stray from a set of 8–20 questions, or at least not stray from the principles. Here's what you need to know:

1. Clean Language is useful for developing metacognition, self-awareness, a sense of autonomy and control over one's scripts.

It allows someone who thinks unusually, to think unusually! CL works at a symbolic level. By this we mean that you ask questions about metaphors, gestures, the structure of *how* they are describing their outcome or problem, not *what* it is. The premise is that the way we describe the outcome is indicative of the journey we need to take to get there and that, by pausing, we can give our coachees the time and space they need to tap into their own innate wisdom.

2. Now before you even start thinking about autistic people who often don't 'think in metaphor', let us direct you to the naturally occurring symbolism in everyday speech:

- I want to move forward with the project.
- We're drifting apart.
- My anxiety will go down when this event is behind me.
- The next step feels out of reach.

We use metaphoric language all the time. What CL does, is make use of these relationships that we inadvertently insert into our speech in order to talk about dynamics without needing the 'he said/she said' details that can be distracting, time consuming and riddled with biases and misremembered content. Equally, some people think in direct metaphors:

- It's like I'm carrying a millstone around my neck.
- I'm feeling wobbly.
- The work is a piece of cake.
- The office is like Piccadilly Circus.
- I like to go with the flow.

The joy of CL is that whatever your coachee says is the right thing to say. If they have spoken in metaphor or not, if they have answered with a sigh instead of a word, you can work with it. They cannot get it wrong, and you can always ask a question about their communication. The use of direct metaphors and analogies is not necessary, it's more about the way we can use CL to enquire about the relationships between ideas and uncover meaning from their proximity and symbolism. This is called 'modelling', which broadly means making a mental model or map of the situation. Analogies are fun and easy to remember, but they are not the goal itself and in working with neurodivergent coachees you need to remember this.

3. The CL approach tips the power dynamics of the coachee and the coach from unequal to balanced.

Instead of the coach being the 'expert', who brings prior knowledge and wisdom (e.g. a technique such as ACTA), the coach becomes a reflector, someone who simply repeats the coachee's words or gestures and invites them to consider their own words more deeply to create their own framework for understanding their patterns. Instead of the coachee being the 'novice', who is a passive recipient of the coach's insight and steering, the coachee becomes the source of the wisdom. This power shift is exceptionally useful for neurodivergent people who have negative experiences of therapy, coaching or indeed any sort of authoritarian control.

4. It is not easy to learn.

CL takes a lot of practice to get good enough to 'unleash' your clean questions on a coachee. If you are not feeling confident at it, don't practise on people who are vulnerable, practise in groups with fellow learners or with willing friends/colleagues. On the other hand, once you have learned CL, it is incredibly easy to bring into your practice as a way of slowing down your own thoughts and challenging yourself to really listen to your coachees.

Using the basic Clean Language questions

The following questions are what most CL practitioners would consider the 'basics' and are taken from a book that described how CL's originator, David Grove, arrived at the work (Wilson, 2017). You will note that the questions don't conform to the typical structure of questions in the English language, as prepositions such as 'what' appear at the end. This is quite deliberate, as this encourages the coachee to respond to a prompt directly, in their own words and terms. Where we have typed [XXX] is where you would insert a coachee's words, gestures, sighs etc.

An outcome focused question:

• And what would you like to have happen?

Questions that are likely to elicit a metaphor or some sort of symbolic response:

• And that's [XXX] like what?
• And does [XXX] have a shape or size?

Questions to explore the metaphor:

- And what kind of [XXX] is that [XXX]?
- And where abouts is [XXX]?
- And is there anything else about [XXX]?

Questions to explore the sequence of a metaphor:

- And what happens just before [XXX]?
- And where could [XXX] have come from?
- And then what happens?

Questions about relationships:

- And when [XXX], what happens to [YYY]?
- What does [XXX] know about [YYY]?
- Is there a relationship between [XXX] and [YYY]?
- Is [XXX] the same or different to [YYY]?

Looks easy, doesn't it? It is a deceptively simple approach, but the difficulty is restricting yourself to those questions. Originator David Grove was a man who brought unusual insights to his practice, which may be interesting for you to learn about. He was a Maori psychotherapist who worked with trauma in the 1980s, 1990s and 2000s. When he started practising, received wisdom was that, in order to heal, a client had to revisit the trauma and talk about it. However, David observed that for some of his clients this was unachievable and so, when they weren't able to go to their trauma, he met them where they were.

If they said, "I can't talk, it's like a volcano about to erupt in my torso", he would simply ask, "and what kind of volcano?" or "and what happens just before there's a volcano about to erupt" and "and what would you like to have happen?". His client might say, "I would like it to rain to cool the lands around the volcano". He could then answer, "and rain, where could rain like that come from?". The client then begins building a sense of their resources, an understanding of a script they might be running around their temper or frustration, but without having to break confidentiality and talk about the actual events that occurred. To be clear, Grove was working with Vietnam veterans and people who had experienced child sexual abuse. This was not easy work and he was not tinkering around the edges. Note that "how does that feel"/"what is that like", "what does that look/sound like" are NOT on the list. These questions may or may not be answerable – humans have different sensory experiences of feeling, seeing and hearing, Grove was wise to this and developed CL to be suitable for a much wider variety of human experience than the neurotypical norm.

Grove was adamant that CL was his gift to the world, that he was a 'launch pad' for the work of CL to be shared freely. It has been adopted into coaching practice by numerous leading coaching schools and practitioners and we can therefore share how to practise it without veering into therapy. However, it can go deep, quickly, which is why you need to be skilled before you start. The best way to explain CL is to show you what happens.

Audrey and the Dam. Whilst Audrey was delighted to come across assistive technology, she had a lot of emotion tied up with learning how to use it. She said one day in her coaching, "this feels just like my dyslexia, I know I should be able to learn it, everyone else can do it, but I can't". I asked her if we could spend some time exploring "my dyslexia" to find out if there was anything particular about it that was stopping her learning, using a questioning technique that asks about the process and symbols, rather than the events. She agreed.

Nancy: And when this feels just like my dyslexia, does my dyslexia have a shape or a size?

Audrey: It's like a dam [she was seated in a comfy armchair and she indicated the height of the dam by moving her hands in front of her, across the top of the dam. It was about the same height as her chest].

Nancy: And is there anything else about that dam? [Nancy also gestures towards where Audrey has indicated the dam is located]

Audrey: Yes, it's blocking all the water.

Nancy: And whereabouts is the water?

Audrey: It's all around me, it wants to flow forward but it can't get to the other side.

Nancy: And when it wants to flow forward, is there anything else about flow forward?

Audrey: Yes, there are trees on the other side and they are thirsty. If the water could get past the dam the trees could grow.

Nancy: And when there's a dam, which is blocking all the water, and the water wants to get past the dam, where could a dam like that have come from?

Audrey: Well, I suppose it's like when I was five and I started school. . . .

Nancy: And it's like when I was five and I started school, and when there's a dam that's like five and started school, is there anything else about that?

Audrey: Well, yes. I'm not five anymore. I'm forty. And I'm bigger than that dam and I can step right over it now!

Nancy: And when I'm bigger than that dam and I can step right over it, what happens next?

And with that, Audrey stood up from her seated position. She saw that the dam, which was so tall that it was chest height on her as a child, was only leg height as an adult. She stepped over her metaphoric dam and learned to use her assistive technology.

Reflecting on the event later in the coaching, Audrey relayed that she had always carried this huge shame from school, a moment in time where she realised that all the other children could do something that she couldn't. She recalls being in a classroom, learning the alphabet, and suddenly realising that she was different. She felt totally powerless and incapable for the first time. The event had created a script for her, which played out every time she tried to address her literacy difficulties and it had branched out into trying new technology or other complex tasks. She would freeze and be unable to take in the new information. However, in the CL session she realised that at the age of forty she had overcome many complex learning events and she simply didn't need to feel intimidated anymore.

Her journey reflects some complex coaching psychology – she was updating her self-belief and internalised narrative about what is possible, she was moving from learned helplessness into a state of self-efficacy. She was also unpicking her inhibition that arose from growing up in a Black community where asking for help or adjustments from white spaces was harder for her than her peers and not encouraged at home. Marcia Brissett-Bailey, author of the book *Black Brilliant and Dyslexic* (Brissett-Bailey, 2023) commented to us when reading a draft of this book, how the story highlights the importance of understanding the impact of culture for neurodivergent people:

> This story highlights the impact of school and workplace culture, the importance of embracing stories and sharing ownership in white space. A person can belong and be able to effectively communicate one's needs and use their voice to be heard, providing tools to empathise and empower others.

We could have got there by Nancy asking for examples of times she has learned something well, by unpacking the approach she has taken since adulthood for developing new skills. Notice how the CL approach can take a short cut through incredibly detailed conversations and work to just 'arrive' at the right outcome, without needing to dredge up all that history. Also notice how Nancy repeats back exactly what Audrey has said rather than summarising or changing the words in any way and how she includes the gestures in her repetition, rather than ignoring them. This allows space for the individual story to emerge untainted and solely owned by the storyteller.

Wes and the Team. Wes came to CL to understand how he could relate better to his team. They worked in shifts and Wes was usually on shift with the same people, who he liked but felt uncomfortable with sometimes. They regularly went for a drink on their way home, into a noisy pub that Wes didn't like. He found it awkward to speak up in meetings and when he needed to collaborate. He wasn't able to work at his best, or collaboratively when he needed to because he was unsure about whether or not he was annoying them. This caused substantial self-consciousness and anxiety. Nancy asked him if he would be okay exploring these issues using CL to let his intuition lead the conversation. He agreed. Nancy wondered where to start on all this. Should they make a model of his anxiety, the team or should they start with an ideal scenario, to which they could compare the current one? She decided to go with the latter. Starting with an ideal scenario is a helpful CL tool. It's not particularly clean, because it assumes that there **is** an ideal scenario! But it gets the modelling started.

Nancy: An ideal team for you, in which you can work at your best, it's like what?

Wes: An ideal team. . . . I suppose it is one that is easy to talk to.

Nancy: And when easy to talk to? What kind of talk is that?

Wes: I don't know really, I don't really like talking when I'm working and focusing, it breaks my concentration. I find it easier to think in pictures, words disrupt my flow.

Nancy: And when you don't really like talking, what kind of team is an ideal team that's easy to talk to?

Wes: One where I can do my own thing, and only talk when I need to.

Nancy: And when there's an ideal team where I can do my own thing, and only talk when I need to, what kind of 'I' is that 'I'?

Wes: Yes, I don't really like working in a team. I like to work on my own projects.

Nancy: And when I like to work on my own projects, that's like what?

Wes: It's like everything around me is still and can't disrupt me and I can see it through to the end.

Nancy: And when everything around me is still and can't disrupt me, and I can see it through to the end, what kind of me is that 'me'? Is it the same or different to 'I'?

Wes: It's different. Me knows that it gets lonely if it is on its own for too long, but the chatter is so noisy that it shuts down my thinking. Me wants company but only if it's quiet. I just want to get on.

Nancy: And when there's a me that gets lonely and an I that wants to get on, what would you like to have happen?

Wes: I want them to stop talking so loudly and so quickly so that I can focus. Maybe they could let me join in the meeting for the first 45 mins and then leave. Maybe they could let me wear headphones when I'm concentrating so that I can get on.

Nancy: And maybe they could let me join in the meeting and maybe they could let me wear headphones. What happens just before 'they could let me?'

Wes: [laughs] Well I need to ask them I suppose!

Nancy and Wes then role-played a discussion with his manager to ask if he could have a dedicated early slot at the weekly team meeting so that he could leave rather than being present during the whole meeting and if he could wear his noise defending earphones when he didn't want to be interrupted. His manager agreed and together they decided how to introduce this to the rest of the team as a plan. The team welcomed the idea, they were aware that Wes wasn't comfortable being spoken to when he was focused on something, and they had individually worried about how to interrupt him if needed. The team agreed that if there was something unforeseen or urgent, they would write a note on a post-it and place it on his workstation rather than tap him on the shoulder or speak loudly. Wes found this made such a difference to his anxiety levels day-to-day, that he could absorb more conversation between shifts and started engaging in conversations in the break room and occasionally even went for one drink after work with his shift. Wes's team were happy to accommodate his differences, they understood that he thought differently, they just hadn't known what to do differently to help. Having the conversation had made everyone more relaxed. By spending more time with them, Wes learned that they were all in awe of his technical skills in assembling equipment.

Eliciting mastery using Clean Language

These examples, and the one from the introduction of Mo and their military father, show how close to therapy CL can bring a coachee. Staying in a coaching focus depends on (a) keeping the conversation work focused and (b) keeping the conversation focused on the positive, the coachee's mastery experience. Nancy used the question "what would you like to have happen" to bring Wes back to thinking about solutions and ideas, rather than unpacking the word "lonely". With Mo, "what would you like to have happen" didn't quite work, so Nancy linked the conversation back to the very first thing that Mo said, in order to avoid going further down the chain of information. This takes CL skill, where the coach needs to maintain an awareness of the coachee's narrative and the psychological safety at all times. This is why you need to practise before you use this technique, because if you are busy worrying about what question to ask, it is difficult to 'hold the space' for your coachee to explore their conceptual landscape safely.

With that warning provided, CL used competently in this way can help a coachee develop an understanding of where they have 'mastery', which is the precursor to self-efficacy, which is an essential outcome for this client group. The positive frame on the starting questions demonstrated above 'flip the narrative' rather than dwelling on a perceived inability. It invites the coachee to explore the possible. In doing so, it taps into our creativity and allows us to understand the conditions that would need to be true in order for us to achieve a more reliable performance in memory/organisation/time etc. – whatever you are modelling with your coachee. The point about those opening questions is that they draw our attention to positive states and this is helpful for coachees who have spent much time ruminating on what they do badly and where they went wrong. One of the lovely things about CL is that you can use it as much or as little as you like. To the uninitiated it can seem a bit odd, but you don't have to dive right in. You can open up a topic with simple questions like those used with Wes and Mo:

"When you are organised at your best, it's like what?"
"An ideal team for you is like what?"

These can be substituted for whichever topic is at hand, something they'd like to improve, an area they need to understand more about:

"When you are remembering/concentrating/managing time/ communicating/working/learning/managing boundaries at your best it's like what?"
"When you are remembering/concentrating/managing time/ communicating/working/learning/managing boundaries at your best you're like what?"

Asking "it's like what" might get you different information to asking "you're like what" – you can use your judgement and knowledge of the coachee to decide which is best. Following their answer, you can choose to explore further with simple CL questions such as, "is there anything else about that?" which are quite straightforward and sound like normal conversation. That can be enough for some coachees. You could also use the clean openers to get coachees thinking before they come to a coaching session, and invite them to respond with diagrams, sketches or words and bring these to their session. The CL process works really well in images and, indeed, after the session with Wes he spent more time working on spatial maps rather than talking through his plans and outcomes. Many neurodivergent coachees will find working in diagrams and pictures a relief if they find conversation arduous. You can bring a bag of symbolic objects to coaching and ask them to choose one that represents them remembering/working/communicating at their best. Nancy has run that exercise in groups with young people who were not in education or training, with senior managers in a manufacturing company – all sorts of people who you would think might turn their noses up! They can choose a song, a movement or gesture. Nancy once asked the clean openers in an email before meeting a coachee and when she arrived to coach him in person, he had painted two oil paintings of his dyslexia – one as it was and one as he wanted it to be! The current state painting was dark and full of sharp angles, the desired state painting included round soft lines and lots of green. He spent the first coaching session with Nancy just listening to what he had already learned through the process and what he was planning to do next with the information. Modelling mastery and inviting people to capture their self-insights in creative ways really plays to the neurodivergent style of thinking. You will be pleasantly surprised by how easily this sort of thinking comes to people and how much they can enjoy it!

This is a good way to bring a CL session to a close:

"and take all the time you need to just map out on a piece of paper what you've just described, the [XXX] and the [YYY], the [ZZZ] and their relationship. You can do this in a list, a diagram, a sketch – whatever comes to you".

Avoid the word "draw" as some people have triggers about not being good at art. Often the coachee will gain further insight when doing so, and the paper serves as a memory aid to the experience, something they can pin on the fridge to remind them of a goal or pathway they've created.

As well as inviting positive models to work out how to transform a difficulty, it's also valid to spend time modelling the strengths that the coachee brings to their work. This might be their creativity, their language ability, they might be hyperlexic, have exceptional design skills, be more reliable and consistent than their colleagues, have an ability to hyperfocus – whatever it is! Spending time modelling strengths adds to the sense of control and mastery that a coachee has over their work and career. They might identify ways in which they can bring those strengths to bear in areas where they are weaker, they might learn more about how to create 'flow' and 'focus' when they need to. Time spent working on positive states and towards positive outcomes is the foundation of good coaching psychology and, in this, CL is a wonderfully flexible and helpful tool.

Top tips for using Clean Language

- Ask your coachee where they would like to be, and where they would like you to be, before you start. People who use gestures and spatial memories to process their thinking need to be seated in the right space before they start and you need to not be in their way! Audrey's mental mapping of her dam would have been difficult if she was seated at a table or if Nancy had been in front of her, because this is where she placed her conceptual dam. By asking, even if your coachee thinks they are fine, it opens up the possibility of moving as they get into it; you can assure them that if they want to move, or ask you to move that is fine. David Grove was reported to have said that "space is my co-therapist" and certainly for some coachees that is true.

- Eye contact is sometimes destabilising for people who are answering CL questions. The process is not like a conversation, it isn't an exchange between you and them where you are co-creating meaning. They are making their own meaning. Just as inserting the phrase "tell me more about" makes it all about you, so can looking at someone directly. Many CL practitioners look towards the same direction that their coachee is looking towards, this feels more in line with the process. This is of course very relaxing for some autistic people who report direct eye contact as intense to the point of painful.

- You need to have built rapport with your coachee. Rapport is the most important ingredient of any coaching, and for them to feel safe enough to explore their mental models with you, there needs to be trust.

- You also need to build that same rapport with their mental model. There is something incredibly joyful about watching someone's mental map unfold into a landscape. People are creative and wise. That dam which was causing Audrey angst in her forties was a resource in her primary education as it protected her from being overwhelmed with all the information that she couldn't capture. Dr Caitlin Walker's book *From Contempt to Curiosity* (Walker, 2014) has lots of stories about metaphors that began as self-protection but became inflexible – these are truly inspirational to read. Clean Language helps us identify the wisdom of how we got ourselves into binds, and through that knowledge we devise our own escape. This is more respectful than telling someone they need to stop their anger overflowing or speak up when they are anxious. It considers the idea that people don't deliberately set out to cause themselves harm – most of us do the best we can in the situation we're in with the resources we have at the time. The volcano of anger could have been needed to keep someone alive – we can't dismiss it. By staying in rapport with the inherent wisdom and beauty of people's mental models, by accepting them without question or judgement, you are creating a wonderful safe space for your neurodivergent coachee to explore their neurological profile and develop self-knowledge.

Combining Clean Language with other coaching styles

Clean Language works well as a coaching technique to create shared understanding and facilitate authenticity and engagement. But it is likely that the coach and coachee will need to look to complementary techniques to facilitate behaviour change.

Clean Language *and goal setting*

There's a lot more to CL than described here; for example, using CL can augment existing coaching practices such as the GROW model (Whitmore, 1992) and goal setting (Locke & Latham, 2002). James Lawley and Penny Tompkins, two world class coaching practitioners and early developers of this work, outline a "clean framework for change" (Lawley & Tompkins, 2012) which is a step-by-step journey, using CL questions. The framework for change first challenges the coachee to consider their outcome as opposed to the absence of a problem. For example, in response to "what would you like to have happen", they might say that they hate feeling stressed. You might ask again, "and when you hate feeling stressed, what would you like to have happen?" They might say that they want to stop feeling stressed. According to Tompkins and Lawley's framework, neither of these are outcomes, they are both descriptions of a problem. The first statement (hate feeling stressed) is a pure problem state. The second (stop feeling stressed) indicates a desire to change, but it has no detail about what that change might entail. Your coachee may be stuck. They describe how you can use CL to move a coachee from a problem or remedy to an outcome.

"When you have stopped feeling stressed, what happens next?"

"And when you would like to stop feeling stressed, what would you like to have happen instead?"

Once you have moved your coachee through from a problem to an outcome, you can develop an outcome to orientate the coachee in the positive state.

"When I stop feeling stressed, I feel productive".

"And that's productive like what?"

"Does productive have a size or shape?"

"When you feel productive, whereabouts is felt productive?"

"What kind of feel productive is that?"

And once the outcome is well formed, you can begin considering the process.

"And when feel productive is like a steady train at a sustainable pace, where could sustainable pace come from?"

"What happens just before steady train?"

And when you have the antecedents, you can orientate the coachee in their wider goals and connect them to their aspirations and social contextualisation.

"And when feel productive, steady and sustainable, what happens next?"

"And then what happen?"
"And what would you like to have happen?"
"And can that happen?"

The framework for change is particularly useful for learning CL and incorporates the essential solution-focused nature of coaching, as opposed to therapy. There's also Clean Space and Emergent Knowledge. These involve using space rather than words to unpack a conceptual landscape. It works best in an open space like a training room or if you are outside for a coaching walk. For example, you might ask, "find a space that knows about not feeling stressed. Move there now. What do you know from there?" Clean Space can work with perceptual positions practices – where the coachee takes a literally different chair to consider the position of someone else in their life. Clean Space is absolutely perfect for those who have strong spatial skills and like to move in order to think, Nancy does!

Clean Language and group coaching

In Nancy's PhD research, we compared group coaching to one-to-one coaching in order to establish which one worked best compared to a control group who did not receive coaching at the time. This was important to Nancy because her company provides group coaching to unemployed people, where resources are fewer. She wanted to find out if they were getting a worse service and, if so, challenge the ethics of this with her funders. Well, she was surprised to discover that the group sessions were in fact more successful than the one-to-ones! They all improved on every measure – self-efficacy, working memory performance, use of behavioural strategies and stress management. However, the group participants made larger gains that were sustained over a longer period (Doyle et al., 2022). Almuth and Nancy wracked their brains on this, but we have the following hypotheses:

• Group coaching reduces shame and stigma – "I'm not the only one who struggles".

- Group coaching reduces the dependency on the coach because the group are using each other as role models.
- Group coaching increases access to role models who are "like me" and therefore accessible.

Using group coaching with CL is great fun. You can start with the modelling mastery approach, asking them to come with an example/time/metaphor for when they have remembered/concentrated/planned/organised at their best. If you have six or more in the group, you will find sufficient diversity of styles – the verbal planners, the spatial memory people – and they can listen to each other's stories and models. The facilitator asks a few CL questions of each person and they start to spot things they have never tried before or used to do but are out of practice. They begin developing cognitive flexibility by 'trying on' each other's models. They learn what they definitely don't want, as well as what might work better. Group coaching is a short cut to developing metacognition and a deep sense of one's own unique way of processing the world. The attention of the group stays on each other and not on the coach because the coach stays clean and doesn't bring their own experience into the room. This reduces dependency and builds confidence across the peers. The camaraderie across the group persists afterwards and they may develop accountability circles, peer mentoring relationships – all based on modelling their skills, which avoids a moaning culture.

Conclusion

We offered Clean Language as a framing for neurodiversity coaching because it is premised on very authentic language and acute listening. It avoids "how do you feel" or "what do you see" type questions as we cannot assume people know, or that such questions relate to their sensory preferences and modalities. Yet some coachees may not take to CL at all and need a lot more structure, at least to start. They might find it hard to know how to answer a clean question and need examples. If this happens, give them a few examples (make sure they are very different from each other) and then move on if it's not landing. Other coachees might find it the only style of coaching that has ever worked for them! We reiterate that it takes practice. Find an introduction to CL course and a practice group to build up your skills. Try it for yourself! Find a CL coach and have a few sessions. The beauty of CL is that you can add it into your practice easily, you can still apply the other coaching techniques we describe in the rest of this book and just choose to gently expand coachee lines of thought with one or two CL questions.

All in all, CL is a flexible and strong technique for working with neurodivergent coachees. It holds us in check as coaches and helps us to learn where we may be inserting our own narratives into the conversation so that we can hold these back. If you find yourself desperate to share something, or ask a leading question, perhaps this says something about you, and your motivations, rather than your coachee? CL will teach you an intense self-awareness of your own boundaries and metacognition – you will know when you are overlaying your own experience on another and when you are not. This is a vital coaching skill to build, particularly for working with neurodivergent people. You may still choose to bring in your own ideas, but you will do so deliberately rather than accidentally, based on your judgement rather than your inexperience. Clean Language is a great process for helping you remain neutral, and not inadvertently pushing your coachees towards neurotypical norms. That alone is important for your coachees' experience of being heard as unique individuals.

Reflective questions

Have a little practice by asking yourself the following CL questions about your own coaching practice.

- When I am coaching at my best, it's like what?
- When I am coaching at my best, what kind of coaching is that coaching?
- When I am coaching at my best, does coaching have a shape or size?
- And where does coaching come from?
- What happens just before I am coaching?
- When I am coaching at my best, I'm like what?
- When I am coaching at my best, is there anything about the 'I' that is coaching?

- And when I am coaching at my best, what happens next?
- And then what happens?
- And knowing all that, what would I like to have happen now?

And then, take all the time you need to list, to sketch, map out or to find something to represent what you have just expressed.

References

Brissett-Bailey, M. (2023). *Black, brilliant and dyslexic: Neurodivergent heroes tell their stories*. Jessica Kingsley.

Doyle, N. E., McDowall, A., Randall, R., & Knight, K. (2022). Does it work? Using a Meta-Impact score to examine global effects in quasi-experimental intervention studies. *PLoS ONE, 17*(3), 1–21. https://doi.org/10.1371/journal.pone.0265312

Dunbar, A. (2017). *Clean coaching*. Routledge.

Lawley, J., & Tompkins, P. (2000). *Metaphors in mind: Transformation through symbolic modelling*. Developing Company Press.

Lawley, J., & Tompkins, P. (2012). *A clean framework for change*. https://cleanlanguage.com/the-evolution-of-the-problem-remedy-outcome-pro-model/

Locke, E. A., & Latham, G. P. (2002). Building a practically useful theory of goal setting and task performance: A 35 year odyssey. *American Psychologist, 57*(9), 705–717.

Sullivan, W., & Rees, J. (2008). *Clean Language: Revealing metaphors and opening minds: Revealing metaphors and opening minds* (1st ed.). Crown House Publishing.

Walker, C. (2014). *From contempt to curiosity*. Clean Publishing.

Way, M. (2013). *Clean approaches for coaches: How to create the conditions for change using clean language and symbolic modelling*. Clean Publishing.

Whitmore, J. (1992). *Coaching for performance*. Nicholas Brealey Publishing.

Wilson, C. (2017). *The work and life of David Grove: Clean Language and Emergent Knowledge*. Troubador Publishing.

Chapter 6

Transactional analysis

Nancy Doyle and Almuth McDowall

Introduction

While the last chapter focused on questioning and conversations, this chapter focuses on dynamics. Transactional analysis (TA) is a way of understanding relationships between people in families, communities and workplaces. It allows us to focus on the dynamics of power, dependency and hostility that can emerge when we are in conflict. It's a relatively simple and straightforward model to underpin coaching processes. It is helpful to share the models about relationship dynamics with coachees to help them develop their understanding of how they can get into difficulties with relationships and how they can extricate themselves. We outline how any dynamics can play out in neurodiversity-affirming coaching, in the coaching relationship itself as well as the relationship between coachee and their colleagues/employer. TA provides a framework for unpicking emotional issues at work. The chapter closes with notes on healthy social dynamics through a neurodivergent lens by outlining examples of the unspoken rules of social communication that might not be obvious to everyone.

Charting its history, transactional analysis (TA) was designed as a therapeutic process, developed in the 1960s by Dr Eric Berne and his collaborators, Dr Stephen Karpman and others (Berne, 1964). It has been frequently adapted to coaching and workplace coaching, as the underlying principles speak to how we relate to others throughout our life span. There is a very useful chapter in *The Complete Handbook of Coaching*, edited by Drs Elaine Cox, Tatiana Bachkirova and David

DOI: 10.4324/9781003368274-8

Clutterbuck (Newton & Napper, 2010), which outlines the main principles of TA and how they apply. It's a lovely tangent to go on to improve your coaching practice in general, and is an effective coaching model with strong evidence of impact (Vos & van Rijn, 2021). Fundamental to the philosophy underpinning TA is humanism, and an unwavering belief in positive psychology. It upholds that people are not broken, that the vast majority of us are doing the best we can in each moment, with the resources that we have available to us at the time. The point of TA as a coaching framework is not to change people, but to provide insight that brings more flexibility and choice to an individual coachee around how they respond to their situation. In this way, it is inherently neurodiversity affirming, because it is not basing the change on a deficit or naming a person as problematic in and of themselves. It can facilitate metacognition regarding relationship dynamics, an area that many neurominorities find difficult and the source of much distress and career derailment. To summarise in brief, there are three main concepts that are helpful for our purposes in coaching neurominorities.

1. Ego states – the parent, the child and the adult. These explain how we can default to an archetypal role in our communication, assuming the role of a parent or a child in relationships for which we are neither. The premise is that at work, we need adult-to-adult relationships and not to be drawn into behaving like parents or children.[1]
2. The OK Corral – This is a quadrant dynamic in which we relate to another person from a position of feeling that we are 'okay' or 'not okay' and that they are 'okay' or 'not okay'. The premise here is that healthy communication operates from a position of 'I'm okay, you're okay', as opposed to finger pointing (I'm okay, you're not okay), shame (I'm not okay, you're okay) or paralysis (I'm not okay, you're not okay).
3. The Drama Triangle – this is where three people in an interaction take a position of persecutor, victim and rescuer. The premise here is that each role has the ability to maintain a drama or conflict by acting in a dependent way to the others and that to break free, the roles have to move into a calmer space where a persecutor can articulate a problem/solution without aggression, a victim can

discover agency and a rescuer can facilitate without taking over. Later work also identified a fourth role – bystander – developing the drama triangle into the drama diamond (Clarkson, 1993).
4. These concepts overlap. A parent role can look like rescuing or persecuting, from an I'm okay, you're not okay position. A child role can look like victimhood, from an I'm not okay position. They also overlap with our fear mechanisms – a fight response is similar to a persecuting role, a flight response is a bystander role, a freeze response is a victim role, and a fawn response is a rescuing role.

Transactional Analysis in the coaching relationship

Our chapter on contracting (Chapter 11) outlines how some coachees approach coaching from a position of victim and are quite wedded to the idea that you might be their rescuer! This particular dynamic is common. You will be able to pick it up straight away when you are contracting and setting expectations and goals. We cannot stress enough how important it is to avoid slipping into these roles. Many neurodivergent people have a lifetime's history of being 'helped' and feeling vulnerable and disempowered. As a group, we have much lower 'self-efficacy' – this is defined as your belief in your own ability to act and be successful (Gillespie-Lynch et al., 2017; Nalavany et al., 2017). Self-efficacy is improved by taking action (in small steps that are achievable) and focusing on what you are good at, experiencing 'mastery' over a situation or task and then building confidence in your ability to repeat the success (Bandura, 1986). No one is going to achieve that if their coach swoops in with their rescuer cape on and tries to save them from their problems.

In practice, this goes right back to the way you set up your contract and remit with your coachee and their employer, who may be the fee-paying client. What is in your remit and not in your remit? The first flag is if you are being invited to do things *for* the coachee – such as 'have a word with a colleague for them' or review/edit a piece of work. These are obvious invitations to rescue, but there are more subtle occasions where you might not notice, for example when a coachee is consistently late or unprepared for coaching and you are invited to repeatedly tell them that it 'doesn't matter', when in fact it is potentially a problem that they have at work more widely and should be discussed as a coaching topic. You might also be drawn into agreeing that someone at work is a persecutor, and therefore you are validating the drama triangle without your own evidence. These dynamics play out in all workplace coaching, but because neurodivergent people experience marginalisation, it is more likely that the victim role has become what we term in TA a 'script'. A script is a storyline template that follows a similar pattern across many relationships in the individual's life and work history. If a coachee has experienced receiving support before, from a teacher, a specialist teacher, a colleague at work or a different coach, they may have a 'script' about how you are 'supposed' to help them. They may bring great expectations of your ability to do things for them and validate their experiences. This could backfire spectacularly when you don't follow the script. Sometimes when a victim is expecting rescuing, and they don't get it, they can place you in the persecutor role. This is why contracting is such an essential part of good coaching. If you have contracted well, you can revisit it as a way out of a drama, and openly discuss whether the request or behaviour is in remit or out of remit.

Staying in adult-to-adult, I'm okay/you're okay language is the best way to avoid being drawn into a script. Stay 'above' the storyline, comment on it, about it, ask questions about it. This technique is called 'meta-commenting' – like metacognition only instead of thinking about thinking patterns, we are commenting on the patterns of the discourse. This will be particularly tricky for coaches who have their own internalised scripts about being needed (rescuer) or taken advantage of (victim) or being surrounded by people who aren't trying hard enough (persecutor). Drama roles are exactly why you need supervision to work in this space and we have devoted our entire last chapter to professional principles. Supervision helps you to understand how your own lived experience of archetypal roles could influence how you react to and communicate with your coachees and their employers.

Transactional Analysis in neurodiversity at work

When working with a coachee on their relationships at work you will also come across scripts. As a coach you can listen for scripts and draw them to the coachee's attention to facilitate their understanding and self-insight about dynamics. Your coach may take a victim, persecutor, rescuer or bystander role. We now explain some common examples of drama patterns we have seen with coachees of all neurotypes, including neurodivergent.

When victims are persecutors

Your coachees won't always be in the victim role, but they may tend to see themselves in the victim role, even when they are persecuting. This is a TA paradox – when someone is being very rude, unsupportive, aggressive, insensitive to others (i.e. persecuting) they typically feel that they are defending themselves (victim). A very tricky course to navigate is unpicking these behaviours with one person at a time, when you have no access to the other people in the dynamic. This is where the OK Corral can be most useful. Encourage your coachees to approach a situation from a position of I'm okay, you're okay – giving the perceived persecutor the benefit of the doubt. "What could they mean? What could be a positive intention behind their behaviour?" It really helps to separate the actual words said, or actions taken, from the inferences made of them. Someone standing up at the start of the meeting could come from a position of relaxed confidence, a need to regain control, a domineering stance, or a bad back. We don't truly know each other's intentions, and when we overlay our own inferences upon other people's behaviour, sometimes these tell the story of our inferences alone. We'll remember how we felt, but how we feel is biased by our scripts, which could be unduly hostile. Unpicking this with neurodivergent coachees is highly skilled work and comes perilously close to counselling if you start to enquire as to where those scripts come from. We advise staying strictly within the confines of workplace experiences and working to a positive outcome – what would be a new script that would enable you to see your team as supporters, not detractors?

A great example here is Wes. When his manager approached him to try and find a more positive way to have meetings, Wes didn't understand him. The manager said that he needed to "play the game" more in the meetings, so that they could both get what they needed. Wes's first reaction was a victim style "he's okay, I'm not okay", as he experienced shame in not knowing how to deliver the request and embarrassment that meant he couldn't ask. He was distressed and didn't know how to approach the situation. His second reaction was a flip. He became angry at the request itself, and assumed that his boss was being deliberately obtuse, trying to alienate and undermine him. Wes was thus playing the persecutor role – "I'm okay, he's not okay". He had assumed hostile intentions, without checking. This flip is common – when one person feels victimised and so becomes a persecutor of the other. In working with them both at the same time, Nancy held the space of adult. She didn't allow herself to be drawn into deciding who was 'right' and who was 'wrong'. She focused on understanding the pattern of communication, without judgement. Having practised Clean Language for over 20 years, Nancy is able to hold the space for meta-commenting on the pattern, rather than being drawn into the content.

Nancy, having worked with Wes for a while, guessed correctly that Wes had taken "play the game" literally and was wondering why his boss wanted him to play games at work. Literal interpretation is a common trait of autistic people. She also suspected that the manager wasn't trying to be obtuse, he just had no idea what to say to unlock the behaviour he sought. Both were increasingly frustrated. She asked clean-ish questions of the manager until he was able to articulate a more concrete request – come to the meeting with a record of what you did last week and what you plan to do next week, around 10–12 tasks on each list, no more than one or two sentences to describe each one. She used questions such as:

"What will you see or hear that will let you know he is playing the game?"

"Wes will be more proactive".
"And when Wes is more proactive, what will you see and hear from him?
What will he be saying or doing?
Have you got an example of a time he's done what you want before?"

But this was a struggle for the manager! He used management-speak lingo so well that he sincerely didn't have a clue that he wouldn't be understood by Wes. Wes watched him wrestle with Nancy's clarifying questions and understood that his intention was not malevolent. Nancy and Wes reflected afterwards on Wes's rush to judge his manager as intentionally withholding information from him. The experience opened the door for Wes to realise that other times he has interpreted his manager as a persecutor might not be true either, and they began to see each other as communicators of different languages (autistic and allistic) rather than enemies. Hostile attributions are a defence mechanism, but left unchecked they can poison relationships and lead to states of embattlement, where the neurodivergent person feels alienated and alone. Helping a coachee to unpick a few occasions like this can be transformative, holding back on the rush to defensive attacks will preserve allyship in careers. Misunderstandings are a normal part of life and conflict is not the same as abuse.

When a coachee is a rescuer

This pattern happens for two reasons. Some neurodivergent coachees will be running a script that they are not valued unless they are indispensable. They will overwork and over-commit themselves in order to feel wanted, and to buffer potential rejection. Other coachees will not have the cognitive skills to plan their time properly and, out of a desire to help, will end up promising too much and delivering only by sacrificing their own wellbeing, then flipping into a victim role. Both patterns can be resolved through understanding the script patterns and drawing a coachee's attention to the start of the pattern when they can make different choices if they are self-aware. This last point is the critical belief of TA – that people are reasonable and, given the right resources and self-awareness, they will make appropriate choices. You can work in coaching from this premise quite happily, but when coachees are continually making choices that cause them or others harm, despite being aware of scripts, this is when we start to cross into counselling and therapeutic territory. It is time to refer.

A coachee that updates their rescuing behaviour needs a health warning – other people may find this annoying! Sometimes a whole ecosystem evolves around someone who rescues by default, their colleagues and friendship groups become dependent on them. When over-helpfulness is withdrawn and boundaries reset, they perceive this as a deficit, rather than the removal of an excessive benefit. It is not unusual for people moving on from rescuing to be abandoned by people with whom they felt they had strong bonds and to need to form new relationships upon more reflexive, equal footings. It might even require a new job role. These changes can be destabilising to say the least!

Mo fell into this category with their colleagues at a clinic. As a trainee counselling psychologist and therapist, Mo had spent a lot of time working on their drama roles and scripts. So they were alert to it in a formal, client to client setting. What they hadn't banked on was how their rescuer tendencies were sneaking into other relationships. For example, they would regularly find themselves in charge of the 'office housework'. These are the sorts of tasks that everyone finds boring but need to be done, otherwise the office doesn't run – putting ink in the photocopier, organising the Christmas party, planning the rota for clinic space, checking the health and safety related documentation, updating the website. Mo had really struggled with admin as a junior and was holding onto some shame about being a drain on other people, having had to ask for help. They were overcompensating. But now, they were getting very stressed by the additional workload and so when they reviewed, in coaching, where these stresses came from they realised they had taken up way more of the jobs than was their fair share. Partially this is a gender issue – people assigned female at birth often have a lifetime of being expected to do unpaid unglamorous tasks and observing those in their gender perform the helper/rescuer/martyr role. As Mo had recently come out as non-binary, having been assigned female at birth, they recognised the weight of this expectation.

In coaching, Mo expressed frustration with their colleagues and Nancy asked them if they saw any drama triangle issues here. Luckily Mo's experience with TA meant that they could very quickly act on this issue without drama. Mo realised that they had taken on more responsibility than necessary (rescuing) but was now feeling hard done by (victim). A great clean question for those in the victim role is "what would you like to have happen?". Often this generates a response of what your coachee would like other people to do. However, your coachee is not in control of other people, so the response needs to be unpacked.

"I'd like my colleagues to do more office housekeeping."
"And when you'd like them to do more, but they are currently not doing more, what would you like to have happen?"
"I'd like to speak to them about it and ask if they have noticed."
"And can you speak to them about it? Speaking to them would be like what?"
"Oh, I can ask for office housekeeping to be on the agenda of our next meeting. I'll keep track of what I've done between now and then in case they aren't sure what I mean."

Do you see how the coaching conversation empowered Mo, to move from child to adult? They started in a parent role (uninvited rescuer) then child (powerless victim) and then moved to adult (negotiator). They called a clinic meeting and presented a list of all the things they were doing that needed to be shared and their colleagues jumped right in. The colleagues, also well versed in TA, appreciated the gender-bound issue and the complex neurodivergent dynamic of needing to feel valued but taking on too much. They agreed who would share which tasks and the timelines in which they would be completed, they stuck to a rota.

When a coachee is a victim

We issue a note of caution – not all colleagues are as responsible as Mo's. It was perfectly possible that their response could have been to nod and agree and change nothing. They may have disagreed openly. They may have said very little in the meeting and tried to brush it aside. At this point, Mo still has choices. They don't have to stay in the role. If your coachees are working with people who won't move off the drama triangle and are wedded to being a rescuer, victim, persecutor or bystander, this is not psychologically safe. In coaching, your role might be to reinforce that there are other options and to explore safe alternatives. Holding the line between this, and inadvertently validating a script that the individual is being victimised when it is actually a hostile attribution, is very complex coaching work. These are the times we are reminded that coaching is hard graft. These are the times we need supervision and reflective practice sessions.

However, we also issue a note of hope – if you can gently steer someone through the thorny side of a drama triangle loop at work, it is life changing. Many of our coachees and mentees who have mastered this have gone on to develop their careers, to maintain and sustain solid work foundations. The beauty of transactional analysis is how clear and relatable the models are, they bring clarity and focus to problems that have caused us anguish. Once coachees learn them, they start to pick themselves up on their own patterns: "Oh, I'm doing the thing where I've assumed they intended me harm again", "Oops, took everyone else's jobs on accidentally again!", "Oh,

I recognise this pattern as persecution or rescuing. I'm going to try to resolve from an adult place and if it doesn't settle, I am going to take steps to protect my boundaries."

Developmental tasks are a great way to get people to change behaviour patterns. Developmental tasks are where you create a simple, discrete objective to stretch into a new pattern. They have to be concrete, time bound and observable. Here are a few examples:

- Go to two meetings and leave without accepting any action points in the next two weeks.
- List five times this individual (who you have disagreed with) has been an ally or aligned with you before your next meeting with them.
- Say "I have observed that" instead of "I feel that" three times in the next week.
- Let three other people speak before you talk in the morning meeting.
- Turn down two requests in the next month in order to protect your time.

Transactional Analysis and exploring emotions at work

TA is a great framework for exploring strong emotions and unwanted emotions at work because we can approach the same topic with a new frame. It is a starting point to look at stresses through the lens of the coachee as rescuer. Have they set themselves up with a pattern of creating additional stress because they have taken on too much? Can they declutter their to do list without an emotional pull or feeling that they won't be welcome or included if they are not over-delivering? Do they have a good sense of comparison between themselves and their peers in terms of workload? Has this intersected with other marginalised identities, such as gender, as described above? When stress piles up because of ongoing rescuing, whether that was invited or played out via an individual's script, the coachee can find themselves veering towards the victim role. And, once there, a persecutor tends to be assigned. That might be the person or team who they have been rescuing, or it might be a colleague who 'should' have been doing more to help as well/ instead. Working through the dynamic of everyday stress through TA can lead to insight and an improved sense of control.

It's not fair

Everyday stress at work can also be about fairness, people doing their fair share of the hard work, the fairness of being supported with adjustments and more. Neurodivergent people are known for having a strong sense of justice, and for seeking equity and balance in very detailed ways. This is pathologised as 'justice sensitivity' and has been linked to increased anxiety for some neurotypes (Bondü & Esser, 2015). Further, being a neurominority is linked to a very real sense of 'epistemic injustice' (Chapman & Carel, 2022). This means that methods of diagnosis, research and knowledge pertaining to neurodiversity are one in which the truth and lived experience of the neurodivergent is overruled and perceived only from the frame of 'normal' and 'abnormal' cognitive and emotional thinking. Epistemic injustice includes systemic racism or patriarchy. The highly tuned fairness radar of the neurodivergent person can be put to good use in a coaching framework. It can help a coachee weigh up evidence of input and output, comparing whether roles are fairly distributed and therefore whether they can avoid running a 'script' in which they have to give or take more. However, it is this orientation towards fairness that can also create strong emotions when unfairness is perceived. Your job is to support them to consider the situation from an adult perspective, wherever they may be sitting in the relationship itself. You can use the parent/child/adult and the OK Corral models to assist your coachee into moving themselves into a less intense frame of mind where they can make decisions about the best course of action – even when this is leaving.

Audrey had an experience like this with her boss. Audrey had been unaware of how far off the mark her spelling and grammar were for her role before having coaching, which included input on goals from her manager. The manager, we'll call her Estelle, had been rescuing her, repeatedly, for many months and was at breaking point. She could no longer edit Audrey's letters before they went out because it was compromising her ability to do her own work. She had got into this habit during Audrey's first few months, thinking she was being 'helpful' to a new member of staff. She had assumed that Audrey would improve as she became more familiar with the language related to the job. Audrey did not. By the time of the coaching, Estelle was in a total bind, should she tell Audrey that for nearly a year Audrey had been underperforming and risk a difficult, emotional conversation, or should she just try and carry on? She was caught in a rescuing loop. When Audrey discovered that this had been going on, she was initially very embarrassed and ashamed. She did not want to have been such a drain – it was not her intention. Estelle was also embarrassed and at first, they had a 'rescue-off', where they both tried to reassure each other that no harm was intended or taken. Both were relieved to learn that assistive technology existed and could be deployed to improve Audrey's writing.

Later on, Audrey became quite upset about Estelle's behaviour. She experienced it as a lack of trust, an undermining of her ability to handle difficult information and improve. She was also cross because, if Estelle had spoken up sooner, she would have had the language to discuss openly. Without the honesty there was just a sense of rising tension that she couldn't put a name to, but she felt that there was distance growing in their relationship. Audrey began to feel that there was a great injustice, that she had been belittled and placed in a child role by a rescuing parent, without her consent. She realised that it had caused her a great deal of anxiety and stress that had bubbled along under the surface for months, without really knowing where it was coming from. She had intuited something was wrong, but without clarity from Estelle had tried to ignore her misgivings. She felt gaslit. Audrey argued that Estelle, as a manager, should have known better and directed her straight to assistive technology. Audrey found it very hard to let go, because it began to chime in with other times that this had happened where friends and family members had just 'done it for her' because they could see she was struggling. She started running a script, where Estelle was an imperfect parent, and started interpreting every offer of help in normal day-to-day interactions as patronising. She built up quite a lot of resentment concerning Estelle. To resolve, Audrey and Nancy worked through the OK Corral. Nancy asked Audrey:

"What could be some positive intentions behind Estelle's behaviour?"
"From an 'I'm okay/you're okay' position, what might have happened?"

Audrey came up with plausible reasons why Estelle may have continued to cover up the literacy difficulties. They discussed the time drains of working in a busy environment and feeling like there was no time to have an in-depth conversation. They considered the strong customer service skills that Audrey had and how Estelle may have wanted to avoid draining her time away from customer focus. Audrey conceded that the large organisation in which they worked did not provide disability inclusion training for managers and that Estelle wouldn't necessarily know about assistive technology, just as Audrey did not. Audrey agreed that Estelle probably didn't mean to humiliate her and was herself a human being with limits who doesn't get everything right.

Nancy also asked Audrey "could the perspective of race and gender be a factor in your relationship?" Audrey agreed that it was. Audrey and Estelle were both Black women and had relied on each other for cultural safety in a predominantly white space, where both had experienced microaggressions. This had made it even harder for Audrey to voice her experience of being undermined by Estelle. She did not want to betray her boss, but she also considered that she had had her on a pedestal. Audrey admired Estelle's tenacity and courage to lead. However, by allowing Estelle to be human and not expecting her to be the perfect boss, Audrey moved into an adult-to-adult role with her boss.

Nancy asked Audrey how she would like to resolve the situation. Audrey arranged a conversation with Estelle to clear the air. She started by saying that finding out her performance had been poor for such a long time had really destabilised her, and she was now worried about finding out something else was bad, that she didn't know about. Estelle assured her this was not the case and they had a very good conversation about what Audrey did well at work, and how Estelle could approach her next time she had a concern. They also had a conversation about the impact of race and being raised in a culture where they had been trained to not challenge authority, as well as being women raised to be deferent and avoid saying difficult things. They considered the impact of racism on their careers and ambition and resolved to be thorough in their feedback to each other ongoing, using the Clean Feedback Model as outlined in Chapter 7, in order to provide a safe and respectful challenge, so that they could both progress in their careers.

Healthy relationships through the lens of Transactional Analysis

The example above with Estelle and Audrey shows the journey of an unhealthy, parent–child dynamic at work transforming into an adult-to-adult relationship of mutual respect. Audrey and Estelle had a good relationship with mutual respect, which was a good basis for resolution, but this is not always the case with employee/boss dynamics. Further, we need to be mindful of and acknowledge dynamics that could possibly play out with white colleagues/middle managers, and how that may trigger trauma, feeling misunderstood, lack of belonging, or simply being made to feel different (Roche &

Passmore, 2022). If you are a white coach you might feel this might be out of your realm of expertise, you may feel the need for supervision. However, as a white coach, it is still within your remit to acknowledge a racial lens, as to ignore it denies another person's reality and attempts to override any responsibility to address it in our practice (Bryant-Davis & Ocampo, 2005).

Your coachees may want to work through social communication that is normal at work, what to expect and how to respond in healthy, psychologically safe ways. So many neurodivergent people are taught to ignore their sensitivities (you're so fussy) to quiet their internal instincts (you need to sit still) and to feel that their problem is a personality deficit (she has such potential, but she doesn't try hard enough). As a result, many of us arrive in adulthood and careers without a strong internal reference for what is right and wrong, when we are being manipulated or disrespected. Some neurominorities are vulnerable to abuse and exploitation. Talking your coachees through TA also gives you a forum for discussing healthy relationships at work and what these look, sound and feel like.

The following section shows a range of adult-to-adult behaviours at work that can easily tip into unhealthy ones. These were devised by Nancy's neurodiverse team at Genius Within and written into a business etiquette policy in order to spell out unwritten social norms of communication. They are based on the typical difficulties that cropped up for the team and caused drama and hurt. Nancy's team are around two-thirds disabled and/or neurodivergent staff, with different life experiences of healthy communication, trauma recovery, trauma bonding and intersectional overlaps. The list might be worth running through with your coachees if you hear any of them cropping up. Remember that a fundamental issue for many neurodivergent people, particularly those with ADHD or autistic traits, is not 'getting' social conventions. The unspoken rules of what is 'okay' and 'not okay' in work relationships is a minefield for many of us. These explanations might seem obvious to you but having the opportunity to talk them through might be eye-opening for your coachees. It was certainly a very settling experience for Nancy's team to clarify where there were boundaries being overstepped and how to walk them back without losing respect for each other. Never assume that social etiquette is obvious!

Being friends with your colleagues, talking about work projects and plans at work

Having colleagues who are also friends is a bonus. It becomes an overstep when you are talking negatively about colleagues without addressing any issues directly, or when you are agreeing that other people in the business are at fault when you only have one side of the story. The risk is that you place an undue emotional burden on each other, exacerbating drama, which can lead to tension and tone in meetings. If group conversations take this turn, it is okay to ask colleagues to stop, and to withdraw from the conversation. It's also completely fine to *not* be friends with colleagues outside work. If you find it easier to maintain strict boundaries, do that.

Being in contact on social media with colleagues at work

A great deal of camaraderie and rapport can be built when you communicate through less formal channels. It becomes an overstep when you are expecting each other to respond out of hours, chastising each other if a prompt response is not forthcoming, complaining about work on social media where your work friends can see it. Work boundaries become blurred; putting pressure to be "always on" to colleagues when they may be trying to relax of an evening leaves colleagues fearful, wondering what upset you and if it will affect them. If you are feeling pressured by social media contacts at work, it's okay to let them know you'd prefer less contact out of hours.

Listening to distress and signposting support

Listening to distressed colleagues is helpful and to be expected in everyday work situations, occasionally. Telling your colleagues what to do when you are not responsible or don't have the full facts is an overstep. You risk getting it wrong, leading your colleague to an inappropriate action, taking on emotional responsibility for your colleague, which can be draining. You can instead simply ask them what they would like to have happen or signpost them to a manager or HR to deal with the issue. If it is a regular event, and you have tried asking colleagues to resolve it elsewhere, it is okay to tell a manager or HR what is happening and ask for them to intervene.

Having friendships with colleagues who may hold different levels of responsibility than you at work (seniority)

When there are friendships at work, these naturally become split across hierarchies as people get promoted. Employers can't and shouldn't police friendships, but this needs careful management, and an agreement between the friends not to discuss work out of work. It's not okay to ask friends to resolve difficult things on your behalf because they have influence or, vice versa, burdening colleagues who have less influence with problems they can't resolve. Whichever side of this you are, it might be tricky and it's okay to talk about it openly with your friend, letting them know when you feel that it's gone too far.

Asking friends to support you in an HR meeting, making it very clear that they can say no if they are worried it might create tension

If you have a difficult meeting to attend, perhaps about performance, it's okay to ask a colleague to attend to support you but give them an out. Telling them you will be upset if they say no, or passive alternatives such as "I don't know who else to ask" puts them in a very awkward position which risks the friendship. If you are asked this, it's okay to say no.

If you are worried about a colleague, talking to them directly or discussing it in supervision with your manager or practice supervisor

If you are worried about a colleague, sharing this confidentially is the right course of action. Talking to other colleagues about it, outside formal confidential conversations creates tension, overwhelm and breaks confidentiality. Direct and within confidential settings is best for concerns. It's okay to ask for advice on a situation confidentially or anonymously.

The occasional bubble over of emotion or worry

It's okay to have a rant now and again to let off a bit of steam. Most employees have a few colleagues with whom they do this occasionally. It's important to make sure that this doesn't become a habit of regular outbursts, gossip and complaint about colleagues behind their back. The latter creates tension, cliques and ostracism. If you are finding that you are regularly complaining, it means you need to take more formal action, be that a complaint or whistleblowing, or moving roles. It's okay to name a situation as a hostile environment and seek an out, if you have tried to resolve from an adult perspective.

Discussing your fears and concerns about work and relationships in your management relationships, with human resources or at reflective practice sessions, coaching and co-coaching

These are the boundaried spaces in which you could discuss complaints and whistleblowing events. When you have serious concerns, using only work friends and colleagues leads to doubt, fear and insecurity that doesn't get resolved. It brings risk to you, your colleagues and won't solve your problems. It is okay to request a meeting with HR or another company representative for help with relationships at work.

Connecting deeply with people who work with you on projects you care a lot about

If you work in a values-driven role, it is likely that you will form strong bonds with your colleagues as you contribute to a shared mission. This is great. Where it goes wrong is when you inevitably find that you don't agree on everything. If you think your colleagues are 'perfect' and put them on a pedestal, they can only fall off. All or nothing relationships are not safe, be mindful that one disagreement doesn't negate all the good things that you have in common. It's okay for your colleagues and boss to have different ideas.

Feeling upset when a close colleague behaves in a way you don't expect but letting it go or engaging in a feedback exchange to resolve if you are struggling to move on

Your colleagues are going to let you down at some point. Expect it. Seeking perfection from colleagues or your boss is not healthy, it signifies a power imbalance, a parent/child relationship rather than adult-to-adult. If you are let down, don't blank the person or talk trash about them, invite them to resolve it with you directly, from a position of trust. You may have misunderstood, or it could be an area in which you disagree. It is normal and okay to disagree with people on some matters and still hold them in high regard.

Giving each other the benefit of the doubt, assuming that there are misunderstandings arising when in conflict and that with feedback, supervision and support we can unpick these

Conflict and disagreement at work are normal. Intervening before we get to the place where we don't believe each other anymore is a preventative strategy. All parties can be responsible for initiation, as adult colleagues – you don't need to defer to your boss as the only person who can start a resolution conversation. You are an adult too. If your boss won't engage, even after a short break to calm down, you have a different problem and it is perfectly okay to approach a different manager, their manager, or human resources.

Withdrawing from everyday communication for a day or two, to process a difficult interaction or event

It's okay to take time to process, particularly when you have a neurotype that compromises your ability to think clearly in the moment. Where this can be difficult is when you expect others to come chasing after you to pull you back into the conversation and, further, if you get mad at them when they don't. These are parent/child expectations. If you need to withdraw for a while, this is fine. If it's going to be more than a few days, or mean that you will miss deadlines or events, you need to negotiate this. At minimum you can send or expect to receive a 'holding email' that lets someone know you are processing and will come back to them soon. Processing is healthy, taking time to calm down and thinking something through is a good indicator of boundaries. Sulking is not healthy and you don't have to accept it in your work relationships.

Being 'in process,' not giving ourselves or each other a hard chastisement when we fail at relationships

Acknowledging that we all fail sometimes, as employees, as managers and as coaches is okay. To err is human, and we can behave responsibly and from an adult perspective afterwards by communicating directly with those we may have let down, taking it to supervision and trying to resolve. Or we can decide that it's time to move on, but that doesn't mean we are leaving villains, we can hold people in respect even when we are no longer able to work with them. Sometimes it takes a bit of time to get here and you should feel able to take this time. If you have failed on this, it is not reasonable for people to ostracise you or talk trash about you. You don't have to accept this at work.

The value of practical exercises based on Transactional Analysis

The list above is compiled from Genius Within, but chimes with wider professional experience. Nancy and Almuth both hold over 20 years of practice and research in the neurodiversity community and beyond. We have travelled our own paths of progress in cultural norms, gender norms and more. The list represents typical difficulties that we have navigated with our coachees and colleagues. We have found our coachees really welcome the opportunity to debrief relationship difficulties with someone who won't jump on the drama triangle with them and will help hold a space for them to reflect and learn. The learning could be that they are tolerating unsafe and unacceptable behaviour because they are so anxious about rejection, in which case this could help them repair their boundaries. It could also be that they are actively participating in a drama that they need to resolve. It is difficult to know, sometimes, where the drama is coming from and it is rarely 100% one-sided. It's even harder to identify when you have a history of being told you are wrong and being socially excluded. Coaching neurodivergent people who are at higher risk of trauma and abuse, from unhealthy to healthy relationships at work requires you to acknowledge your own relationship patterns. If you think you've never had any issues, you might need to take part in some coaching to develop your self-awareness. Negotiating relationship boundaries is a unifying human experience, even though it may be easier for some people than for others. This is where intersectionality really matters and where you need to take account of cultural safety, legal safety, experiences of being medicalised and pathologised, as well as excluded by poverty and finding authority a risk rather than a safety mechanism (Kendall, 2020). Intersectionality also matters for realising ambition and career aspirations. Many workplaces remain neuronormative and purport engrained, white, cisgendered, heterosexual, male stereotypes for leadership and management. TA allows coach and coachee to illuminate potentially toxic dynamics.

Conclusion

TA is a non-judgmental and empowering technique to use in neurodiversity coaching as it allows reflection on relationship dynamics. This is particularly helpful where coachees have established roles and behaviour patterns such as a rescuer or where relationships at work have become fraught or difficult. Clear developmental exercises encourage practice between sessions. Negotiating relationship patterns and understanding convention can be challenging for some neurodiverse coachees, therefore we provided you with concrete examples to share with your coachees, but we invite you to collate your own.

Reflective questions

Here are some questions for you to work out your current understanding about TA and relationships:

- Identify the last time you have been in each of the drama diamond roles. Make some notes about what sparked each event.
  - Persecutor:

- Victim:
- Rescuer:
- Bystander:

- When you were last in each of the drama diamond roles, how did it resolve? What steps did you take?

  - Persecutor:
  - Victim:
  - Rescuer:
  - Bystander:

- Can you identify scripts in your life story? Are you usually misunderstood? A scapegoat? The only one who can manage? The one who can make difficult decisions? Forgotten about and overlooked?
- Can you think of any times where your script turned out to be untrue and you made a mistake?
- Do you have any good experiences of leaving work relationships? Where the goodbye was respectful and drama-free? What allowed that to be the case?

Note

1 Note that the use of parent, child and adult are metaphors here for power. TA does not seek to assert that all children behave thus, or that all parents are unskilled.

References

Bandura, A. (1986). *Social foundations of thought and action*. Prentice Hall.

Berne, E. (1964). *Games people play*. Grove Press.

Bondü, R., & Esser, G. (2015). Justice and rejection sensitivity in children and adolescents with ADHD symptoms. *European Child & Adolescent Psychiatry*, *24*(2), 185–198. https://doi.org/10.1007/s00787-014-0560-9

Bryant-Davis, T., & Ocampo, C. (2005). Racist incident–based trauma. *The Counseling Psychologist*, *33*(4), 479–500. https://doi.org/10.1177/0011000005276465

Chapman, R., & Carel, H. (2022). Neurodiversity, epistemic injustice, and the good human life. *Journal of Social Philosophy*, *53*(4), 1–18. https://doi.org/10.1111/josp.12456

Clarkson, P. (1993). Bystander games. *Transactional Analysis*, *23*(3), 158–172. https://doi.org/10.1177/036215379302300307

Gillespie-Lynch, K., Bublitz, D., Donachie, A., Wong, V., Brooks, P. J., & D'Onofrio, J. (2017). "For a long time our voices have been hushed": Using student perspectives to develop supports for neurodiverse college students. *Frontiers in Psychology, 8.* https://doi.org/10.3389/fpsyg.2017.00544

Kendall, M. (2020). *Hood feminism: Notes from the women white feminists forgot* (1st ed.). Bloomsbury Publishing.

Nalavany, B. A., Logan, J. M., & Carawan, L. W. (2017). The relationship between emotional experience with dyslexia and work self-efficacy among adults with dyslexia. *Dyslexia, 24*(1), 1–16. https://doi.org/10.1002/dys.1575

Newton, T., & Napper, R. (2010). Transactional analysis and coaching. In *The Complete Handbook of Coaching* (1st ed., pp. 172–186). Sage.

Roche, C., & Passmore, J. (2022). Anti-racism in coaching: A global call to action. *Coaching: An International Journal of Theory, Research and Practice, 16*(1), 115–132. https://doi.org/10.1080/17521882.2022.2098789

Vos, J., & van Rijn, B. (2021). The evidence-based conceptual model of transactional analysis: A focused review of the research literature. *Transactional Analysis, 51*(2), 160–201. https://doi.org/10.1080/03621537.2021.1904364

Chapter 7

Positive communication in coaching

Almuth McDowall and Nancy Doyle

Introduction

We've taken a deep dive into Clean Language (CL) and Transactional Analysis (TA) as two core coaching methods for working with neurodivergent coachees. These are the two with which we conducted the majority of our neurodiversity affirmative coaching research. However, there are other workplace communication models that also lend themselves to a person-centred and positive psychology coaching framing.

Firstly, we introduce Appreciative Inquiry (AI) which is relevant in neurodiversity coaching because of the emphasis on language and discourse to speak about what works. We next discuss reflexive coaching, which looks at loops and patterns in language and how to recognise and examine these to encourage solution-focused thinking. The chapter then outlines the principles of feedback, including the 'feedforward', which combines AI principles with feedback theories to offer a model for structuring conversations around what the individual can achieve. Thus, this chapter references specific techniques to use in neurodiversity coaching, but also general portable principles about good feedback to share with coachees to implement in their current work context.

The coaching models we're presenting are not meant to be exhaustive but based on what we find relevant and helpful in this context. For those of you who are trained coaches, many of the tools you already use can be deployed for neurodivergent people,

DOI: 10.4324/9781003368274-9

such as goal setting, the GROW model, acceptance and commitment coaching. For those of you hoping to move into coaching, there is a wealth of models that form a baseline of good practice. Any recognised, externally verified coaching qualification will give you a strong baseline from which to practice.

Appreciative inquiry in coaching

AI was conceived as a method to guide a range of organisational change initiatives that encompass organisational development, training, restructures and mergers, training and leadership development and coaching (Cooperrider et al., 2008). The basic premise is that every organisation has aspects that are 'right' and give it life; therefore, the starting point of a conversation is to identify what is positive. AI takes an open-system approach, which means that organisations rely on their social and human capital, the people in it, to bring it to life. In many traditional organisational development approaches the focus has been on problem-solving and troubleshooting, for example identifying why an established process or structure does not work so well and then how to make it better. In contrast, AI frames "organisations as a mystery to be embraced". While we might believe that we know everything about an organisation at a surface level, there are likely to be things that everyone needs to discover, and then harness, together. This can be a very empowering stance to adopt in neurodiversity coaching. As we outlined in Chapter 2, neurodivergent coachees often bring a history of perceived failure to coaching due to lack of affirmative experiences in earlier life; for example, lack of success in education or continuously being judged for things that others consider different or jarring. Such prior experience can mean that, even where coachees do well at work overall, so have a role that suits their capabilities, they get discouraged and lose confidence when things don't quite go to plan. This is where coaching conversations that focus on the positive can be helpful and encourage reflection.

AI-based conversations loosely structure around four questions which we have adapted from Cooperrider et al. (2008) using CL.

We have put some additional prompts in brackets as sometimes you have to be very explicit with neurodivergent coachees:

- When you think of a 'high-point' experience in your workplace, when you are most alive and engaged, this is like what . . .?
- What is it that you value most about:

  - You? (you might need to gently but firmly bring this back to a work context if coachees go off on a tangent!)
  - Your work? (prompts might be: the tasks you do? What you have been trusted to do?)
  - Your organisation? (prompts might be: the environment, the way that things are done in general, etc.)

- The things that give life to your organisation/career (so without these, it would no longer be there), they are like what . . .? (you might need to explain this more concretely – for example 'the things that make your organisation unique, that you notice a lot')
- A miracle has occurred. Your organisation/career became exactly what it wants to be. You go in and look at this change. Imagine what the entire picture looks like in your head. This is like what? (You might need more prompts here: what is new? What has changed? What has become better/more effective/more inclusive? What's the first thing you see/hear that you don't see/hear now?)

The idea is that such questions stimulate change; where dialogue leads to discovery to dream about the future, then co-create or design what could be, which creates a new destiny. The AI interview works well particularly in group coaching. In neurodiversity coaching, our experience is that you might want to tone down the language a little from the original writing originating from the US, particularly when you work in countries such as the UK, where people talk in less flowery and positive language. You might also need to spend more time clarifying what exactly you mean by phrases such as "something that gives life" – for example wording such as "the kind of things that give people energy where you work" are more precise. We outline an example below.

Almuth used an AI framework when she was working with a micro enterprise, who were people working in an arts and design context as a cooperative; several identified as neurodiverse. One of them confided in advance of a briefing call that some members of their cooperative feared that they "had fallen out beyond repair". They had come to Almuth for support to help them better understand each other. Almuth facilitated a day's workshop and group coaching, which the group wanted to be held somewhere other than their usual work to "allow them to start afresh". Almuth asked each of them to answer the AI questions in turn, answers were noted on a flipchart, to help people remember what was said. This also helped accommodate their preferences – they were all comfortable looking at the chart and the words, but less comfortable looking at each other. All five agreed that the high point for them at work was setting up their collective. They told each other how much they liked their common purpose which "gave others a space to be creative". Almuth asked the question, what did they value about how they worked with each other, and their creative endeavour, first. She could sense that some were reluctant to talk about themselves, so this helped to make everyone comfortable with these questions. She then asked what they valued about themselves and each other. The group shared how much they valued each other but for very different qualities – each of them had a unique contribution to their community. This conversation made it clear how much they loved their creative work. They really liked that they "gave each other room" and "freedom to be creative". When asked the miracle question, they said that the one thing that would have changed was for them to be more connected to each other. Almuth asked them, "being connected is like what . . .?" – "Asking each other questions about how we are and what we are doing!" was the spontaneous answer. The group then did some action planning about how they would apply these insights, and how they would know that the change that they wanted was happening. They made "questions about each other" a focus of regular team meetings, which were going to be about their human connection and celebrating difference and not just focused on how they ran their business. They are still working with each other! Notice how Almuth used CL questions to develop the group's conversation seamlessly and without interference, whilst holding the AI model in mind. This is what we mean by modelling, instead of using models when you are coaching – the fluency to move seamlessly between approaches in order to best fit what your coachee needs at the time.

Reflexive approaches

There are situations when a reflexive rather than purely appreciative approach is more helpful as set out in reflexive coaching (Oliver, 2010). Reflexive coaching puts emphasis on the power of communication and interpretation. This approach helps to think about the following aspects of communication and our typical responses to what is being said to us:

1. Our **emotional response**: this usually depends on our work context and our personal context. We can all think about things that raise emotions in us. For example, Almuth finds that she has strong negative reactions when people talk over others in meetings. She finds this hard to observe.
2. Our **interpretive response**: our emotional responses impact on how we interpret events, and we tend to have rules for interpretation (Oliver, 2010). For example, we can all think of situations that prompt particular reactions in us, where we fall back into habitual patterns of interpretation. Almuth's interpretative reaction about people talking over each other in meetings might be that people are being disrespectful, and she feels a pain-like sudden jolt when she witnesses this happening.
3. **Action**: our interpretations shape how we act. We tend to rely on 'rules', which are schemas or scripts for doing things. So, if Almuth interprets that people are being disrespectful, it is likely that she

would 'default' to a defensive behaviour pattern. This pattern could be withdrawal – people are disrespectful, so not wanting to be part of this, getting frustrated and showing this frustration, or playing back to people what she heard and saying how this might affect others.

Such patterns and rules have usually developed over time, and reflexive coaching focuses on what it says on the tin – encouraging thought about reflexive choices in conversations. We always have a choice between applying our usual rules and blueprints, or stopping and thinking about our interpretation. CL questioning is helpful to demystify what has been heard and identify reactions and interpretations, and gently challenging these in conversation, observing and playing back very closely what has been said. TA can help us understand the default positions we adopt when we think we have been slighted. Here is an example.

Ned works in a senior role in a knowledge management organisation where he has to do lots of reporting. He is being coached because others at work said that he was "often angry" and "difficult to work with". His coach used the framework of reflexive conversations to unpack the emotion, the interpretation and the action.

Ned: "My boss told me yesterday that my client report fell short of expectations – this made me feel angry and upset [emotional response] so my boss doesn't like me [interpretative response]. I gave them a piece of my mind [action]."

Coach: "What did they say about the client report?"

Ned: "That I had not used the template which they had agreed with their client for reporting. Because I had written it different this made it hard for the client to pull out the key information. Could I please make sure I use it next time to make everyone's life easier."

Coach: And when you think that your boss doesn't like you, what did your boss actually say or do?"

Ned: "Well, nothing really, but they said that they didn't like my report the way I had written it."

Coach: "And is there anything else about 'giving them a piece of your mind' . . .?"

Ned: "I was angry and hurt that they didn't like my report because I had worked hard and it had a lot of detail and relevant information. I started shouting quite a bit and said this over and over again. This sometimes happens, that the angry inside me comes out."

Coach: "The angry inside you, when it comes out, it's like what . . .?"

The coach then worked with Ned on awareness about the link between the emotional response, as the negative feeling influences how we interpret, and how this sets up a default response of getting angry. The next step was for Ned to identify ways to help him recognise emotional reactions – for him, these were very physical, so, starting to feel hot and bothered. Ned learned to notice and observe these, and then ask internal questions about "what have I really heard?" rather than jumping to conclusions. Over time, this helped him manage his emotional reactions and create different response patterns.

As shown in the example above, reflexive coaching is about identifying interpretations and response patterns – so the default patterns for actions. You can do this using CL, TA or just free form. The work context can also be very important to consider in coaching. It might be worth exploring what the team culture is like; in the example above it is potentially very task focused, hence the boss might have offered their view on Ned's report without an introduction, or a conversation opener to put Ned at ease. It might also be good to clarify the relationship between Ned and his boss. What is it like now, and what could it be like? In all likelihood, the emotional response is an important starting point. How often and in what context has Ned observed strong emotional reactions in himself? When has he noticed different reactions? Conversely, imagine that you are working with the boss in this example. From their point of view, it could be important to understand what led them to offer very direct feedback without an opener and setting context. Was there no time, or is there a wider expectation for managers to be so direct? What have they noticed about reactions in others, any patterns? Reflexive coaching is focused on doing inquiry together, asking questions and observing what has been said jointly to help identify patterns in communications and in relationships. It is possible that Ned and their boss strengthen each other's patterns – the more defensive and upset Ned gets, the more the boss will react strongly to the next client report. What could help to foster mutual understanding? Looking at the patterns and loops in communication is a good starting point. This approach helps to contain potentially strong emotions in coaching, as the focus is on looking at the patterns and 'loops' together.

An AI perspective encourages us to focus on what already works well, but it can be helpful to combine this with a reflexive perspective from different angles of the system in which someone works. Though the boss might have been rather blunt, they have nevertheless been clear and directive about what needs to improve. Is there a reason why Ned does not adhere to the set structure? This can be a behaviour pattern, either because coachees don't like being told, or because they have forgotten the set structure (see Chapters 2 and 3). Noticing such patterns will facilitate insight. Sometimes these are what Christine Oliver (2010) calls paradoxical reflexive patterns. For example, in unstable organisational environments, such as when a lot of change or restructure is going on, there is often an underlying feeling of fear, and fear of loss. To manage this, people micro-manage as the meaning is that they must control something ("I've done something!"), and if necessary argue this out or simply shout people down. Doing so gives temporary relief from their fears, but in the long run perpetuates a culture of fear. This is because the system only works if things and people are being micro-managed, it becomes unstable when it is not. There might be a really good reason Ned did not use the standard template but there is no room for this discussion in the way the feedback has been dispensed/interpreted. This is a 'hexed loop', where people usually remain in this kind of situation and environment longer than is good for everyone.

A 'charmed loop' has a different view on relationships at its heart, namely that we all get fearful and anxious – it's natural. People care and have good intentions, and we value learning, as well as difference. Charmed loops and relational systems are resilient because everyone is allowed to learn and grow. The difference between such loops is not always easily explained in coaching, particularly where coachees bring a history of being stuck in toxic hexed environments. The analogy of a plant is helpful – all plants can thrive as long as you care and nurture them. You cannot keep a plant well by watering them as you like to and when it suits you – this might lead to over- or underwatering. Plants need the right amount at right times. If you look carefully and learn over time to look after your plants, you can spot warning signs which are often subtle at first – leaves changing colour, a little white mould on the soil. In hexed loops and systems, these signs are ignored, and it's unlikely the plan would thrive in the long term.

While in coaching you only have access to the microcosm of the individual and their experience of their relationships, with reflexive conversations you can start building a conceptual map of the wider system. This is essential for coachees to determine the extent to which they fit with the values and mission of their employer. If the system level is a match, but they struggle with one or two relationships/tasks, that is a very different situation to when the system level is a mismatch. A good coaching outcome is sometimes finding a new path and a graceful exit.

Giving and receiving feedback

Inquiry is based on communication processes, feeding back and feeding forward. Feedback is information that is provided regarding our performance and/or understanding (Hattie & Timperley, 2007). While AI and reflexive enquiry focus a lot on asking, feedback theories and concepts are more focused on the transmission of information. We tend to assume that feedback, broadly telling people how they've done, is a good thing in organisations, in education and of course in coaching. Surely telling people how their actions 'benchmark' against expectations, or conveying how others perceive and react to behaviour, is a good thing? Yet empirical evidence is sparse and somewhat sobering. The seminal meta-analysis by Kluger and DeNisi (1996) remains relevant several decades on: feedback has only modest effects on performance and in one-third of cases people do worse once they have had feedback. To disentangle why this might be the case, it is useful to go back to first principles. Feedback is a communication process (see McDowall, 2012) and coaching relies on communication. Coaching is a safe space to model good feedback and feedforward practice. These are the distinct aspects involved in the process of relaying information:

- **The feedback source** (or indeed multiple sources): the coach, the line manager, the task itself, other people at work.
- **The feedback message**: the information that is being relayed, for example about work behaviour, or about the level of progress over a series of coaching sessions.
- **The feedback recipient**: usually the coachee, but you might also be talking about others in the coachees' working environment.
- **Feedback as a loop**: it's a two-way process where learning takes place both ways.

Where neurodivergent coachees struggle with making sense of feedback or giving feedback, a simple diagram or chart which makes these different categories clear is a good way of taking any emotionality out of this topic and observing processes and dynamics together.

Feedback literacy

Focus on relevant skills has been a big movement in higher education. Educators over the years have spent much time and energy on giving feedback to students, but much less effort has gone into equipping students to use this feedback. The principles behind feedback literacy sit well with a coaching approach (Carless & Boud, 2018; Carless & Winstone, 2023). The first principle is to consider, and where possible pre-empt, emotional reactions to feedback and ask people to review what was being heard. Just like the example of Ned above – he inferred that the boss, who had said that he needed to adhere to better structure in client reporting, did not like him. Ned's reaction was to become angry and frustrated. In such contexts, the coach might need to use their judgement. It can be helpful to 'sit' with such emotions, notice, calm down and then go back to the feedback after some time. But such an approach can have the unintended consequence of coachees 'dwelling', in which case it is better to move on to action. Helping coachees craft action-planning logs is helpful in this case: can they develop a blueprint for turning feedback into action and tracking progress? For Ned, the next step would be to apply the feedback from his boss to the next report. What will help him adapt the common report structure? How can he utilise this to best effect to make the report clear? Where and how can he make sure that his report is 'owned'? Is there some insight that Ned has about the utility of the standard report structure that might be a learning for the whole team? Coaching can help coachees make sense of feedback and become more literate in interpreting clear feedback or asking for more detail if not clear.

In time, the next step would be to share learning with the boss, for example that it helps when they are specific about feedback. Ned might want to ask for feedback to be conveyed in a specific way. So rather than saying, "you didn't use our template which we had agreed with our client for reporting, which makes it so hard for our client to pull out the relevant information", can you try and generate neutral feedback? For example, "I noticed that you took an independent approach with your last client report. What will help you next time around to shape this further, using our template for added clarity?" This way, the boss opens the conversation and opportunity to agree shared understanding. However, this still assumes that the boss is right and Ned is wrong.

Often when neurodivergent people have avoided sticking to a rule, it is because the rule was not helpful. Ned might want to accept the feedback and ask for a time to explore in more depth "Thank you for that feedback, I understand that changing the template without warning made it difficult for others. I have some ideas about changing the report templates that I'd like to discuss, can you let me know a good time?"

We also need to look at feedback-seeking behaviour (FSB, Anseel et al., 2015, for a thorough review in the organisational literature) as it is important to understand how people monitor information at work. The perceived cost/benefit is important. The higher the perceived value of feedback, the more likely people are to actively enquire. Value is less important for how we monitor feedback which is a more passive process (ibid.). People with a high learning orientation and an external feedback propensity think that feedback is pretty much always a useful thing, and are likely to seek feedback more often. How credible the feedback source is also matters – people are more likely to take feedback on board and change their behaviour if they think that someone knows what they are doing. Perhaps soberingly, this study also did not find a strong link between feedback seeking and any improvements in performance. But does this mean that feedback does not matter? Oh yes, it does matter, because feedback is an important 'ingredient' and process for shaping our self-concept and self-beliefs (see the section on self-efficacy in Chapter 4, or the section on self-confidence in Chapter 8). Feedback seeking and literate interpretation of feedback is a useful coaching goal for coachees who have low levels of self-confidence and need reassurance.

Performance feedback and neurodiversity

Most workplaces, to a greater or lesser extent, have some processes and structures in place, for letting people know how well they are doing, and/or benchmarked against any targets. Such processes might also be linked to other decisions about promotions and rewards, for example, or training and development opportunities. This is called performance management.

Academic writers have started to look at performance feedback specifically for neurodivergent workers. Hamdani and Biagi (2022) set out seven feedback principles for giving performance feedback. They make the case that relevant conversations need to acknowledge potential variation in needs and preferences. Neurodivergent people have considerable strength, but might have difficulties with social interaction, remembering things and interpreting language. We have separated out/added an eighth point, as this is crucial in our experience in coaching and other contexts. These eight principles align with what we signpost in our other chapters about clarity and respect. These principles also question the myth of the effectiveness of the feedback sandwich, which is often bandied about as a good model – to say something positive first, then offer critique, then end with something positive. We have experienced that such set structure can be trite and lack authenticity.

The eight principles below are useful in two ways. Firstly, they are a reference for coach and coachee during coaching. Secondly, they are generally useful for the coachee to learn what kind of performance feedback is going to help them thrive at work. Coach and coachee can explore to what extent these are present. Depending on what this conversation elicits, the next step could be to work together on priorities where they could ask for and instigate changes. Performance conversations with the line manager are often a good starting point – the eight principles might help your coachees define what they need to ask for.

1. **Build rapport as a baseline**: build trust, be sensitive to others' needs and empower them. Give people the opportunity to explain their needs and challenges and how others can support.
2. **Time feedback well**: positive feedback works best if given immediately – constructive criticism needs to be well timed. For example, giving feedback and instruction right before a task can help clarity and reduce anxiety – but of course this depends on the task! Well-meant constructive feedback before someone is going up before a crowd to deliver a client presentation might be counterproductive. Be careful about any constructive criticism at the end of a coaching session or end of a working day, so that people don't dwell.

3. **Be specific and relate feedback to the job and task**: make feedback data driven and use examples. For example, many organisations use rather vague competency-based systems and behaviour descriptions. But what does 'good leadership' or empowering others' look like? Instead, feedback should be specific and future focused – for example setting a goal that conversations with direct reports are completed and recorded monthly, or practising engagement by asking questions in meetings.

4. **Feedback should be continuous**: affirming and regular feedback is assuring, particularly for neurodivergent people (but benefits everyone!). Constructive criticism needs to be conveyed and not held back – remember how destabilised Audrey was when she realised she was under par? Ensure calm and uninterrupted environments for feedback and agree a rhythm for speaking and listening. If you only engage in feedback when there's a problem, this makes feedback an anxiety-inducing event.

5. **Sequence mixed feedback so that it works**: we have all heard about the feedback sandwich – that the constructive criticism is the filling in the middle. But there is no evidence that this works any better than other sequencing. There can be situations where it is important to give constructive criticism straight away (imagine for example a safety-critical context, say in emergency services!). Sincerity and specificity is the best strategy paired with unconditional positive regard. By this we mean that we assume any negative events were not malicious. Feedback is given in a spirit of working together and making progress, rather than pointing out a character flaw or bad attitude.

6. **Set goals and create an action plan**: that goals help us regulate attention and direct behaviour is one of the most established findings in psychology. For neurodivergent coachees, this might mean giving support with action planning without taking away agency. Let's say a coachee had been referred because they were struggling to meet deadlines and also because there was conflict with co-workers. Both issues will need addressing – which one do they want to tackle first?

7. **Training feedback skills**: we outlined above that feedback is more complex than it seems and takes skill and attention to get it right – remember that otherwise feedback can be counterproductive

and leave people worse off. Ensure that there is shared language and understanding. For example, asking 'clarifying questions' or encouraging neurodivergent coachees/workers to ask their question of the day or week – in other words signposting that it's okay to ask.

8. **Feedback is about pacing**: ensure good pacing with ample opportunity for checking understanding. So the coach/manager starts, then the coachee/worker repeats and checks understanding, pausing where necessary, one or both take notes, and then the end of the conversation is devoted to action planning and transferring learning – as well as agreeing on how 'success' can be benchmarked.

Feedback styles

When Almuth did some professional development training on coaching years ago, one of the simple (and effective) exercises was for attendees to consider their feedback style: were they a sledgehammer or a pussycat? Almuth reflected that this 'depends'! When she is stressed, she becomes the proverbial sledgehammer – 'out with it,' and there you have it. She can also be a pussycat, for example when she senses that someone is vulnerable or might react strongly. Surprisingly, people's feedback styles seem to have been of little interest to researchers, people have been much more concerned with other aspects such as the timeliness. Zhou (1998) undertook a rigorous experiment some years ago. They looked at the impact of three variables, which were feedback valence (i.e. was it positive or negative), task autonomy and feedback style, on creative performance. Feedback style captured whether this was informational (so gave people constructive information about their behaviour and gave them a sense of how to do this) or focused on competence (in a more controlling style, emphasing a standard or outcome that had to be achieved). The outcomes of this study showed that when people were given informational feedback that was positive and gave them task autonomy, this resulted in the most creative ideas.

Although there is not much research on feedback style from a work context, colleagues in educational research have concerned themselves with the topic. Pitt and Norton (2017) asked students about their reactions to feedback and debunked the myth that students are only interested in grades – qualitative feedback matters a lot and directly impacts students' reactions. They invite readers to consider the concept of emotional maturity carefully and any unwanted 'emotional backwash'. This brings us back to feedback literacy – it is very important to develop and empower those receiving feedback so that it can be held in a positive psychology frame. Thus, Almuth is still working on keeping her internal feedback sledgehammer in the cupboard under lock and key, but instead spends more time on explaining and preparing for feedback. Bearing in mind previous chapters on maintaining the I'm OK/you're OK positioning, in order for feedback to be experienced as positive, you may need to unpick the relationship dynamics as part of this process.

Clean Feedback

As well as asking for and positively digesting the feedback they have received, you might want to explore giving feedback with your coachees. They might be the blunt or sledgehammer style themselves, which is causing difficulties with colleagues who perceive them as insensitive, even though they are trying their best to be clear. A mismatch in style does not have to be a case of someone being

Table 7.1 Clean Feedback observations, interpretations and impact

Observation (what was objectively seen or heard)	Interpretation (what you took the event to mean)	Impact (how you felt or the wider implications)
You stood up during the meeting. Your voice was louder than normal, and your speech was faster than normal.	You were experiencing a strong emotion and needed to feel in control.	I felt intimidated. I was worried about coming to the next meeting.
You asked me where I would like to sit when I came into the room.	You were thinking about my needs and wanted to make me comfortable.	I immediately relaxed in your company because actually, sitting with my back to the wall is really important to me.

wrong or right, just different. We have used the Clean Feedback Model (Walsh et al., 2015) to help our coachees work through their feedback before sending it, to make sure it is concrete, observable and that the inference/emotional biases have been separated from the actions. This gives room to discuss intention rather than prejudging the situation as hostile and it is particularly useful for unpicking ambiguities with literal thinkers. Table 7.1 explains the components of cleaning separating observation from interpretation and impact and is a useful coaching exercise.

An important tenet of Clean Feedback is that the interpretations we make are not necessarily true. The observations can be true, but we have to accept that the interpretations reflect our own experiences more than the sender of the communication. For example, standing up in a meeting and talking louder and faster than normal might convey excitement and passion, rather than aggression. Asking where someone would like to sit might be a power play rather than an invitation, it might mean someone is asserting control of the room. Separating observation/interpretation/impact gives coachees a chance to unpack some of their default assumptions. Unlike Clean Language, where you keep the interpretations out, you can add them to Clean Feedback, but on the proviso of knowing that they are not necessarily a reflection of the individual to whom you are feeding back. Your feedback is, in fact, indicative of your own values and beliefs about social interactions. You can learn a lot about yourself from reading back over feedback you have given! This is a lovely coaching exercise.

It is our experience that few managers and colleagues know how to give feedback at the observation level and tend towards interpretation. They say things like "you were very clear in that meeting" – what does 'clear' refer to? It might be the handouts, the slow delivery of information, the pausing for questions and then pointing back to the materials. Who knows? In normal circumstances, the receiver has to do what Kluger and DeNisi (1996) called 'cognitive elaboration' – that is the tracking back of the interpretation or impact to the actual behaviour. In Clean Feedback, the sender has to do the cognitive elaboration and ensure that feedback is concrete and observable before they share. Coachees might find it useful to learn this model in order to ask questions of their managers and colleagues. Remember when Wes's manager told him to "play the game?" Nancy taught Wes how to ask questions until this feedback was observable behaviour. They asked questions like "can I have an example?" and "what would you see or hear if I was doing this well?" Giving coachees the agency to develop feedback into a format they can understand can transform relationships and end a multitude of confusions.

Feedforward

We value the feedforward interview (FFI, Kluger & Nir, 2006; 2010) as a way of structuring coaching conversations (see McDowall et al., 2014) that brings together principles of AI and feedback intervention theory (Kluger & DeNisi, 1996). This interview does not require anything other than very attentive active listening skills:

1. **Eliciting a success story**: telling a story of choice when the coachee felt at their best to focus on positive episodic memories. This could be context specific – for example a story of when the coachee felt that they were doing their best and most effective work.
2. **The peak moment**: this is about the 'highlight' of experiences at the time, which strengthens positive self-evaluation and emotions.
3. **Clarifying the conditions**: coachees describe what the self, others and the environment contributed to the success story to clarify what optimal conditions are like.
4. **Further conversation and the future**: coachees work on how they can use insights gleaned (for example, about their strengths, about working conditions that are important to them in the future). It can be helpful to do a gap analysis first, and then set concrete goals to stimulate action.

With Tamsin Crook, who is a career coach in private practice, we researched the feedforward interview (FFI) to understand

ADHDers' career strengths based on her postgraduate research project (Crook & McDowall, Crook & McDowall, 2023). There is a dearth of studies that report on how we can better support adult ADHDers at work, as a lot of research is based on the effectiveness of drug treatments and there are few psychological intervention studies (Lauder et al., 2022). We used the FFI protocol and added specific prompts asking participants to talk about their strengths, as well as specific questions about the link between their ADHD and their respective successes. We identified two core themes. The first theme was that strengths can be paradoxical: they are both 'core' and essential but can also be overplayed. This quote from one of our participants illustrates this well:

> "the paradox is that if you're ADHDish [sic], the most responsible thing to do is to make sure that you're stimulated [. . .] from my experience, most people with ADHD aren't really motivated by money, I mean, money's boring."

The second theme was that career success is evolving and not static: participants talked about 'hard won' successes despite ADHD and 'authentic successes' because of ADHD. People found career success through their energy, their unconventional approaches and their ability to intuitively connect with others, as well as high levels of intrinsic motivation, but that successes could be sporadic and contingent in context, illustrated by this quote:

> "I'm good at what I'm doing, I know I'm in control [. . .] I've done it for a long time, it's just natural, it flows [. . .] I just feel, it's a bit like a Billy Elliot moment, you know when he says, [. . .] 'I feel when I'm dancing, I'm in a different place'. It feels like that for teaching, you wouldn't know I have all the hang-ups when I'm teaching a class of people."

Tamsin continues to use the FFI in her career coaching work and shares insights from her practice. You might note that some of these insights chime with what we've said in Chapter 8 on psychology and positive paradigms.

Almuth: "Are you still using the FFI?"

Tamsin: "It has become an integral part of a career lifeline exercise that I have always used."

Almuth: "Anything that needs adapting for neurodivergent coachees?"

Tamsin: "When you're asking people to dig deep and identify strengths it can be quite a vulnerable thing to do, particularly when they may have had negative feedback in the past. So the job of the coach might be to reflect back positive things you've noticed. It can be hard for some ND coachees to remember positive experiences so I give them time to prepare and combine with the lifeline exercise. Writing down experiences chronologically helps to trigger episodic memories. ND coachees can struggle with strengths-based psychometric assessments – the length and repetitiveness of the questionnaires, and the ambiguity of the questions asked can be incredibly frustrating. The FFI gives them the opportunity to speak authentically. The strengths they name in themselves, in the way that they name them, are more likely to be owned by them – which is a crucially important part of the process. When self-esteem is low, you don't necessarily 'accept' strengths that others recognise in you, or that are 'assigned' to you from a questionnaire that you may not relate to. For some coachees, especially with a history of perceived failure or trauma, I frame this process slowly and cautiously – it may be genuinely difficult to recall a time when they have felt 'full of life' or 'at best'.

Positive psychology can become slightly toxic if nuance and trickier parts of life are not acknowledged and respected. If people are in a genuinely difficult space, to the point where they are unable to recognise any positive experiences or potential for positivity

Almuth: "What does everyone learn with the FFI?"

Tamsin: "These conversations can be very powerful for the coachee, as they may not have had the opportunity to speak in such depth before. For ND coachees who may not feel they have a coherent career narrative, the FFI can help them to recognise themes and patterns from their experiences. The approach really helps to draw out the individual unique perspective, and what they need to be happening around them in order to feel successful. Three elements – strengths, values and environment – are foundational to helping people work out what they need to be doing, and where they need to be doing it. The process of talking about and recognising strengths is incredibly important to build on self-esteem and self-efficacy.

> in the future, then they may not be in the right headspace for coaching and should be supported to potentially explore more therapeutic support."

We never tire of using FFI. It is genuinely a privilege to hear stories time and time again. The gentle light-bulb moments, when people recognise, "I am actually good at this", or "I might be different, but difference is good". When working with neurodivergent coachees, you might want to consider three adaptations to FFI. Firstly, it can be helpful to give coachees a written or oral brief or an exercise such as getting started on a lifeline in advance and ask them to write down or record some notes and thoughts. This gives them more time to prepare and focus on success stories. Secondly, you might want to 'tone down language', particularly if coachees have had a rough time. Thirdly, as we add from our own observations, think about ways to handle the conversation where the pace is either very fast and almost frantic, as it's important to spend some time with the success story, or where the pace is slow and conversation comes to a halt. Ensure that you have agreement in advance on where and how to summarise and reflect back. Doing so will help mutual understanding. It might happen that coachees, particularly when they are unhappy in their current workplace, find it hard to report a success story. In that case, either go further back in time, or ask them to imagine a scenario 'as they would like it', i.e. retell an episode as they would have liked it to happen. Use the Clean Feedback Model to track the experience back to observable, concrete behaviour. If coachees feel put on the spot when being asked to do so, it can be a good idea to give this as homework for the next session.

Conclusion

Coaching is all about communication; feedback and feedforward are essential tools and techniques. We started out with a brief introduction to appreciative inquiry (AI), which has a positive focus on language and dialogue to invite people to discover, dream and design a new destiny through articulating what is precious and gives them energy in their current work environment. Reflexive coaching focuses on context-specific narratives and is suited to inviting reflection on behaviour and language patterns in order to move to a positive frame. Research on feedback tells us that simply giving people information does not lead to behaviour change and can even be harmful. We encourage coaches to incorporate how feedback should take place as part of contracting, in order to stay solution focused. Coaches also need to know what good performance feedback should look like in organisations and offer a framework of eight principles. We concluded by outlining the feedforward interview (FFI), which is a deceptively simple but effective format for structuring conversations. Important issues from this chapter are that feedback is always more effective if it is specific and well timed, that conversations are better with structure for neurodivergent employees and that action planning is crucial to ensure transfer of skill and learning. Feedback and feedforward processes work best when everyone is developed and empowered to make the most of the process.

Reflective questions

- When you think about a high point in coaching (having your own coaching, or when you are engaged with a coachee), when you feel most alive, this is like what . . .? Note down your thoughts.
- To what extent have you experienced different kinds of communication loops in your own context? Any 'hexed' experiences? Any 'charmed' experiences?
- What have your experiences of feedback been, how does this differ from various sources? How do you seek feedforward from your coachees?
- Prepare a feedforward interview and put this into practice: think in advance about allowing pauses and silence – this is often when shifts happen. What was this like?
- What is your feedback style, and your default?
- Give yourself some clean feedback using Table 7.1 as a guide. What works well about your coaching practice? What would you like to do better?

References

Anseel, F., Beatty, A. S., Shen, W., Lievens, F., & Sackett, P. R. (2015). How are we doing after 30 years? A meta-analytic review of the antecedents and outcomes of feedback-seeking behavior. *Journal of Management*, *41*(1), 318–348. https://doi.org/10.1177/01492063134845

Carless, D., & Boud, D. (2018). The development of student feedback literacy: Enabling uptake of feedback. *Assessment & Evaluation in Higher Education*, *43*(8), 1315–1325. https://doi.org/10.1080/02602938.2018.1463354

Carless, D., & Winstone, N. (2023). Teacher feedback literacy and its interplay with student feedback literacy. *Teaching in Higher Education*, *28*(1), 150–163. https://doi.org/10.1080/13562517.2020.1782372

Cooperrider, D. L., Stavros, J. M., & Whitney, D. (2008). *The appreciative inquiry handbook: For leaders of change*. Berrett-Koehler.

Crook, T. & McDowall, A. (2023). Paradoxical career strengths and successes of ADHD adults: an evolving narrative. Journal of Work-Applied Management. Vol. ahead-of-print No. ahead-of-print. https://doi.org/10.1108/JWAM-05-2023-0048

Hamdani, M., & Biagi, S. (2022). Providing performance feedback to support neurodiverse employees. *MIT Sloan Management Review, 63*(3), 1–6.

Hattie, J., & Timperley, H. (2007). The power of feedback. *Review of Educational Research,* 77, 81–112. https://doi.org/10.3102/003465430298487

Kluger, A. N., & DeNisi, A. (1996). The effects of feedback interventions on performance: A historical review, a meta-analysis, and a preliminary feedback intervention theory. *Psychological Bulletin, 119*(2), 254.

Kluger, N. K., & Nir, D. (2006). Feedforward first – feedback later. Keynote lecture delivered at the *26th International Congress of Applied Psychology.* Athens, Greece.

Kluger, N. K., & Nir, D. (2010). The feedforward interviews. *Human Resource Management Review, 20,* 235–246.

Lauder, K., McDowall, A., & Tenenbaum, H. R. (2022). A systematic review of interventions to support adults with ADHD at work: Implications from the paucity of context-specific research for theory and practice. *Frontiers in Psychology, 13,* 893469. https://doi.org/10.3389/fpsyg.2022.893469

McDowall, A. (2012). Using feedback in coaching. In J. Passmore (Ed.), *Psychometrics in coaching: Using psychological and psychometric tools for development* (5th ed., pp. 59–76). Kogan Page.

McDowall, A., Freemann, K., & Marshall, K. (2014). Is feedforward the way forward? A comparison of the effects of feedforward coaching and feedback. *International Coaching Psychology Review, 9*(2), 135–146.

Oliver, C. (2010). Reflexive coaching: Linking meaning and action in the leadership system. In S. Palmer, & A. McDowall, A. (2010). *The Coaching Relationship* (pp. 119–138). Routledge.

Pitt, E., & Norton, L. (2017). "Now that's the feedback I want!" Students' reactions to feedback on graded work and what they do with it. *Assessment & Evaluation in Higher Education, 42*(4), 499–516. https://doi.org/10.1080/02602938.2016.1142500

Walsh, B., Nixon, S., Walker, C., & Doyle, N. (2015). Using a clean feedback model to facilitate the learning process. *Creative Education, 6,* 953–960. https://doi.org/10.4236/ce.2015.610097

Zhou, J. (1998). Feedback valence, feedback style, task autonomy, and achievement orientation: Interactive effects on creative performance. *Journal of Applied Psychology, 83*(2), 261.

Chapter 8

The psychology of coaching

Almuth McDowall and Nancy Doyle

Putting psychology into coaching

Coaches come from a variety of backgrounds and there is currently no unifying framework for professional practice or agreement on 'what works'. Is there a specific kind of professional background and associated knowledge that makes for better coaching outcomes? This is an important question to which there is no easy answer and we have come across highly qualified professionals who we feel practise badly, and comparatively untrained people who are insightful and wise. We're going to outline some of the core knowledge that we have drawn down from our psychological training and leave it to the reader to determine whether you feel your own knowledge base has sufficiently prepared you for coaching in the neurodivergent community.

Nancy and Almuth are registered practitioner psychologists with the Health and Social Care Professions Council in the UK, and are Chartered with the British Psychological Society, have undergone additional psychological training and have doctoral degrees in Psychology. Nancy is a member of the American Psychological Association and a member of the International Coaching Federation, Almuth is an Academic Fellow of the Chartered Institute for Personnel and Development and both are Fellows of the International Society for Coaching Psychology. Nancy continues to work as a coach and oversees other coaches' work, Almuth currently does not do professional coaching as she focuses on research, but she prefers to adopt a coaching rather than supervision approach to working with colleagues and mentees. Is it important for all coaches who work in a

DOI: 10.4324/9781003368274-10

neurodiversity context to have such knowledge and qualifications? We argue that some basis of psychological grounding is important, even where coaches don't have an undergraduate degree in Psychology. This is because psychological approaches combine knowledge of individual differences (the science of the brain and how people think, feel and behave) with knowledge about groups and systems. Such knowledge is at the heart of understanding both neurodivergence and social exclusion, as per our extensive summary in Chapter 2. Psychology also provides explanatory frameworks for our observations and teaches us to test hypotheses rather than assuming our experience is the only way forward; this is an essential aspect of professional practice. Another reason why psychological knowledge is very important is because this helps us spot potential warning signs and refer coachees where specialist input is needed. Let's look at what might happen otherwise.

Almuth has a cautionary tale to tell. One of her acquaintances, who worked in a corporate environment as a day job, retrained as an NLP[1] coach and hypnotherapist some years back. They had been seeing a hypnotherapy coachee over a series of sessions who had self-referred because they had a mental illness. In the last of a series of sessions, the coachee became aggressive and caused physical harm to the hypnotherapist. Their behaviour had been erratic, and some psychological knowledge on behalf of the coach would, in all likelihood, facilitated clear contracting and firm boundaries. Was it actually ethical to see this coachee at that moment in time? What kind of screening should have happened before hypnotherapy commenced and, once it hard started, might have helped to identify potential issues and refer on? What were the safeguarding and risk management processes? Did the coach have a supervisor who would have helped identify warning signals to deteriorating behaviour? As we have highlighted before, coaching is not therapy or a medical intervention, and it is important to have clear boundaries.

Although the above example is extreme, it is not unheard of. Psychological grounding is an important safety factor for coaching practice, but may also lead to enhanced outcomes for coachees. Together with a multinational interdisciplinary research team, Almuth undertook a meta-analysis to consider the contribution of psychological approaches to coaching (Wang et al., 2022). We set out to investigate to what extent psychologically informed coaching approaches are linked to positive work outcomes, including performance and wellbeing. We systematically searched for, and then evaluated, 20 studies. We found that psychologically informed approaches in coaching were linked to a range of outcome measures. Interestingly, the psychologically informed studies enhanced work performance outcomes when they were rated by others, rather than self-assessed performance. An integrative approach that combines different frameworks was linked to the most positive outcomes, including wellbeing, and we found no other (significant) differences between other psychological approaches. From these findings, we learned that wide-ranging knowledge of different approaches, which is likely to facilitate a context-sensitive and tailored approach, appears very important to make coaching work – the breadth of the toolkit matters. So the psychology is important, even if you are not a psychologist. We know plenty of excellent coaches practising without psychological training, but all have done due diligence to their craft in other ways, including attention to supervision, continuous professional development, reading a wide range of materials on their subject and regular attendance in reflective practice. We expand on these issues in Chapter 12 and we now turn to some core coaching psychology knowledge that can equip your practice.

The coaching alliance

Psychology as a discipline provides a baseline knowledge outside one's specific area of practice, from which we can draw portable principles. A consistent finding in therapy is that the therapeutic alliance (the rapport and quality of relationship between the therapist and client) matters (e.g. Horvath & Luborsky, 1993). More recently, this has been found to transfer to coaching practice. Our research found that the coaching relationship is vital and that a professional psychology background and training are important for understanding coachees' emotional reactions (Lai & McDowall, 2014). We offered a broad behavioural framework for coaching psychology, in three categories:

1. Professional knowledge: supporting emotions in coaches; knowing about a range of psychological techniques; supporting diversity; organising ourselves etc.
2. Our attitudes and beliefs: remaining open, non-judgemental, enthusiastic and committed.
3. Core skills: communication; relationship building; facilitation.

All three aspects apply to a neurodiversity coaching context, where we add a fourth category, which is having insight into and appreciation of neurodiversity and how this might affect practice. Hence this book! Managing emotions can be absolutely key, as are communication skills. As the examples in Chapters 2, 3, 4 and 7 on challenges, opportunities and feedback demonstrate, coaches need to be aware of the need to adapt language and tone to support coachees' growth and learning. We think it's better to consider the relationship or alliance as a process of negotiation not collaboration, as therapy researchers have argued (Safran & Muran, 2006). Psychodynamic approaches invite us to recognise that conscious and unconscious aspects will be at play in the relationship. A process of renegotiation is a mechanism for change, where coachees come to observe and understand themselves and others from changing and varied viewpoints. The same researchers also questioned whether the concept of the alliance had outlived its usefulness and become too broad. Let's look at the evidence and highlight what we need to know to inform coaching.

A group of German researchers (Graßmann et al., 2020) set out to investigate to what extent the quality of the coaching relationship matters for a range of coaching impacts. They found that the relationship quality matters hugely for all potential outcomes but was overall twice as important as for emotion-focused and cognitive outcomes and also to prevent unintended negative consequences. These results held up regardless of the types of coachees or the number of coaching sessions. The research team thought that the results were somewhat paradoxical when they compared the effects they observed to previous research from therapy settings – surely the issues that people work through in therapy are usually more severe than in coaching. We reflect that this is the explanation, rather than a paradox; issues might be less 'severe' in coaching, but involve the above referenced negotiation, flexibility and, dare we say, intuition for the coaching to go where it needs to. Coaching outcomes are often broader than therapy goals, and goalposts invariably move during coaching. This is both the beauty and the challenge.

Many years ago, while working with the company Training Attention, Nancy was facilitating a group of new coaches to discover how to build rapport. They were working with unemployed and marginalised groups. A core part of the training was understanding one's own patterns of bias and prejudice. They played a game called "I am a racist and . . ." – a play on the trope "I'm not racist but . . ." – which draws us to acknowledge our own bias, rather than to ignore it. In the game, trainee coaches were invited to notice any negative stereotypes they were holding about groups or people that they could concede were likely sweeping generalisations based on fear or negative messaging. The frame for the session was that we all hold these opinions, our job is to continually work on ourselves to aid us in unpeeling the layers of systemic discrimination to which we are all exposed. The group began identifying their prejudices and biases. One participant identified that he was always nervous around homeless people and found them frightening. He believed they were likely to be on drugs and was nervous about interacting. Given his job, this presupposition would be quite harmful for his ability to build rapport with his client group! Nancy and colleagues set him a developmental task to exchange words with one homeless person during his commute before the next week.

That night he left the course and waiting for his bus, encountered a homeless man selling the *Big Issue* – a newspaper that is deliberately only distributed by homeless people. He tried to pluck up the courage to talk, but his bus came past. He let the bus go and continued trying. In the end, three buses came and went before he was able to speak! He eventually bought a copy of the *Big Issue* and engaged in a conversation. It turned out that the homeless person was on his first day selling the paper and had spent the entire time also trying to pluck up the courage to offer him a copy! They connected over each other's stories and built beautiful rapport.

The moral of this story is about deliberately seeking opportunities to challenge yourself, to be more flexible not less, to build rapport outside your current experience. Nancy used to deliberately work as a training partner with her colleague Emma Dalrymple, who had opposite patterns of communication to her. Nancy would build instant rapport with all the alpha types, the loud and bouncy ones. Emma would notice the quieter withdrawn participants who didn't speak until after lunch. She would deliberately go out of her way to seek them out at breaks to have a one-on-one interchange, which would relax them because they were too nervous to speak in a crowd. Nancy observed this over many years and began to do the same. Now Nancy advocates for trying to catch a new participant or a new coachee over the phone or via text/WhatsApp to start building rapport before in-person communication. The way you handle the logistics and the booking will prime the coaching alliance before it even starts. It is your job, as a coach, to meet your coachees where they are rather than have them dancing to your tune. Even if they don't respond, they will be taking something from your reach out. You are letting them know that you are interested in building a relationship with them. Do not interpret silence as dislike, it might be that they need more time to ease into communication flow. Nancy has, in fact, conducted Clean Language coaching sessions with coachees who do not speak at all. She asks questions like:

"What would you like to have happen now?"
"Take all the time you need to process that question." [long pause]

"And when you are processing, notice what needs to happen for
   your outcome to occur." [long pause]
"And notice what resources you already have." [long pause]
"And notice where they come from." [long pause]
"And notice anything else about your resources, your outcome."
   [long pause]
"Does it have a size or a shape?" [long pause]

Clean Language teaches us that our understanding, as a coach, is
not essential for the coachee to experience catharsis or to develop
self-knowledge. You can sometimes build better rapport by simply
not expecting your coachees to conform to social niceties and
allowing them to be their authentic selves in the coaching. Coaching
psychology, as an academic discipline, has researched the importance
of a good alliance as a definitive factor in coaching success, but it is
professional training and supervision that will allow you to develop
rapport building as a skill.

Dealing with impasse and rupture

The relationships we form during therapy or coaching can start
well but get worse, stop progressing or break down. There is more,
better quality, research on this topic in therapy where academics
have looked at such ruptures and impasses with a range of different
methods. It is a consistent finding that a strong working alliance
always supports good outcomes. However, when clients end
therapy, particularly when this ending is abrupt, this has detrimental
psychological outcomes (see Safran et al., 2014; for an excellent
overview). Ruptures are when therapist and client have different
experiences of the same interaction and become dissociated from
each other. Safran and colleagues have been researching these
over the years through a method called task analysis where they
looked at recorded sessions of therapy (see e.g. Rice & Greenberg,
1984 for the original method). They identified two types of ruptures
which are:

a) confrontation ruptures, when the client expresses dissatisfaction
   with the therapist, the therapy or both and

b) withdrawal ruptures, when the client stops engaging but might find it difficult to say that this is happening and the reasons for this.

The underlying dynamics are due to tensions in human experience between our need for personal agency versus our need for connectedness with others (Safran & Muran, 2000). With confrontation ruptures, the need for agency comes to the forefront and, for withdrawal ruptures, the need for connectedness. Noticing when ruptures happen and making them part of the therapeutic conversation is good for client and therapist – we argue that the same holds true for coaching. The following observations are important, which we have adapted from a therapeutic to a coaching context. They normalise what might be happening and emphasise that both parties have joint responsibility:

a) It is common and normal for coachees to have negative feelings about the relationship. A trusting relationship should allow the space and respect for these feelings to be articulated, and for coaches to respond in a non-judgemental way. Clean Language will come in useful here: "what would you like to have happen?"
b) The coach needs to remember that they have the professional training and that they need to be attuned to subtle shifts in the relationship during sessions.
c) It is beneficial for both parties to work together to notice and solve ruptures because this supports learning and growth on both sides. What are any fears that might be obstructing progress? Are there any dissociated hopes and desires? What might the coach have been contributing?

The concept of 'therapeutic meta-communication' asserts that it can be helpful for the therapist, or (here) coach, to step outside of the direct dynamics in the relationship and examine these together with the coachee, with curiosity but without judgement. Safran and Muran (2000) call this 'mindfulness in action'. (We will allow the term 'mindfulness' here, although Almuth and Nancy don't like mindfulness training; it has been overused in organisations as a 'quick fix' and isn't helpful for everyone.) A useful technique is to adopt a different perspective with the coachee for example looking at what happened in the coaching session from above (e.g. from a helicopter – what do you both notice as you hover above from a distance?); or from the sidelines (e.g. like a line judge – if this was a game, what tactics are currently being used?). This helps to make the (potential) rupture a 'thing', so a third entity in the coaching context, rather than apportioning blame to either party.

Rupture/impasse patterns in neurodiversity coaching

From our experience, there are some common patterns in neurodiversity coaching. Coachees might go off on tangents – so while coach and coachee jointly agreed to work on a particular topic (for example self-organisation), the coachee might be enthused about reporting on issues that are not so relevant to this, or apportioning blame on others (e.g. "I can't self-organise at work because my line manager never listens to me . . ."). Another pattern is that coachees might talk for quite some time as a monologue, even without acknowledging the coach, about certain topics that are important to them. This can make it hard to stay focused and interested in the activities and the relationship. A good tactic is to listen once without judgement and curiosity, then bring the attention of the coachee to this pattern and then ask them whether they communicate like this at work, and what they have noticed when this happens. Like noticing ruptures, you notice patterns together with curiosity and examine them without judgement. Observing together helps the coachee understand behaviour patterns and potential impacts on others. The observation also helps the coach show how such patterns have developed. It could be that the coachee's behaviour might make it unlikely that they get direct feedback from others (see also Chapter 7); for example, if they much prefer to work on their own with noise-cancelling headphones on or are very anxious about receiving feedback and therefore avoid it. Coaching provides a safe space to notice, rewind and practise new patterns – how they are with you is how they are probably also with their colleagues.

Almuth is reminded of working with Nancy during her PhD studies. In UK academic speak, the academic overseeing the work is called the 'supervisor'. Almuth does not like this term because it implies surveillance and uneasy power dynamics. She prefers a coaching/mentoring approach with her doctoral candidates. There was one progress session when Nancy outlined at length how she had been at the university's sports centre ice skating and how much she enjoyed this. Nothing much about the research was discussed! Almuth made futile attempts at first to steer the flow back to the academic work. Then realisation set in. Nancy simply had to get this out of her head at this moment in time – nothing could change this. So Almuth listened. And when the time was right, they picked up the academic conversation again, and refocused on Nancy's research.

What this little vignette illustrates is that there are differences in how we think, feel and act. Nancy talks in tangents when she is nervous and doesn't know what is expected of her. But hearing her out lets her know she is in a safe space and will not be unduly judged. There will be times when you, the coach, need to just 'tune in' in order to build rapport. It was a good strategy in this example to just listen and observe while attention strayed, and a detour happened. But if this happened again, it would have been helpful to reflect and share these observations: "I have noticed that you go 'off topic' and then tell me about XXX and YYY. What can do we do to help you focus?" Nancy passed her viva without any corrections, by the way, which is a testament to the quality of her work, and that there are many ways and strategies that lead to success. Almuth's success here as a mentor was to not be quick to write Nancy off as unfocused and lacking in seriousness. If she had judged Nancy at face value on this one occasion, the work might never have come to fruition. Once Nancy got focused, she was like a steam train, plugging away to get to the destination on time.

The psychology of impasse and rupture may have been developed in the wider context of therapy, but the lessons are transferable to practice and supervision, allowing us to consider the dynamics at work in our coaching and also signposting some strategies to overcome.

Psychological safety

The coaching alliance, and how to manage this in neurodiversity coaching, has been at the heart of what we have outlined so far. Open, curious and candid observations about the 'coaching room' mean that there has to be a high degree of mutual trust. Yet, coachees may have experienced years of having to mask, unable to be their authentic selves. They may have experienced intersectional invisibility in the coaching experience with a neurodiversity expert who has no knowledge of their cultural safety. Their experience may be coming from a Jewish, mixed or Roma heritage – not everyone's ethnicity is obvious. They may have gender dysphoria, have experienced trauma in coming out as gay, lesbian or bisexual, or active discrimination. They may be wrestling with such events right now. You, the coach, might need to take active steps to rewrite such scripts with the coachee by signposting and making it clear that your relationship will be different. You may need to be humble and accept that your own lived experience does not allow you insight, but find other ways to signal that you represent a place of safety. You may not always be able to do this, in which case you need your own supervision time to reflect and unpick your biases.

Psychological safety is important, and goes further than the coaching alliance, reflecting on the wider safety in the individual's team, organisation and even industry. The original work of Amy Edmondson (1999) was focused on collaboration in teams and identified that teams learn more and perform better when there's a shared belief that it is okay to take interpersonal risks. This work has been extended over the years and tested in many studies. The evidence shows that, in order to foster psychological safety, it's more important how we work with each other. For example, focusing on strong relationships with our peers and our leaders before our own characteristics, such as how open we are to experience. Psychological safety is crucial for fostering engagement, performance, satisfaction and commitment at work (Frazier et al., 2017). Coaches have to model psychological safety in coaching, because this belief helps coachees to focus on goals, pre-empt any problems and make us more likely to give the benefit of doubt. Right from contracting, you could make it explicit that you will:

- Regularly check in on each other to see how things are working, through mutual support.
- Be curious and attentive when things don't go to plan and examine what happened together.
- Feel able to ask for help and, in this instance, particularly the coachee asking the coach; neurodivergent coachees will find this difficult. Keep signposting that this is okay and part of coaching.
- Express unconditional positive regard, even where you differ in opinion or style.
- Benchmark progress and explicitly notice shifts, no matter how small or large.

Over time, focusing on psychological safety will also foster metacognition in the coachee by being able to recognise, and eventually challenge, when levels of psychological safety are low in their work environment. If they report relevant observations back into coaching, they can have space to notice, observe and then think through potential actions. For example, has the coachee taken steps to find out if others have noticed similar things? To what extent have they role-modelled at work what they have done in coaching through the principles agreed above? If they haven't done this, what have the challenges been and how far can they be overcome? The sections in this chapter so far have mainly looked at relationships and what psychological science teaches us about the coaching dyad. Let us now turn to the self, given that coaching is a process of learning and self-discovery, and how to foster a positive mindset.

The positive psychology of self

Our earlier chapters made the point that a deficit focus, associated with a medical model of difference, has prevailed in neurodiversity research and practice. The same has held true more generally for psychological research on different conditions, which focused for many years on what makes people depressed, anxious, worried or simply abnormal. A paradigm shift occurred in the early 2000s when Martin Seligman (Seligman & Csikszentmihalyi, 2000) put forward positive psychology as a basis for scholarship, therapy and intervention to harness strengths in people, rather than fix what makes them ill. He highlighted how much of psychological science had been devoted to understanding problems and that, in order to promote happiness and peace, we also needed to devote some attention to positive experiences of self. Very congruent with the neurodiversity paradigm emerging at the same period in history, Seligman's U-turn, given that he had been the one to coin the term, "learned helplessness" in the context of depression (Seligman, 1972), was not without controversy. Other researchers argued that humanistic traditions in psychology, which have always centred on appreciation of the person, had a long tradition of positive regard in psychology (e.g. Taylor, 2001). Regardless, the frame of positive psychological approaches then generated a plethora of studies on the effectiveness of relevant interventions, usually called positive psychology exercises (PPE). Mongrain and Anselmo-Matthews (2012) replicated one of Seligman's studies with two PPEs, namely to:

1. list three good things that went well each day for one week, and;
2. do an assessment of their (signature) character strengths (e.g. creativity, kindness etc.) and then use these strengths for one week.

They compared the impact on people who did this to a control group who were simply invited to think about positive early memories, without the above structure. However, all participants experienced decreases in depressive symptoms over time, including the control group, which thought about positive early memories. There was no "time by condition interaction effect", meaning that the changes did not differ across conditions. Participants' levels of happiness varied by condition, and over time – the signature strengths interventions had the largest gains at time of immediate follow-up and after six months, whereas the three good things activity showed the most pronounced effects at one month follow-up. Overall, this research on positive psychology exercises underlines that a positive self-concept is important and can be fostered – just thinking about early positive memories had an effect, but how long effects are maintained can also vary.

We have observed similar patterns in our own research. Some years ago, we researched a strengths-based group intervention that we had designed to target people's self-efficacy, confidence in their goals (which coachees set as part of the coaching) and strengths knowledge (McDowall & Butterworth, 2014). We found that both the experimental group, who received coaching, and the control group, which wrote down and reflected on goals, improved. It is common to both of these studies that the activities, whether labelled PPE or coaching, were structured. This will appeal to neurodivergent coachees who appreciate structure and clarity. But it can also be a challenge with certain coachees to 'stick' with any plan and actually put the activities into practice. For any coach, it is helpful to think about such eventualities in advance to plan strategies for when to adapt and flex and try different tactics. However, sometimes, a direct approach is helpful to get coachees to reflect on what it means for their work if they find it hard to stick to tasks in coaching. Remember Nancy's coachee Mo and their cooking and recipe example from Chapter 3? It is sometimes necessary to work on more general memory and effectiveness strategies first before approaching PPE exercises in coaching. The other adaptation we would recommend, particularly for the strengths-focused PPE, is to be more explicit. For example, many neurodivergent coachees will prefer a behavioural definition of concepts such as creativity or kindness. What does either mean in terms of doing things? How do you observe that someone is being creative or kind at work, and what is the polar opposite for either? Working together to define vague terms with concrete behaviours will be a helpful starting point.

A positive self-concept

We emphasise again that neurodivergent coachees may often present with a history of perceived failure and lack of successes more so than the coachees you have seen to date. As we explained in

Chapters 2 and 3, this is because we live in a world designed for the 'norm' – it's our environment that can be disabling. Yet, psychological research agrees that a positive self-concept is very important for our wellbeing and success, at work and elsewhere. We can all think of examples, large or small, short- or long-term, of occasions when we didn't like ourselves very much and the inner critic set in. It's not a nice place to be. We replay conversations or thoughts in our heads and put the bits that really didn't work on repeat. We don't like our look in the mirror. We start thinking no one really likes us. Everything seems grey, or slow motion, or both. Conversely, when our self-concept is good, things around us seem brighter, and we are energised. Timothy Judge and colleagues (e.g. Bono & Judge, 2003) have been researching core self-evaluations (CSE) over the years and argue that they are about how we fundamentally evaluate ourselves (internal focus). Following a thorough review of the literature, they identified a compound trait of self-concept made up of four facets that have been known in psychological research for some time (ibid., also for an overview of the original definitions):

1. Self-esteem: our regard or approval for ourselves.
2. Low neuroticism: a degree of high emotional stability.
3. Locus of control: to what extent we think that we are in control of our lives and actions.
4. Self-efficacy: our 'best estimate' belief in our capabilities.

Psychological research tells us that, taken together, these form a positive self-concept that links to job and life satisfaction (Judge et al., 2005) and to coping; so, how individuals react to stress and strain. This is a robust piece of research that combined a meta-analysis and a diary study document showing that people who are high in CSE experience less stress and strain and do less avoidance coping, but also that people's level of emotional stability has a unique influence (Kammeyer-Mueller et al., 2009). It may or may not be helpful in coaching to undertake an assessment of CSE and personality as we note that many measures are not easily adapted in a neurodiversity-friendly way. But it can be powerful to explore the degree of a coachee's positive self-concept in general, and particularly how this might be affected if the going gets tough at work – we tend to fall back into patterns of negativity when we are stressed. Good starting points for conversations in coaching are questions about issues such as:

- To feel confident and competent at work, what needs to happen? You could separate the competent and confident questions out as they are two slightly different things.
- How can you gain control of one thing at work which is important to you?
- What will you do over the next two weeks to plan your career?

It is important that coaches gain a good understanding of the working environment of the coachee in order to frame realistic expectations. There are probably things that the coachee has little control over; for example, they might not be able to influence the scale or pace of any organisational change. When working with neurodivergent coachees, it is particularly important to be clear and not raise hopes that might later on be squashed. This could be counterproductive. That said, there is always room to consider where and how they could play a role. In the organisational change example, one potential consideration is to start or be part of a change coalition at work, i.e. a group of people who have an active role in deciding how best to implement any changes. That said, it is important to remember the focus for CSE is always coachees' inner world and their beliefs. If the conversation strays to, "Oh, but I have no control over X, Y, Z", then gently and kindly bring this back to what coachees think, feel and do. Focus back to issues where they have agency (everyone can plan for their career) and focus on one issue at a time, about taking control about one thing that is important to them above. Again, an intersectional lens will be important here, for elements such as feeling that you have agency over your career or work success take on a different nuance when you are experiencing marginalisation and minoritisation.

Note how the CSE folds into concepts such as the victim archetypal role on the drama triangle, and the use of Clean Language such as "what would you like to have happen?" This is the 'modelling experience' rather than using a model approach that we are aligning to great coaching – it is the underlying knowledge that allows us to make sense of and see the patterns within different coachee experiences. Each model that we introduce allows you to identify different causal mechanisms, applying them with rapport is what allows your coachees to develop their self-knowledge. When you are listening, is this a control/agency issue? An internal script from childhood issue? A cognitive skill issue? Where will the shift come from? What questions can you ask to provide a framework in which your coachee can develop their self-awareness? Reframe the problem as a resource? Set a goal to challenge themselves?

Audrey's company was going through a period of organisational change. They had new software coming in and had to prepare by uploading some existing documents into a specific format. Audrey was at the same time going through some personal issues with her father in hospital and needing to organise home care for him when he was finished with his treatment. She was very stressed and overwhelmed. This was when her relationship with Estelle, her manager, was not quite where she wanted it to be, she had been holding onto some unspoken concerns about whether she was meeting the grade for her role (see Chapter 6). One day, in coaching, she appeared very flustered and expressed that she just "didn't know where to start".

Nancy suggested they start with a download of all the things on her mind. As Audrey spoke, Nancy wrote each worry down on a sticky note and placed it on the desk next to them. When they were all out, there was a lot of sticky notes! Nancy suggested they separate them into things that are 'in my control', 'not in my control', 'not sure'. For example, her father's health was not in her control. But calling three home care agencies and asking for costs for two visits a day was in her control. Audrey placed her relationship with her boss in 'not sure', but together they established that she could 'ask for a conversation with her boss', which might not fix the relationship but would be within her control. Gradually breaking down all the mountain of worries into shorter manageable chunks gave Audrey a sense of control, a plan and a list of things to achieve that would build back her self-efficacy.

Self-confidence

Developing a strong sense of self-confidence is often an issue for neurodivergent coachees; a lifetime of feeling 'different' and 'not quite fitting in' can sap away at self-belief. This can be compounded by other demographics and marginalisation. Curiously, 'confidence' is far less defined in psychological research than 'efficacy'. Our colleague Dr Anna Kane and co-researchers looked at this during her doctoral studies, framing self-confidence as "an overarching skill" (Kane et al., 2021). Based on rigorous interview research with diverse people, they argued that self-confidence has three interlinked dimensions, which are authenticity, competence and connectedness. In turn, these are influenced by people's mindset, working together to produce a confident performance. For authenticity, it is important that coachees can act in a way that accords with one's self-image and values. For confidence, knowledge and skill are important, as is positive feedback. Connectedness is underpinned by a sense of engaging with others, belonging and having support. All three aspects taken together are facilitated by an enhancing mindset that refers to a balanced and positive perspective paired with a sense of control. All of these are important notions to attend to in coaching, with an embodied experience to make experiences tangible, and real.

Almuth remembers working with her own coach during a particularly difficult time at work, which had made her doubt her capability. She was dealing with tricky people issues which had been going on for some time and were not resolved. Her coach asked her what this looked like in her inner world; in her own authentic words, Almuth said, "well, I am usually petite, but I feel really small and short at the moment – like a dancer in the back row on stage" (Almuth used to be a dancer). Hearing this, her coach invited her to rehearse a difficult conversation to start tackling some of the people issues. She asked Almuth what skills (competence) she could bring to this conversation. Almuth said that she was not sure because she felt so small. The coach repeated her words and asked her what would happen if she was in the front row on stage and feeling tall. Almuth said that this would give her confidence. So Almuth practised the conversation by standing up on a chair to make herself feel tall, which she moved forward in the room. The coach gave her direct feedback when she heard that Almuth sounded unsure and started hedging her words with 'maybes', 'I think' and so on. The practice was repeated and Almuth then used this embodied experience of 'feeling tall' as an anchor to engage in the conversation in real life. This helped her even when she got nervous as she could recall the sensation of feeling tall and saying things from a different perspective.

Psychological Capital: when good things come together

Positive psychology has also taken hold with concepts that are specific to work contexts. The most well-known work is by Dr Fred Luthans and colleagues on Psychological Capital (PsyCap) (for an overview, see Luthans & Youssef-Morgan, 2017). Like Seligman's work, this line of research has the underlying premise that it is more fruitful to help people flourish and thrive than to fix what does not work. It rests on the concept of resources that a positive outlook helps to foster. The four components abbreviate to the HERO within:

1. **Hope**: a motivational state that combines energy and planning to meet goals (Snyder et al., 1991).
2. **(Self-) Efficacy**: people's beliefs in their capabilities, which develop through experience of mastery; vicarious experience and

modelling; social persuasion and feedback, as well as arousal (Bandura, 1997).

3. **R**esilience: people's capacity to bounce back from events and progress (Luthans, 2002).
4. **O**ptimism: a positive explanatory style that attributes positive experience to personal and stable causes (Seligman, 1998).

A subtle but necessary distinction to CSE is that the PsyCap components are malleable and can be developed and changed, whereas, for example, neuroticism is a personality trait that remains relatively stable over time. So CSE is a helpful framework for facilitating self-insight in coaching, whereas PsyCap readily underpins relatively short and targeted training and coaching activities. The underlying mechanisms for these are as follows: positive emotions and appraisals are what help people reframe experiences in a positive light. The activities cue positive emotions and energy, which help people to be motivated to achieve their goals. Although the focus is on the person taking personal agency and responsibility for any actions, the activities also have a social component; for example, encouraging people to think about how they can draw on and build social support. PsyCap activities take about two to three hours and readily lend themselves to group coaching, particularly where employees from any one organisation come together, as this encourages transfer of learning. Such activities always have four building blocks:

1. To encourage hope and energy.
2. To strengthen people's belief in their capabilities.
3. To overcome any events and obstacles.
4. To retain a positive outlook.

Let's look at how building PsyCap might work with groups.

Almuth has used adapted PsyCap exercises for groups. This works well when people are physically in a room together rather than online. Use tablecloths or large sheets so that people can draw. Start in the top right-hand corner (where you want to end up – so this is deliberately a little counterintuitive as you don't start the exercise where you are now) and work round clockwise – draw a cloud or 'bucket' which holds the following: "What does 'good' look like for doing your best work? Where can you be your best authentic self?" Ask people individually to write down their answers on sticky notes and then, as a group, democratically decide which sticky notes go in the bucket. Do they all agree on some? If everyone doesn't agree, could some still be very important? Then, draw a group of stick people in the bottom left-hand corner (the starting point) to represent the people doing the exercise. Next consider about milestones and SMART (specific, measurable, achievable, realistic, time-framed) goals: write down clear steps and milestones for how they will get from where they are now to where they want to be. Who do they want and need support from? Who will give them feedback, and how are they going to seek feedback? Then draw out what the journey from the starting point to the cloud/ bucket looks like: a straight line? Some ups and downs? What might any obstacles be? What kind of situations are they? Spend some time on each situation and ask the group to work on solutions together. How can they be overcome? This part of the conversation might need gentle facilitation to shift the focus to solutions rather than problems. Then, at the end, ask each group to describe their journey; does it have a name? How will they embark on this journey in real life? How will the goals be translated into action?

Having introduced you to a range of concepts to foster understanding and development of the positive self, we conclude with a note of caution. We have advocated focus on people's strengths and how these can be developed. But we do not advocate an uncritical, or overly positive perspective that seeks to impose toxic positivity. Doing strength- and self-focused work in coaching needs to be paired with a dose of realism about the level of agency coachees have in their jobs and context in order to keep expectations realistic.

Conclusion

This chapter has brought together different psychological frameworks. We started out by looking at the alliance in coaching and how crucial this is for fostering successful coaching outcomes. We looked to research from therapy how to address ruptures and impasses, before turning to psychological safety. This led us to consider the importance of a positive self-concept and psychological concepts, including core self-evaluations and psychological capital. Self-confidence in coaching is a very relevant topic too, and we introduced you to a coaching model. We cautioned that it is important to set expectations clearly and not 'overpromise'. Indeed, we do not advocate a naïve perspective on positivity. Coachees might have prior trauma. Organisations can be difficult places to thrive in at times. Society still has a way to go to truly embrace difference. But coaching can help to model good working alliances and relationships, to promote considered and positive self-evaluation, as well as identify strategies to gain control and practice efficacy and confidence.

Reflective questions

To what extent do you practice an integrative approach in coaching? What helps you be effective in this regard?

- What have your experiences of coaching relationships been like? How do you handle it when coachees 'get stuck', or challenge you? What have you learned from this chapter to help you deal with such episodes?
- Have you ever worked in an environment where psychological safety was low? What effect did this have on you, and what could have been done to make this better?
- What about the different frameworks for a positive self-concept? Which one has resonated with you most, which one least? Your observations have been like what . . .?
- Have a go at using one of the exercises in this chapter (e.g. the PsyCap example?). How did this go? What worked well? Did you adapt anything to make this 'your own', any learning that you noticed?

Note

1 Stands for Neurolinguistic Programming – a style of coaching that can be controversial in terms of professional standards and research evidence.

References

Bandura, A. (1997). *Self-efficacy: The exercise of control*. Freeman.

Bono, J. E., & Judge, T. A. (2003). Core self-evaluations: A review of the trait and its role in job satisfaction and job performance. *European Journal of Personality, 17*(1_suppl), S5–S18.

Doyle, N. E., McDowall, A., Randall, R., & Knight, K. (2022). Does it work? Using a Meta-Impact score to examine global effects in quasi-experimental intervention studies. *Plos One, 17*(3), https://doi.org/10.1371/journal.pone.0265312

Edmondson, A. (1999). Psychological safety and learning behavior in work teams. *Administrative Science Quarterly, 44*(2), 350–383. https://doi.org/10.2307/26669

Frazier, M. L., Fainshmidt, S., Klinger, R. L., Pezeshkan, A., & Vracheva, V. (2017). Psychological safety: A meta-analytic review and extension. *Personnel Psychology, 70*(1), 113–165.

Graßmann, C., Schölmerich, F., & Schermuly, C. C. (2020). The relationship between working alliance and client outcomes in coaching: A meta-analysis. *Human Relations, 73*(1), 35–58. DOI: 10.1177/0018726718819725

Horvath, A. O., & Luborsky, L. (1993). The role of the therapeutic alliance in psychotherapy. *Journal of Consulting and Clinical Psychology, 61*(4), 561–573. https://doi.org/10.1037/0022-006X.61.4.561, https://doi.org/10.1111/peps.12183

Judge, T. A., Bono, J. E., Erez, A., & Locke, E. A. (2005). Core self-evaluations and job and life satisfaction: the role of self-concordance and goal attainment. *Journal of Applied Psychology, 94*(1), 177–195. https://doi.org/10.1037/a0013214

Kammeyer-Mueller, J. D., Judge, T. A., & Scott, B. A. (2009). The role of core self-evaluations in the coping process. *Journal of Applied Psychology, 94*(1), 177–195. https://doi.org/10.1037/a0013214

Kane, A., Lewis, R., & Yarker, J. (2021). Measuring self confidence in workplace settings: A conceptual and methodological review of measures of self confidence, self-efficacy and self-esteem. *International Coaching Psychology Review, 16*(1), ISSN 1750–2764.

Lai, Y., & McDowall, A. (2014). A systematic review of Coaching Psychology with Focus on the Coaching Relationship. *International Coaching Psychology Review, 9*(2), 135–146.

Luthans, F. (2002). Positive organizational behavior: Developing and managing psychological strengths. *Academy of Management Perspectives, 16*(1), 57–72. https://doi.org/10.5465/ame.2002.6640181

Luthans, F., & Youssef-Morgan, C. M. (2017). Psychological capital: An evidence-based positive approach. *Annual Review of Organizational Psychology and Organizational Behavior, 4*, 339–366.

McDowall, A., & Butterworth, L. (2014). How does a brief strengths-based group coaching intervention work?. *Coaching: An International Journal of Theory, Research and Practice, 7*(2), 152–163.

Mongrain, M., & Anselmo-Matthews, T. (2012). Do positive psychology exercises work? A replication of Seligman et al. (2005). *Journal of Clinical Psychology, 68*(4). https://doi.org/10.1002/jclp.21839

Rice, L. N. & Greenberg, L. S. (Eds.) (1984). *Patterns of change: Intensive analysis of psychotherapy process* (pp. 289–308). New York: Guildford Press.

Safran, J. D., & Muran, J. C. (2000). *Negotiating the therapeutic alliance: A relational treatment guide.* Guilford Press.

Safran, J. D., & Muran, J. C. (2006). Has the concept of the therapeutic alliance outlived its usefulness? *Psychotherapy: Theory, Research, Practice, Training, 43*(3), 286–291. https://doi.org/10.1037/0033-3204.43.3.286

Safran, J. D., Muran, J. C., & Shaker, A. (2014). Research on therapeutic impasses and ruptures in the therapeutic alliance. *Contemporary Psychoanalysis, 50*(1–2), 211–232. https://doi.org/10.1080/00107530.2014.880318

Seligman, M. E., & Csikszentmihalyi, M. (2000). Positive psychology: An introduction (Vol. 55, No. 1, p. 5). American Psychological Association.

Seligman, M. E. (1998). *Learned optimism.* Pocket Books.

Seligman, M. E. (1972). Learned helplessness. *Annual Review of Medicine, 23*(1), 407–412.

Snyder, C. R., Irving, L., & Anderson, J. (1991). Hope and health: Measuring the will and the ways. In C. R. Snyder, & D. R. Forsyth (Eds.), *Handbook of social and clinical psychology* (pp. 285–305). Pergamon.

Taylor, E. (2001). Positive psychology and humanistic psychology: A reply to Seligman. *Journal of Humanistic Psychology, 41*(1), 13–29. https://doi.org/10.1177/002216780141100

Wang, Q., Lai, Y. L., Xu, X., & McDowall, A. (2022). The effectiveness of workplace coaching: A meta-analysis of contemporary psychologically informed coaching approaches. *Journal of Work-Applied Management, 14*(1), 77–101. https://doi.org/10.1108/JWAM-04-2021-0030

Section C

Context matters

Chapter 9

Good work

Almuth McDowall and Nancy Doyle

Introduction

This chapter sets neurodiversity coaching in the context of 'good work' – which is work that promotes health and wellbeing rather than stress and harm – summarising relevant frameworks from practitioner and academic literature to provide reference points for neurodiversity coaching. We draw heavily on the academic field of Occupational, Industrial and Organisational Psychology, in which we furthered our own psychology training. We outline widely-cited models relevant to good job design, including the extended job characteristics model job–demands–resources (JD-R) and job crafting. Next, we include a section on the physical office environment and consideration of sensory sensitivities that are common in neurodiversity – yet good research about how to address them at work is sparse. But an overview is important so that coaches understand what kinds of things might be helpful for coachees to facilitate self-advocacy. Given that successful return to work after a period of sickness absence can be an issue for neurodivergent coachees, we outline the IGLOO model (developed by Nielsen et al., 2018, which integrates different levels of support interventions from the individual to the wider context) for return to work, which is based on conservation of resources (COR) theory. The final section looks at universal design principles at work. These are a further reference point for coaches to understand what 'good might look like', both in their own practice and what coachees could or should expect at work. We conclude by emphasising the concept of resources and how to build these through neurodiversity coaching.

DOI: 10.4324/9781003368274-12

Good work and good jobs

Being in work is good for people, good for organisations and good for society at large. But not all work is equally good – the quality of work experience is important (Weinberg & Doyle, 2017). This observation holds true for everyone including neurodivergent workers. When you are coaching, you will invariably come across coachees who are not enjoying their jobs. Helping them to identify where the difficulties are coming from is part of the process. To help you in the task, mindful that some coaches may have limited experience of human resources and work psychology, we've devoted a chapter to consider what good, healthy work resembles. Not every employer will be capable of achieving perfection on all healthy job measures! Some industries have endemic unhealthy practices based on overwork and unhealthy cultures. However, these principles can be explored with your coachees to enable them to make choices and rationalise their experience. They may seek a career pivot to prioritise their wellbeing, or they may realise that their challenges are not a 'them' thing, but a 'the job' thing, which gives them permission to feel less shame. The Chartered Institute for Personnel and Development, a UK organisation with a global network, undertakes an annual benchmark of job quality (CIPD, 2022) with representative samples of workers from a wide range of industries. According to this guide, good work has seven dimensions:

1. Pay and benefits: people's subjective evaluation of any extrinsic rewards offered.
2. Contracts: appropriate contract types and arrangements for the given context.
3. Work–life balance: the CIPD (somewhat narrowly) defines this as the interface of work time and overwork with people's lives and the provision of flexible working.
4. Job design and the nature of work: this is a wide-ranging dimension including the degree of intensity, autonomy, job complexity, as well as the respective match to people's skills and qualifications, and any development offered.
5. Relationships at work: the quality and cohesion of relationships, how psychologically safe people feel as well as the quality of leadership and management.

6. Employee voice: the extent to which workers can express their views, and to what extent these are taken on board.
7. Health and wellbeing: positive and negative impacts of work on mental and physical health.

These dimensions can be grouped into categories. Some are antecedents (precursors), a baseline that has to be met, such as contracts and pay. In psychology we call these hygiene factors – they're a bit like a basic level of cleanliness – if they are not there, everyone will notice, but if they are there, they become background information and don't necessarily motivate on their own. Our recent research has shown that adjustments and accommodations may be hygiene factors for neurodivergent people (McDowall et al., 2023). The next category are process conditions, including relationships and employee voice which are likely to fluctuate over time. The last categories are outcomes – here health and wellbeing. The annual CIPD benchmarking shows that there are large variations between employers; the last survey (2022) documented that job design, work–life balance and health and wellbeing were rated higher for small employers. People also rate all aspects of work, and in particular work–life balance, more favourably in higher-level occupations than lower level. Key workers (health and social care, teachers etc.) fare low on work–life balance. The 2022 data also points to notable differences by age for wellbeing with younger worker groups scoring significantly lower as a group, who are also more likely to change jobs. Although this job quality benchmarking is broad, it provides framing for coaching discussions where neurodivergent coachees say that their job is not right, or not doing them good, but are less clear as to the issues.

Our own 2023 survey has shown that neurodivergent workers are on average likely to be employed at the right skill level but are less satisfied with promotion and progression opportunities – this means we would consider it more helpful to look at the various aspects of job design in the fourth category in more detail.

Job design characteristics

What does academic research say about good work? The most cited model goes back nearly 50 years to Hackman and Oldham's (1976) seminal work, regarding motivational aspects of work, including skill variety and job autonomy. Curiously, this work and its successors had unintended consequences as it served to highlight what motivates people, but then led to a decline in work design research in high quality academic journals. Humphrey and colleagues (Humphrey et al., 2007) picked up this line of enquiry again. They formulated and tested a more comprehensive model, which brought together the following work design features:

- **Motivational characteristics**: for example the degree of autonomy, skill and task variety; task identity, job complexity and specialisation.
- **Social characteristics**: such as feedback, social support, degree of interdependence and interaction beyond the workplace.
- **Work context characteristics**: how work is set up physically and the actual working conditions.

They examined 'critical psychological states' as mediators, which are variables that can change the relationship between two other variables, namely meaningfulness, responsibility and knowledge of results. As work outcomes they considered:

- **Behaviour**: performance, turnover and absenteeism.
- **Attitudes**: satisfaction with the job, supervisor, colleagues, and rewards such as compensation; organisational commitment, job involvement and intrinsic motivation.
- **Work role perceptions**: conflict and ambiguity.
- **Wellbeing**: level of anxiety, stress, burnout, and overload.

The findings of their robust meta-analysis are wide ranging; we summarise the relevant highlights here. Their analysis showed that both social characteristics and work characteristics matter for how people experience work, but that relationships differ. For example, social characteristics have a strong relationship to whether people will stay in their job, motivational characteristics almost none. Meaningfulness is by far the most important mediator. Another significant finding was that autonomy over your work and social support are the best predictors of job satisfaction. So, we hear you ask, what is the relevance of all of this for coaching in a neurodiversity context?

Firstly, while this might seem obvious, it is important for any coach in a work context to have a reference point of what 'good work' looks like. While jobs and sectors and levels of seniority and specialism will differ, there are some aspects that matter regardless. A simple check list that can be used in coaching as a discussion tool is useful; this could be based on the CIPD dimensions or Humphrey et al.s, framework (2007), a hybrid of frameworks, or an even more comprehensive check list, also integrating some of the research below. You would write out these dimensions on sticky notes and ask questions about each and then note down brief observations. Doing this together can provide valuable insight into which job aspects are currently high, medium or low quality and what contributes to these ratings. Get creative! A simple check list approach can be a helpful starting point to facilitate clarity and shared understanding in neurodiversity coaching.

Meet Haven. Haven worked as a senior manager in a local authority. She was referred to coaching for support with wellbeing issues and had been signed off work because of depression and anxiety for some weeks. She was returning to her job, initially four days out of five, with the view to hopefully returning full-time soon. This is called a 'phased return' and it is an important accommodation for those who have been on extended health absences. In her first meeting with the new coach, she said that she "hated" her current job and appeared angry and flustered. The coach offered a calm, "how about if we look at what the issues are and consider together aspects of your job and how you work?" This acknowledged the importance of the topic, but also served to diffuse the emotion, it provided the opportunity for metacognition – coming above and distant to the situation in order to look at the patterns and features. Coach and Haven then spent half an hour together, looking at a check list of good work and moved sticky notes around to identify priorities.

This process identified a clear issue to work on together. Haven felt frustrated because she had made autonomous suggestions for improving the workflow in their immediate environment, but these had not been taken up. Clean exploration of how she had framed the suggestions elicited that there is a time and place to put forward constructive suggestions – right at the end of a tiring team meeting might not be the best opportunity. Having reflected on this, Haven and coach worked out a homework strategy for identifying allies at work who also agreed that positive changes were needed. Haven then worked together with two co-workers to put together a vision and a plan for effective workflows and took turns to present at the next team meeting. Their suggestions got a 'thumbs up' from everyone in the room and the changes were implemented and followed up. This approach increased Haven's work autonomy, reduced unnecessary job complexity by instigating a simpler process, and resulted in increased meaning in her work because it was satisfying to see the changes in action, but also increased her social support by proactively reaching out to others. Win–win!

This example shows that it can be useful in coaching to consider the different categories that mark good work holistically in coaching, going beyond what motivates coachees to also include their social and work context, and a range of outcomes. Neurodivergent employees often have good ideas about how to improve systems and become frustrated when these are not obvious to others. However, the coach's approach of taking the information seriously by offering a practical framework added detail and structure to Haven's ideas. This then enabled Haven to present the information as a positive force for efficiency, rather than a grumble that the team was doing it wrong.

We note the intersection of gender here, and that women in general are less likely to be listened to at work, more likely to be interrupted and overlooked as the creator of their own ideas (Tannen, 2021). If you are not and have never been female, but you are working with neurodivergent women or indeed neurodivergent people with other marginalising characteristics you need to be aware of the additional hazards some people face when suggesting changes. The dominant group may overlook, dismiss or pass off ideas as their own. It can require significant support and reassurance. Going the route of identifying allies and presenting a joint idea may have been successful here, but it also limits the chances of Haven being seen as a creative innovator in her own right. This is something to revisit in the coaching journey, in order to set Haven up for ambition and growth in her career.

Job demands and resources

You will have noticed that psychosocial characteristics are particularly important for good work, alongside a good physical set-up. Detrimental working conditions are linked to more accidents, lower performance and more sickness absence amongst other negative outcomes (see Schaufeli, 2017). The job–demands–resources (JD-R) model is a useful heuristic to understand good work and wellbeing outcomes. In essence, this model says that effective resources, which can be personal (e.g. energy) or social (e.g. support) are linked to increased engagement, which is a state of feeling involved and absorbed in one's work (for more wide-ranging definitions see Schaufeli & Bakker, 2010). In contrast, demands such as ill-defined work expectations or overwork are linked to burnout (e.g. Bakker & Demerouti, 2007). The central proposition of this model is that job strain develops when demands are high and resources low, and that work engagement is most likely when resources are high, even when demands are high. Although some might say that the model is overly simplistic, it is very flexible, and provides a simple framework for looking at jobs and their 'fit' in coaching.

We would encourage sharing a simple summary with coachees – so when demands (the things that you find hard) are high and resources (what helps you) are low, then people's energy is drained over time and burnout more likely. This isn't good for anyone. Conversely, job resources make us feel motivated, give us energy and thus help us do good work, which benefits everyone. A helpful anchor is that good job resources contribute to engagement (not low demands), whereas high levels of job demand paired with poor resources are linked to burnout. Thus, increasing resources is always a good thing, whereas getting rid of or decreasing demands will only affect potential burnout – it won't build motivation or engagement on its own. This can be important for neurodivergent coachees, as Nancy has seen many examples in her practice where well-meaning managers have tried to slim down a role to make it easier, without considering how patronising this can be. Although a questionnaire exists to measure people's Energy Compass (e.g. Schaufeli, 2017), in coaching it can be more helpful to use visual illustrations; in our experience this brings a more visceral element to any session. For example, you might want to create worksheets where coachees can indicate what helps them to dial up their energy and charge their batteries and, conversely, what saps their energies most. In Haven's case there was a link between two aspects – autonomy and being 'heard' was crucial, but this had to be paired with good social support to put things into practice.

Job crafting

Another useful concept relevant to increasing of resources and decreasing job demands is job crafting (Tims & Bakker, 2010; Wrzesniewski & Dutton, 2001). This fits into a wider body of research on proactive job behaviours – that is, things people do out of their own accord – in this instance to change the characteristics of their job. We always think of this as 'chipping away at your job' to make it into something that you like. In many work contexts, this might be more feasible and realistic than undertaking an entire 'job re-design'. When thinking of job crafting, Almuth is always reminded of her paternal grandfather. He was trained as a master carpenter – his parents expected this so that he could take over the family business. Yet he was an artist at heart, incredibly good at playing the piano and he loved painting and sculpture. So, he taught himself how to do beautiful wood inlays. His masterpiece was a wooden trinket box, inlayed with a scene of children playing, rather than the big piece of furniture everyone expected him to do. Making occasional decorative pieces remained his way of expressing art in his work – quite literally chipping away at wood.

So how can job crafting happen in contemporary work environments? In essence, people make changes, whether large, medium or small (or all of these!) to better balance job demands and resources with their own needs and capacities (see Rudolph et al., 2017). Research tells us that individual differences such as personality and demographics are precursors, but so are job characteristics including autonomy and workload. Crafting behaviours can be grouped as those that are structural or social and those focused on resources or demands. The outcomes include feeling happier at work, increased engagement and better performance. It can be empowering to get coachees to think aloud about how they can increase their capacity to job craft. We are suggesting a list of reflective question prompts below, which draw on previous research and questionnaires (see ibid):

The Job

- **Task crafting**: to change the scope or tasks at work, where is your flexibility? To ring-fence time to concentrate on specific tasks, what do you need to make happen?
- **Cognitive crafting**: to give deeper meaning to what you do, how do you think about the overall mission and how each task fits in?

The Self

- **Increasing challenging job demands**: identifying something at work that is challenging that you'd like to try, you will do what ...?
- **Seeking resources**: how will you ask for feedback on your performance?

The People

- **Collaborative crafting**: to decide together with co-workers about things that are not productive or can be done better, what's the first thing you will do?
- **Relational crafting**: to enlarge your network at work by one person next week, who can you reach out to?

Note how all of these prompts, with the exception of cognitive crafting, which is more akin to reframing in terms of adjusting one's mindset, actively cue action on the part of the employee. This is important. Neurodivergent coachees can bring a history of a sense of failure to coaching, which can result in learned helplessness (Seligman, 1972), where they think that trauma is uncontrollable, and they learn to stop trying. Focusing the conversation is important to reinstate a sense of personal agency and convey the message that coaching is 'work', for everyone involved, and success contingent on personal action. It is not therapy to resolve deep trauma. Please note that job crafting does not mean giving up the tasks you hate and only doing the things that you love. There needs to be balance across the team and certain aspects will just simply need to be delivered. Nancy loves mentoring emerging leaders, but hates writing up one-to-one notes. However, it is important to keep records to help each other's memories and for governance. So, Nancy has learned to type while she listens, in order to keep her focus and ensure that there is a record for her to quickly tweak rather than start from scratch. Almuth on the other hand finds that writing whilst listening disturbs her flow, so she asks her mentees to write their own notes, which additionally helps her monitor their understanding. Job crafting is what we do to our roles to make them fit us, rather than a wish list where we ask for all the fun stuff to come to us and ignore some of the less glamorous aspects.

The environment and sensory sensitivity

Given the importance of recognising good work and a healthy environment, we need to include some reference to physical workplace adjustments. Neurodivergent coachees who have declared a disability qualify for reasonable adjustments or accommodations at work including alterations to the space people work in. These can include physical workplace adjustments such as design solutions including quiet zones, or control over noise and heat. Both hypersensitivity (reacting strongly to any stimuli) and hyposensitivity (little or no reactions) feature in neurodivergent populations with regard to noise, sound, smell, lighting and also balance (for a good overview see Weber et al., 2022). Environmental changes can be an important accommodation and, if implemented well, have great potential for improving and supporting physical health and wellbeing. Therefore, they are often talked about as best practice, but there is very little longitudinal data to establish what actually works. It is hard for us to definitely argue for one accommodation rather than another. The following two points are drawn from Weber et al.'s review (2022) and serve as a guide to understanding the role of environmental accommodation and flexibilities:

- Adjustments to the workspace need to be tailored and based on need, not on compliance. This means that employer representatives have to be trained/and or seek expert advice to implement accommodations well.
- Physical environment changes need to go hand-in-hand with good psychosocial support: one without the other is always less effective.
- Expectations have to be managed so that the effectiveness of any accommodations, and the immediacy of any effects, is considered appropriately.

Refer your coachee back to HR, their manager or Occupational Health (as appropriate) but be very wary of being drawn into a discussion about what should or should not be provided as you only have one view – the employee. Adjustments must be 'reasonable' and that involves cost and the impact on others who may also have their own disability protections to which your coachee may not be privy. Instead, help your coachee to rationalise their experience of the sensory environment and consider small, incremental buffers that are within their control, as well as empowering them to negotiate directly with their employer, for example about local adjustments in their immediate environment.

We want to be clear that as a coach you are not engaged in the remit of advising on accommodations and need to avoid getting drawn into relevant discussions for self-protection. Nancy has seen employees use aside comments from their coaches presented as evidence to their employer for disability discrimination – "my coach said you should have provided a permanent desk for me". You cannot advocate for your coachees like this, sad and annoying as it might be. Your best port of call is to return to the person who referred the coachee to you, if you want to advocate – this might be an HR department or Occupational Health.

Return to work, COR, and the IGLOO

It is not uncommon for neurodivergent coachees to have been in and out of jobs and have had prolonged absences from work (see Chapter 2 and 3). Mental health conditions (MHC) such as anxiety and depression are common in neurodivergent populations (see Doyle, 2020). Having any MHC has serious consequences for work, including low employment prospects (e.g. Prang et al., 2016. Returning to work is often problematic and a highly anxious and worrying time, as workers are likely to relapse and have repeat periods of absence (see Nielsen et al., 2018, for an overview). Therefore, it is important for coaches to have some understanding of what it means to work towards creating an environment that promotes healthy and sustainable return to work even if this is a complex issue. But let's look at the individual – which is where the concept of resources comes in handy again, just as it did in the JD-R model. Conservation of resources theory (Hobfoll, 1989) proposes that people are motivated to protect and accumulate valued resources. Resources can be pretty much anything that is helpful to people such as energy, time, status and so on. Positive and negative loss spirals can occur. Once the first resource is depleted, say when energy levels are low, then it is more likely that people won't cope with the demands of future situations. If you miss a deadline, then you must catch up to work towards the next one, but you are already tired, which means that you are more likely to miss the second one – this in turn makes you more tired.

Positive gain spirals are the opposite but also rely on 'resource caravans' from multiple sources: say you recognise early that you are going to miss a deadline – you talk to the team, divide up responsibilities but also compromise and drop an aspect of this task that is non-urgent. Therefore, you have increased resources through social interaction, but also gained shared understanding about what is important. Dr Karina Nielsen and her colleagues (Neilsen et al., 2018) have been building these notions into their IGLOO framework for sustainable return to work. We summarise the model here:

Level 1 – Individual: this level is about what people think, feel and do (cognitive, affective and behavioural), which is helpful to them at work, including job crafting, believing in their capabilities and lifestyle behaviours, such as rest and recouperation.

Level 2 – Group: this level is about attitudes at work and from friends, family and others, including the overall supportiveness, specific attitudes to return to work, but also frequency of contact – so how groups and teams engage with each other.

Level 3 – Leader: this level is about line managers', leaders' and also healthcare professionals' attitudes, behaviour and support, including the presence and positivity of role models, the decisions that are made and supported, and how people approach conversations.

Level 4 – Organisation: this level is about the presence of practices and policies at work, and the degree of involvement of occupational health, and support outside work from voluntary and community organisations; for example, about reasonable adjustments, phased returns to work, or implementation of training and development.

Level 5 – Overarching/social context: this level is about the respective legislation and welfare policy, for example the level of generosity of the welfare system (e.g. is absence from work paid for and by whom).

Conversations in coaching are likely to centre on Levels 1 to 3. But it is important for the coach to have some insight of Levels 4 to 5 also because they reference the wider context. Coaches working in the neurodiversity context, particularly when the initial referral had a wellbeing focus, will touch on relevant issues at some point in their practice.

Coaching in the IGLOO. Remember Haven? She had been off work and then returned, initially as a gradual phased return to work. The coach asked "when you returned to work it was like what . . . ?" Haven said that she felt really overwhelmed when she returned to work as "things had moved and changed in their absence". Together, coach and Haven focused on the 'I' in the IGLOO, to look at what would help her feel less overwhelmed.

Haven had always really liked checking others' work and was good at spotting typos. So she offered the team help proofing and finishing reports. This meant that she could spend some time reorientating in her strongest skills. Reading the reports had the add-on benefit of learning what colleagues had been doing in her absence. During coaching Haven also voiced that she needed 'quiet time' to do this. She negotiated with her co-workers that someone else would take any inbound enquiries for Haven while she was proofing – this helped to address the 'G'. Having then admitted that she was anxious that colleagues thought it was nevertheless difficult to integrate Haven back into the team, the coach asked questions about what was challenging. Haven said that she felt lonely and out of her depth when she returned and thought that "my manager is really judging me". The coach questioned whether there was any evidence for this, and it turned out Haven hadn't had a return-to-work meeting. Haven asked for a one-to-one and she and the coach prepared for this meeting together as Haven said it helped them to have an agenda. The meeting with the manager turned out to be very positive as they said that they should have a regular process of checking in with each other and put dates in the diary. This made Haven feel more secure and heard – addressing the 'L'. Lastly, the coach suggested to Haven building a resource caravan together. A big caravan was drawn and Haven seated different people in the caravan, drawing 'speech bubbles' to outline why these were important people to engage with and how she would do this. The driver seat remained empty. The coach asked, "so who will be driving the caravan?" Haven said that she'd have to be the nominated driver, as the others were being busy doing what they do. This proved an empowering metaphor, helping Haven to re-establish herself as a leader in a busy department. Haven wears a small badge of a caravan to this day.

We have found this type of problem to be endemic in our coaching – coachees worrying about what others will think of them, assuming the worst and then acting accordingly. Nine times out of ten when we coach neurodivergent people to "just ask" or "make a suggestion" it lands well and resolves the situation. And, on the small number of occasions where it doesn't, this tells your coachee everything they need to know about their workplace. A useful aspect of coaching is unpicking those worries and self-conscious doubts about what others are thinking. Just like feedback, it can say more about the coachee than their colleagues. Facing it head on takes courage and the support of the coach, but it prevents conflict **or** reveals a toxic scenario. Both outcomes help a coachee to move forward.

Universal design and coaching

In a previous paper (Doyle & McDowall, 2021), we used the metaphor of the diamond in the rough to describe neurominorities as people who may have talented qualities and are likely to become valuable with appropriate care and attention. How should such care and attention manifest at work? We mapped the principles of universal design (e.g., Story, 2001) onto the employee life cycle in a comprehensive table. The employee life cycle typically has seven stages including exit, which comprise the following six aspects to support neurodivergent workers during their employment:

1. Work should be designed to focus on outputs, not inputs – if people get their job done well, it should not matter how they do it, as there are many routes to success. Craft roles for specialists and generalists.
2. Organisations should ensure that everyone can give their best during hiring and match the recruitment technique to the job at hand rather than interviewing everyone or making everyone take an online test.
3. Terms and conditions of work should be inclusive to increase access for everyone in contracting and the psychological contract should be made explicit.
4. Any training or development should have inclusive principles from the design stage on, to ensure equal access for neurodivergent people, such as sending reading materials well in advance and having remote options.
5. The review of performance needs to be inclusive and clearly communicated with good feedback principles.

6. The provision of wellbeing should be inclusive and include specialist provision, rather than a blanket panacea like mindfulness courses for all.

Universal design juxtaposed against the employee life cycle might include the following examples:

Equitable use:

- Job design to avoid social constructs in 'essential' criteria, such as team skills for jobs where performance will be independent.
- Use of work sample tests in recruitment to measure performance in the actual role rather than social expectation – loaded interviews or proxy measures such as timed intelligence tests.
- Provision for: remote working; flexible hours; general reduction in commuting obligations as standard in all employment contracts where feasible.
- Ensuring access to standard training through best practice in preparation and delivery for all in-house provision, details as below.
- Provision of personal performance training as standard company offer, e.g., time management, planning, prioritising and other performance issues common to neurodivergence, but also relevant to a wide range of employees and those newly promoted.
- Ensuring a variety of wellbeing initiatives, including mental health as equal to physical health. Signposting access to wellbeing supports into standard onboarding and reviewing protocols so that they are standard; reviewing the design of work to include elements of control, autonomy, support and collegiality, as above.

Flexibility in use:

- Craft roles for specialists as well as generalists, for example permitting senior roles without supervision responsibilities.
- Offer a menu of adjustments as standard in recruitment, which signals that organisational intentions are welcoming of difference. Invite candidates to contact recruiters if they would require time extensions or location flexibility, for example.

- Provide flexible options for standard systems such as frequency of supervision and feedback, which may need to be increased during onboarding for some neurominorities.
- Ensure adjustable pace in learning programmes and allow additional time for preparation in any post-training testing.
- Permit mentors in performance reviews, provide feedback written in advance to allow reflection, and ensure appraisal scoring to avoid penalising where employees excel in specialist areas but are average in others.
- Ensure wellbeing provision incorporates specialists, as standard advice may not be appropriate for some neurodivergent people who have additional cognitive and medical needs.

Simple and intuitive use:

- Over time, roles develop 'creep' and become overlaid with sometimes inconsistent responsibilities, so regular review of performance output variables and team structures helps to ensure that jobs are designed simply and intuitively in line with the business goals.
- Clear instructions in recruitment on how to complete applications and what to prepare for assessments using simple bullet points or numbered steps.
- Well laid-out terms and conditions, signposting to relevant policies and procedures, covering note, using read ability score to assess language accessibility.
- Consistency of formatting and training scheduling to avoid confusion or absence.
- Standard format for assessing and reporting performance that is consistent and clearly communicated in advance.
- Well-advertised wellbeing provision with information clearly presented in both simple step-by-step format and as an overview.

Perceptible information:

- Role descriptions to be accessible in format, e.g., multisensory, adjustable text size/background colour, sans serif font, printable, editable.

- Language to be behavioural and output driven, avoiding ambiguity and gender/culture-bound statements such as "influencing skills".
- Application process in accessible formats, e.g., multisensory, adjustable text size/background colour, sans serif font, printable, editable.
- Understanding the additional needs for psychological contract – what seems obvious may need to be explicit to avoid misunderstandings. Multisensory options for ensuring policy compliance, e.g., safeguarding videos.
- Written contract in accessible format to augment written policies.
- Training materials to include accessible written pack and opportunity for discussion, reflection, and action before completion of training.
- Feedback to be factual and not interpretative, guidance and training provided to supervisors about reporting performance feedback clearly with examples.
- Transparency on purpose of wellbeing initiative, ensuring that it is perceived as optional help rather than mandated acquiescence – many neurodivergent people have had negative experiences with mental-health practice.

Tolerance for error:

- Ensure that safety, risk and customer-facing deliverables have second checks built into the role design to reduce the need for 100% accuracy.
- Allow candidates to review and edit application information before online submission. Encourage applicants to pause or take breaks in interviews if required. Give clear instructions on directions and login details, as many neurodivergents have significant impairments in way finding. Do not penalise this specifically.
- Provide standard contract process to include reviewing verbally as well as written, giving opportunity to ask questions.
- Set a tone in training for the permission of 'silly questions' and create an environment of positive regard. Permit multiple attempts at knowledge tests and allow practice tests.
- Allow for appeal or negotiation where performance ratings resulted from misunderstanding.

- Create feedback loops for employees to submit their experiences, both negative and positive, to ensure employee voice regarding wellbeing is captured and acted upon.

Low physical effort:

- Understand the additional burden of commuting and busy workspaces for some neurodivergent people; for some this causes physical pain and extreme fatigue, leading to poor performance. Design roles with minimal sensory load and travel requirements in mind.
- Ensure provision of assistive technology (AT) or materials that are in formats compatible with AT. Consider timing of interviews and offer flexibility around location and need to commute in rush hour.
- Create as much time as possible for reviewing and completing the contracting process to avoid slow processing speed anxiety.
- Use AT in training.
- Have regular comfort breaks to accommodate sensory overwhelm and aid processing.
- Ensure proximity of support to reduce travel, and that wellbeing services also meet multisensory design and AT compatible standards.

Space and size for use:

- Seek specialist input into the design of workspaces and, where possible, allow flexibility or compromise (shifts) in attendance on busy work sites.
- Match the recruitment environment to the job performance so that you can assess in context with the caveat that there should be a quiet environment for preparation and recruitment tasks, as there is likely to be additional anxiety for neurodivergent people.
- Define location of workstations, provision of dual monitors, sit/stand desks, and acoustic barriers as standard options in contracts.
- Provide flexibility around onsite versus remote delivery, group size and familiarity in training.
- Ensure performance reviews are conducted in a friendly location and quiet, calm environment, with sufficient notice of who will be present.

- Ensure flexibility of remote access to tertiary wellbeing support via app, video, phone, or face-to-face. Avoid reliance on single delivery method.

Although universal design is a blunt heuristic, it's a helpful set of principles that state that environments should be designed in a way that is fair, intuitive and accessible to everyone. Not all employers or coachees are aware of this framework, therefore it is a useful coaching activity to share the principles, and then invite coachees to share how their work experience compares. It may not be possible for an employer to make all the accommodations, given the limits of their resources, so this shouldn't be an exercise in seeking perfection. But responsiveness, compromise, a desire to support a neurodivergent employee who reaches out is a solid green flag for a positive work environment. Similarly, being immediately shut down is a red flag. In coaching you cannot control your coachee's employer, but your coachee can choose how they respond to their employer, and bringing a more informed perspective to any conversations can be empowering.

Universal job design as a lens for work experiences. Some years ago, Almuth was part of a team delivering an assessment centre for promotion. Candidates invited to the centre were mainly neurotypical generalists but occasionally also neurodivergent specialists. The specialists were assessed against the same criteria as everyone else, the only exception was that they were not rated on the observed quality of line management-specific behaviours but on specialist knowledge. This is because they were being hired into specialist roles and would not have line-management accountability. This is an excellent example of good job design, here facilitating access to leadership roles without the need for line management.

However, to demonstrate their specialism, they had to deliver a technical presentation. On one occasion, a particular candidate was the only specialist being assessed with five generalists, and the assessors observed what they had prepared. One assessor rated them very low, as they were "not making eye contact, talking quickly, and failing to read the audience's attention". The other assessors challenged this, saying that presentation style had nothing to do with their technical expertise demonstrated in the structure and content of their work. At the final assessor conference when results were discussed, these candidates' performances were much debated. It was decided that they were not ready for promotion based on the observations.

But had the assessment centre (i.e. review process) really been designed with universal design principles in mind? Was it actually fair for everyone to be assessed at the same time? Why was making eye contact seen as being relevant to a role that requires in-depth and specialised expertise? Imagine you would be seeing this specialist in coaching – they feel bruised and discouraged by their experience. They think they will never get promoted. What would your starting point be? Are there are also ethical tensions – to have a better chance of success next time, is it right that the person must adapt? Or is there a way they could make it clear that their presentation style will be unusual? Could they ask to submit a report instead of talking through the ideas?

You can also take active steps to model universal design in coaching, this is always a good thing, but particularly assuring for coachees who currently have or have had unhappy work experiences. Three phases from the employee lifecycle are particularly relevant to the delivery of coaching, namely designing, contracting and wellbeing. We have summarised these here, the first two under the same heading:

Equitable and flexible use: how can you design coaching that is accessible for everyone? How will you accommodate different preferences for space, format and location in contracting? To what extent have you considered wellbeing as an integral part of your coaching offering, and can you refer issues and topics that warrant specialist advice?

Simple and intuitive use: have you checked your standard contracting policies and documents for accessible format and language? Are you actively seeking feedback from coachees to what extent your approach is clear? Are you addressing wellbeing in accessible and step-by-step approaches during coaching?

Conclusion

This chapter has offered several frameworks to help coaches and coachees understand what makes jobs and work 'good'. These can inform several approaches in coaching, and are a helpful reference point at all times, but particularly so when coachees need to negotiate the experience of transitions, such as settling into a new role, applying for promotion, or navigating return to work after sickness absence. They share common features:

- That it is always good to **boost resources**, such as people's energy and social support. So address the boosting of resources first, so that coachees can tackle any demands that sap their energy.
- Although job contexts and sectors differ, there are dimensions that are always important. Research tells us that the **psychosocial environment**, that is, how people interact, always matters.
- If people can't change their job role, there is always an opportunity to **craft**, and to make our jobs 'our own'. Thinking about relevant strategies can be very empowering for coachees and boost resources.
- The physical environment is important, as neurodivergent workers are likely to have particular sensitivities. There is rarely a solution that works for all. Coaching can be a helpful and safe space to explore, and then model 'what works'.
- The principles of **universal design** tell us that work should be designed and implemented with principles of equitability and fairness to all in mind. Coachees are likely to have varied

experiences – knowing what 'good' could look like is an important motivator to instigate change.

In short, there are principles of good work relevant to everyone. Neurodivergent coachees may, however, have specific preference for when and how they work. Coaching might not be able to solve or address all of these, but awareness raising and strategies to tackle job crafting and enhance the psychosocial environment are likely to bear fruit for everyone.

Reflective questions and practical exercises

- Which of the frameworks describing good work and job design did you find most insightful and accessible to inform coaching? To what extent do you currently actively address or come across good work and job design in coaching?
- Prepare a check list or exercise (resource caravans, anyone?) to use in coaching. How can you ensure that this complies with the principles of universal design?
- To what extent do you job craft in your work? What gives you energy? Have you noticed positive job crafting strategies among your coachees which you could note and share?

References

Bakker, A. B., & Demerouti, E. (2007). The job demands–resources model: State of the art. *Journal of Managerial Psychology, 22*(3), 309–328.

Chartered Institute for Personnel and Development (2022). *CIPD Good Work Index 2022. UK Working Lives Survey.* www.cipd.co.uk/Images/ good-work-index-survey-report-2022_tcm18-109896.pdf

Doyle, N. (2020). Neurodiversity at work: A biopsychosocial model and the impact on working adults. *British Medical Bulletin, 135*(1), 108–125. https://doi.org/ 10.1093/bmb/ldaa021

Doyle, N., & McDowall, A. (2021). Diamond in the rough? An "empty review" of research into "neurodiversity" and a road map for developing the inclusion agenda. *Equality, Diversity, and Inclusion: An International Journal, 41*(3), 352–382.

Hackman, J. R., & Oldham, G. R. (1976). Motivation through the design of work: Test of a theory. *Organizational Behavior and Human Performance, 16,* 250–279.

Hobfoll, S. E. (1989). Conservation of resources: A new attempt at conceptualizing stress. *American Psychologist, 44*, 513–524. https://doi.org/10.1037/0003-066X.44.3.513

Humphrey, S. E., Nahrgang, J. D., & Morgeson, F. P. (2007). Integrating motivational, social, and contextual work design features: A meta-analytic summary and theoretical extension of the work design literature. *Journal of Applied Psychology, 92*(5), 1332.

McDowall, A., Doyle, N., & Kisleva, M. (2023). *Neurodiversity at Work 2023: Demand, Supply and Gap Analysis.* Neurodiversity in Business, 1–60 pages.

Nielsen, K., Yarker, J., Munir, F., & Bültmann, U. (2018). IGLOO: An integrated framework for sustainable return to work in workers with common mental disorders. *Work & Stress, 32*(4), 400–417.

Prang, K. H., Bohensky, M., Smith, P., & Collie, A. (2016). Return to work outcomes for workers with mental health conditions: A retrospective cohort study. *Injury, 47*, 257–265. https://doi.org/10.1016/j.injury.2015.09.011

Rudolph, C. W., Katz, I. M., Lavigne, K. N., & Zacher, H. (2017). Job crafting: A meta-analysis of relationships with individual differences, job characteristics, and work outcomes. *Journal of vocational behavior, 102*, 112–138.

Schaufeli, W. B. (2017). Applying the job demands–resources model. *Organizational Dynamics, 2*(46), 120–132.

Schaufeli, W. B., & Bakker, A. B. (2010). Defining and measuring work engagement: Bringing clarity to the concept. *Work Engagement: A Handbook of Essential Theory and Research, 12*, 10–24.

Seligman, M. E. (1972). Learned helplessness. *Annual Review of Medicine, 23*(1), 407–412.

Story, M. F. (2001). Principles of universal design. In W. F. E. Preiser & J. K. Smiths (Eds.), *The Universal Design Handbook* (2nd ed., Chapter 4). McGraw-Hill.

Tannen, D. (2021). Three decades in the field of gender and language: A personal perspective. *Gender and Language, 15*(2), 232–241. https://doi.org/10.1558/genl.20312

Tims, M., & Bakker, A. B. (2010). Job crafting: Towards a new model of individual job redesign. *South African Journal of Industrial Psychology, 36*, 1–9. http://dx.doi.org/10.4102/sajip.v36i2.841

Weber, C., Krieger, B., Häne, E., Yarker, J., & McDowall, A. (2022). Physical workplace adjustments to support neurodivergent workers: A systematic review. *Applied Psychology*, 1–53. https://doi.org/10.1111/apps.12431

Weinberg, A. & Doyle, N. (2017). *Psychology at work: Improving wellbeing and productivity in the workplace.* British Psychological Society. www.bps.org.uk/psychologist/bringing-healthy-workplace-heart-government

Wrzesniewski, A., & Dutton, J. E. (2001). Crafting a job: Revisioning employees as active crafters of their work. *Academy of Management Review, 26,* 179–201. http:// dx.doi.org/10.5465/AMR.2001.4378011.

Chapter 10

Wellbeing and work–life balance

Almuth McDowall and Nancy Doyle

Introduction

This chapter outlines research on wellbeing at work, including the role of leaders and managers. Our first section acknowledges potential physical health difficulties linked to neurodiversity, as coaches need to be aware of these, and where necessary refer on. Wellbeing is a key concern for neurodivergent coachees for several reasons, including: (a) the frequency of co-occurrence of mental health conditions; (b) links to health conditions such as Ehler's Danlos syndrome; and (c) links to behaviour patterns that may impact health and wellbeing at work. We introduce the concept of and include specific notes on Pathological Demand Avoidance in this chapter because it can be a crucial wellbeing concern. As many neurodivergent employees will hyperfocus and work in intensive bursts or periods, we introduce our readers to frameworks about burnout, stress and work–life balance in the light of empirical research. We affirm holistic and intersectional perspectives to inform organisational and coaching practice. This leads to consideration of flexible and hybrid working, which is often touted as the solution of choice for making reasonable adjustments for neurodiverse workers, but also as a work–life balance management solution.

We reiterate disclaimers about remit and boundaries in coaching for wellbeing as typical contracting concerns to facilitate strategy, performance or wellbeing coaching – NOT to offer health advice. Nancy has stopped referring work to associate coaches who insisted that nutritional advice was part of their coaching remit. However, it is important to know that physical health issues are likely to be

DOI: 10.4324/9781003368274212-13

prevalent. It is beyond the remit of this book to unravel why this is the case, but suffice it to say that these can include co-occurring conditions such as hypermobility, epilepsy, sleep disturbances and difficulties in coordination, regulating appetite, gastric distress and more. A heartening and consistent research finding is that exercise ameliorates some symptoms even if most of the evidence is focused on children and young adults. Specific studies have shown that exercise improves cognitive functioning in autistic people and/or ADHDers (Tan et al., 2016) and improves fitness, stamina, muscle strength and social functioning as well as motor skills (Healy et al., 2018) for autistic youth. Another meta-study documents that functional outcomes improve with exercise for children with ADHD, and more so for longer exercise interventions (Vysniauske et al., 2020)

Sleep is good for everyone as a recovery process, helping us to replenish resources and in turn aiding our wellbeing, which helps us perform better at work. Sleep quantity and quality are important (see Litwiller et al., 2017). Sleep disorders such as insomnia and narcolepsy are common across neurodivergent people, but are often undiagnosed and untreated for example in adult ADHDers (Wajszilber et al., 2018). Psycho-education is important – people need to know about sleep hygiene and how to address this, but medical referral and treatment may also be warranted, for example via the GP to a specialist sleep clinic. Research in this area still lags behind or has been overly focused on children and paediatrics. Good sleep is one way of recharging our batteries but there are also other things we can do to help our recovery processes. Many neurodivergent people have experienced a lifetime of sleeplessness. For those who haven't explored strategies, signposting to investigate good sleep hygiene is helpful. For others, including those working shift patterns or with demanding caring roles at home, a helpful position is empathy and acknowledgement of the disruptive role of poor sleep and/or identifying varied means of self-care.

Intersectionality may have an impact on physical health too (see Chapter 2), as research shows that: (a) women and people of colour are less likely to have received diagnosis for instance, or appropriate early health support (Roman-Urrestarazu et al., 2021); and

(b) the long-term effects of systemic injustice and previous trauma in marginalised groups (e.g. Tujague & Ryan, 2021), which can have significant, ongoing impacts on wellbeing. Although coaching is not a health intervention, it is the right forum to work on self-help strategies addressing topics such as:

- Knowing yourself and the warning signs: when to recognise signs of burnout, and how to put in place early remediate strategies such as increasing rest or decreasing levels of stimulation for a while.
- Self-advocacy and healthy living: setting clear boundaries with others and making 'leading a healthy lifestyle' a daily task, but not an obsession.
- Reducing load: staggering or structuring work and other loads by scheduling in breaks, downtime and so on.
- Support: actively reaching out and negotiating support – psychosocial support is often as helpful as structural adjustments.
- Being authentic: behaving as you are without having to mask and explaining to others why this is important.

Wellbeing: from surviving to thriving

The World Health Organization (WHO) provides this definition:

> Mental health is a state of wellbeing in which an individual realizes his or her [or their] own abilities, can cope with the normal stresses of life, can work productively and is able to make a contribution to his or her community.[1]

Mental health has been a concern to governments and policy makers because of the potential economic and societal impact of ill health. In the UK, the report *Thriving at Work* (Stevenson & Farmer, 2017) outlined such issues as the huge cost of poor mental health to employers, the economy and society and stressed that stigma and lack of knowledge prevails. Poor mental health is implicated in neurodivergent conditions and, even on its own, can create a spiky profile. We think, feel and act differently if our mental health is impaired and this impacts our capacity to manage our lives (see Weinberg & Doyle, 2017). Across situations and time, probably all of us fluctuate to some degree between thriving, struggling, being ill/burnt out and possibly off work – this is likely to be true for coachees in any role or job level.

Almuth had been invited to run a session for a senior leadership team. They had asked if she could share her wellbeing expertise so that they could apply this to their organisation. However, when Almuth walked into the room, people looked grey, low in energy and oddly disconnected. Usually, when Almuth runs a session where people already know each other there is some chatter, some banter. There was none of this. They were in the room because they were not well themselves. Almuth decided to use an exercise to ground them in their own experience and precedents to elicit the principles of wellbeing at work.

Almuth used a simple line graph on a flip chart, which she annotated with the words surviving, middle and thriving. She invited everyone to go up and indicate where they were currently on this line, not with their name but just a mark. The visual representation was revealing, as this indicated that few, if any, of the team thought they were thriving – most were clustered in the 'surviving range'. Seeing this together opened the conversation. It was the first time that they had openly talked about their wellbeing with each other. The realisation set in – how can we lead a thriving organisation, when we are not thriving ourselves? Almuth then asked them to repeat this simple exercise – to imagine where they would like to be in two years' time. There was unanimous agreement to collectively change towards thriving. This recognition underpinned a discussion about joint responsibility to make change, and how everyone should play a role in creating a culture that puts wellbeing at its heart, free from stigma or prejudice, through a change in culture as well as bottom-up employee-led initiatives. By working on themselves in a group-coaching context, they were able to see how they were asking their staff to 'do as I say, not as I do', which was creating a culture of overwork and poor health throughout the business.

What does good wellbeing practice look like in an organisational environment? The *Thriving at Work* report advocates the following five key markers, called the mental health core standards (Stevenson & Farmer, 2017, p. 6):

- Produce, implement and communicate a mental health at work plan.
- Develop mental health awareness among employees.
- Encourage open conversations about mental health and the support available when employees are struggling.
- Provide employees with good working conditions and ensure they have a healthy work–life balance and opportunities for development.
- Promote effective people management through line managers and supervisors.
- Routinely monitor employee mental health and wellbeing.

Building on these core standards are more ambitious 'enhanced standards' signposting that employers who take mental health seriously should accelerate and embed good practice by:

- Increasing transparency and accountability through internal and external reporting.
- Demonstrating accountability with specific targets and Key Performance Indicators (KPIs) for managers.
- Improving relevant disclosure processes.
- Ensuring provision of tailored in-house mental health support and signposting to clinical help.

In neurodiversity coaching, it can be advantageous to translate relevant standards (similar standards exist in other countries, e.g. Australia,[2] Canada[3]) into a check list as a reference point when coachees report that they are not feeling mentally well at work. In organisational practice, there are three levels at which you can intervene. Primary wellbeing interventions have a preventative focus on working conditions – hours and shift patterns, environmental factors like noise and comfort, organisational policies and culture. Secondary interventions focus on prevention at the individual level, such as encouraging healthy behaviour – cycling to work schemes and regular reflective practice for those handling emotional labour, for example. Tertiary interventions happen when wellbeing is already poor, such as Employee Assistance Programmes (EAP). Many wellbeing interventions have focused on secondary or tertiary interventions that centre on people rather than the root causes (see e.g. Lamontagne et al., 2007) such as the growth in mindfulness programmes. Although there is some evidence that mindfulness-based interventions reduce stress in non-clinical samples (e.g. Querstret et al., 2020), they will not make you better if there is a wider issue in your organisational environment – for example, if neurodivergent people need to reduce noise distractions and have struggled to adjust to hot-desking. A joint pulse check (asking targeted questions) of the current environment can open up coaching conversation and help to de-individualise the issue. The enhanced standards (above) are highly relevant to neurodiversity, as there is fear of disclosure at work due to stigma and prejudice. Tailored support can be wanting – it is important that occupational health or other professionals are appropriately trained in neurodiversity-affirming care.

It can be complex to address wellbeing issues in coaching because many such issues are systemic, rather than individual. There might be a genuine lack of support in the environment that coaching cannot target or change. But it can also be empowering for coachees to ask for appropriate support, then gain strength and momentum together with relevant allies to instigate change. It is important to ascertain priorities and how ready coachees are to address these issues. Conversely, such a pulse check can explore what is happening. It could equally be that a coach encounters a coachee who thinks that "no one understands my difficulties, so I remain unwell". Yet the coaching conversation documents that there is policy and support in abundance in the organisation. This leads the coach to enquire with curiosity why the coachee thinks that no one is being supportive. "Because I have not dared to ask". "But how do you really know if you have not asked – let's consider what insights can be gained from asking?" Readers will note the careful framing on the part of the coach. They don't imply in their question what will happen as a result of asking. Instead they put the focus on what can be learned and observed with curiosity.

Conceptual models of wellbeing at work

There are several conceptual models of wellbeing at work, which provide a reference point for coach and coachee. Dr Peter Warr's (1994) Vitamin model says that nine psychosocial aspects of work come together just like vitamins affect people's wellbeing at work, together with other aspects such as the differences between people:

1. The level of autonomy a person has at work
2. Opportunities to use and develop poor skills
3. How clear goals and rules are
4. Task variety
5. The level of performance expectations and feedback
6. (Good) Social support and contacts
7. Financial rewards
8. Physical comfort and sense of security
9. Position and status.

The Vitamin model also says that we can take too much of a certain 'vitamin'; for example, too much resource, too much autonomy or too much variety. More recently, researchers have also considered levels of autonomy 'fit', and that there are different types of autonomy. The results show the level of autonomy 'fit' predicts wellbeing better than the degree of autonomy as such (Stiglbauer & Kovacs, 2018). This means that some employees do not seek as much autonomy as others. Some coachees might find autonomy stressful and want clear instructions and a format to follow. This observation underlines that it is important to understand wellbeing issues for coachees in their respective context and ascertain what helps coachees thrive at work – what might work for you, or other coachees, might not be the right fit for the coachee in front of you right now.

While none of the research was undertaken with explicit reference to neurodivergent people in mind, we can surmise that many participants were neurodivergent, given prevalence rates in the general population. The model is a useful and simple reference point in neurodiversity coaching. First, ask people how well they feel overall, physically and mentally. Next, ask them to describe their work context – how do people know that they are doing a good job, who is there to support, how are people rewarded? Then ask specific questions to consider the nine aspects in turn, to identify positive work features as well as those that need attention. Recall Audrey's experience of laying out all her problems and then sorting them into what she could and could not control. This exercise could be repeated with examples of experience using the Vitamin model as a framework.

Stress, strain and burnout

We have to talk about stress and burnout as these are omnipresent concepts when we talk about wellbeing at work. There are several theories of job stress and strain that are well established. Karasek's (1979) Job Demand Control model (JDC) holds that how individuals experience stress depends on the level of demand as well as control or decision latitude – individuals are better at tolerating stress if they have some control, which aligns with the research on job characteristics (see Chapter 9). This was developed into the Job Demand Control Support model (JDCS) to encompass the buffering role of social support – individuals can tolerate stress better where support levels are high (Johnson et al., 1989). Neither model is particularly clear on what stress or strain actually is, work stressors can take many different forms, including the level of workload, how ambiguous or clear a role is, as well as actual physical, emotional and psychosocial demands. The challenge–hindrance stressor framework (Cavanaugh et al., 2000) groups stressors into two different categories:

- Hindrance stressors: for example, how ambiguous a job role is, or the level of bureaucracy to get a job done (very salient to us working in academia!)
- Challenge stressors: for example, the level of workload, and cognitive demand.

Hindrance stressors are linked to losses so people will perform and feel less well, but challenge stressors can result in individual gains such as motivation and growth. However, more recent research

(Kubicek et al., 2022) documents clearly that this prediction does not hold up when carefully examining two different challenge stressors. Workload as well as cognitive demands were negatively related to learning and motivation and positively related to strain, and the negative impact of workload was even stronger for some workers including in care and social work. These findings go hand-in-hand with what we set out in Chapter 9 on healthy work – it is not always the case that individual reactions to pressure need addressing – it can be the job itself that needs looking at. Your role as a coach is to facilitate reflection on priorities and core issues so that coachees develop awareness of how they work at their best.

Depending on the level of knowledge of the coachee, you might also want to explain stress reactions and where they come from. Our reactions are often very physical because of hormone changes. They create changes including an increase in heart rate and blood pressure – which is why psychologists often research stress reactions with blood pressure monitors and saliva tests! Stress is common, all of us experience strong reactions at some point. It's prolonged exposure, and lack of resources that puts us at risk.

Much has been said about a global burnout epidemic and how this is negatively impacting people's working lives. Burnout was first seen as a social problem, rather than something that should concern researchers and health professionals, and researchers and practitioners alike have been arguing whether it exists. Maslach and Schaufeli (2018, p.9) make the point that you can only determine burnout in a "relative way" (p. 9) by comparing it to other psychological constructs. While stress is a short-term reaction, burnout is prolonged and is marked by a breakdown in adaption – body and mind can no longer cope with pressures. Exhaustion of mental and physical resources is a key marker, the probably most cited definition is: "Burnout is a syndrome of emotional exhaustion, depersonalisation, and reduced personal accomplishment that can occur among individuals who do 'people work' of some kind" (Maslach & Jackson, 1986, in Maslach & Schaufeli, 2018, p. 14). While a lot of the original research was done in a care or service context, we can equally argue that most of us do 'people work' in some way – there are very few jobs, if any, where we never need to talk to others.

Burnout in neurodiversity

Burnout is a much-discussed issue in neurodivergent communities, and in particular in the autistic community. The Academic Autism Spectrum Partnership in Research and Education (AASPIRE; https:// aaspire.org/) conducted qualitative research with autistic adults and analysis of internet data (Raymaker, 2022, p. 141), and put forward this definition:

> Autistic burnout is a syndrome conceptualised as resulting from chronic life stress and a mismatch of expectations and abilities without adequate supports. It is characterised by pervasive, long-term (typically 3+ months) exhaustion, loss of function, and reduced tolerance to stimulus.

The difference between general burnout and autistic burnout is that the latter is linked to experiences in various life domains, not just at work; for example, masking autistic traits, the expectations from others, sensory overwhelm and the impact of life changes and transitions, as well as barriers to getting support. We urgently need more research on burnout, across all neurodivergent conditions. A single study on dyslexia and burnout, for example, found very similar experiences to the autism cohort (Wissell et al., 2022). Mantzalas and colleagues (2022) formulated a conceptual model of burnout, which provides a starting point for discussions in coaching based on sound research, including the JD-R and COR theory (see Chapter 9). We surmise that across neurodivergent conditions the following merit attention:

- **Personal demands**: these will increase the risk of burnout and decrease personal resources and wellbeing.
- **Personal resources**: these will decrease the risk of burnout, can increase or decrease personal demands, increase wellbeing and decrease mental strain.

- **Mental strain**: this will increase the risk of burnout and decrease wellbeing.
- **Wellbeing**: prioritising self-care will decrease the risk of burnout and decrease mental strain.

Conversation about these four issues will help identify root causes and priorities for action. Bear in mind our note about intersectionality here – encouraging de-masking is contingent on levels of privilege. Our research in 2021/2022 reported significantly more social obligation to mask and anxiety about de-masking at work for female, non-binary and neurodivergents of colour (Doyle et al., 2022). De-masking when cisgendered, heterosexual, white and male poses less risk. Consider your coachee's context when discussing de-masking and disclosing needs at work.

Coping, acceptance and self-compassion

When we talk about stress it is important to consider how individuals react, as well as the actual sources of stress or strain. This is because people react differently. One of the most widely known models is Lazarus and Folkman's (1984) transactional model of stress, which posits that stress occurs when the demands are greater than individual resources. Stress is our internal reaction to external influences that we judge as harmful – but that the strength of our reaction depends on our interpretation, rather than the act itself. Reactions to stress can be acute and in the moment – 'flight or fight' – but also chronically affecting us physically, psychologically and psychosocially in the long term. Stress hormones change our body chemistry, producing more adrenaline and more cortisol. This can affect our nervous system through increased blood pressure, heart rate and blood sugar levels and make us more likely to become ill (e.g., Davidson & McEwen, 2012). Stress can also change our brain activity and, for example, affect our cognition negatively, such as a negative impact on our memory and processing speed. Applying the transactional model, we can assess to what extent potentially stressful events or actions impact us. They could be:

- **Irrelevant**: have no impact at all.
- **Benign–positive**: have a positive impact (but see our cautionary note about challenge stressors above).
- **Stressful**: result in harm or loss of resources.

Reviewing what we experience in each category is revealing. When there are many things under the 'stressful' heading, there is call for action to look at resources swiftly. Does the coachee have the resource right now to handle situations? If not, how can they solicit support, and engage in solution-focused coping, such as delegation, dropping tasks, or reorganising work? When working with neurodivergent coachees, simplicity is often key and concentrating on 'easy wins' first to free up mental capacity and manage strong emotional reactions. Emotional coping is all about managing our own reactions but needs cautious and careful consideration. Emotion-focused strategies, such as seeking support, taking ownership, trying positive thinking, can potentially spark a cycle of negative coping such as blaming the self, anger or frustration. By and large, initial solution-focus will be a better strategy. Noticing how we react, without judgement, is a helpful principle for dealing with any stresses; psychological flexibility, which we describe in the next section, is a useful concept to share with coachees.

ACT based approaches

Acceptance and Commitment Therapy (ACT) based coaching lends itself to develop psychological flexibility and acceptance. Unlike Cognitive Behavioural Coaching (CBC, a variant of Cognitive Behavioural Therapy or CBT), which focuses on identifying and removing psychological blocks and goal-focused action, the start point for ACT is noticing and accepting. So, rather than practising to eliminate a limiting belief, it invites curiosity and acceptance of such beliefs (see Skews & Palmer, 2016). ACT focuses on patterns of thought and behaviour due to psychological inflexibility; such as avoidance of our internal world or being overly involved in one's thinking, lack of value clarity and absence of behaviours that accord with our values.

There is an engaging case study of a singing teacher who used ACT principles to train a student vocalist and 'treat' performance anxiety (Shaw et al., 2020). Performance anxiety can be crippling. Many famous artists have publicly spoken about this, such as Lana Del Rey who stopped touring because of her fear of the stage and crowds. In this case study, the singing teacher developed psychological flexibility to permit their students to persist with behaviours that were of value, even where there was some 'unwanted discomfort' (Shaw et al., 2020). Through this lens, the goal was not to reduce anxiety symptoms as a primary focus but the 'ACT Hexaflax', which is a model summarising six processes, and relevant actions and reflections. These include identification of one's values, being present in the moment, cognitive diffusion, being comfortable with the self as context and committed action. The coaching process for the performance-anxious student detailed in the paper (ibid.) combined a behavioural approach where the teacher, once trained in ACT, drew on the GROW model (goal, reality, options and will; Whitmore, 2010) to benchmark progress in each session with exercises such as thought labelling, identification of values and mindfulness. The student learned to categorise their behaviour into 'away moves', that is, things they did to avoid performance and anxiety and 'towards moves', moving towards sources of reward and/or value, and were encouraged to use more 'towards moves' during their performance.

Such exercises are valuable in neurodiversity coaching because they aim to develop self-acceptance rather than changing the way you think or feel, which has potential pitfalls for a community who might have been told about being 'wrong' or 'disordered'. ACT exercises are tangible, easily understood and provide structure. To embody the experience you can work with the coachee to take steps back, the 'away moves' (safely of course, watch the cupboard behind them!) and the 'towards moves' by stepping forward. Coachees often notice that steps forward are bigger than steps backward! To set expectations, it is important that it is made explicit in contracting (see Chapter 11) that some deliberate discomfort can be part of coaching – as we outlined in our introduction, we do not judge coaching as 'soft'.

Self-compassion

A lack of self-care and low self-confidence (see Chapter 8 on coaching psychology) are common issues for neurodivergent workers. Coaching needs to address how to make the 'self' a legitimate entity that deserves care and thought in the same way as the people around us. Based on Dr Kristin Neff's work (for a good summary see Neff, 2022), self-compassion has the same principles as having compassion for others, but the noticing is turned inwards to the self. Thus, you notice your own suffering, difficulty and/or being unwell and respond with a feeling of warmth and care, recognising that we are all human and noticing our feelings with curiosity and openness. This is *not* self-pity ("poor me", "no one could possibly relate to what I am going through") and getting wrapped up in emotional drama – it is about noticing with care that struggle can be real. There is now compelling research that self-compassion is linked to lower levels of psychopathology, including reduced anxiety, depression and negative affect as well as loneliness (Lee et al., 2021; Stutts et al., 2018). Self-compassion is also good for physical health, including enhanced immune function and reduced cortisol levels (Bellosta-Batalla et al., 2018; Kirschner et al., 2019 in Neff, 2022) and better sleep quality (Brown et al., 2021, in Neff, 2022). We turn to the issue of sleep below, as this is very important for neurodivergent populations. Neff (2022) is very clear about the distinction between self-compassion and self-esteem, and indeed cautions that there can be too much valuing of the self – where this becomes a somewhat ego-focused end goal rather than a conducive way of thinking, feeling and behaviour – cuing evaluations such as "How good am I at this?", or "In comparison to others, how good am I?". How "good" we judge ourselves to be depends on our experiences, so it is a state that is unstable, rather than an enduring trait (see Kernis, 2005, in Neff, 2022). It is heartening that self-compassion can be developed and trained. While full compassion-based therapy goes beyond coaching, there are several behaviour-based approaches that can be adapted in coaching; for example, there is SCHC which is Self-compassion for Health Care Communities (Neff et al., 2020). While the precise method for this intervention is not easy to backtrack from the publication, we took away from this research that for busy workers it is more conducive to practise self-compassion *on the job*, rather than engage in extensive programmes, which might ultimately just add to the workload. With careful priming and setting up, you can work with coachees to implement self-compassion on the job, and report back.

Specifically, we like the concept of 'compassion with equanimity', which informs a simple practice. Caregivers, or indeed a range of people at work, think of wording that describes how they care for others (or work with others) where they are not in complete control of outcomes to gain perspective. Then, using one's breath rhythm, on the inbreath the person imagines that they are taking in compassion for themselves, validating themselves, and on the outbreath that they are distributing compassion to others. This validates experience, but also cues the person to put attention on themselves first. Almuth worked with health-care professionals during the pandemic. Doctors reacted strongly to such suggestions "I am under such time pressure; I have to focus on patients and the wards!" Almuth gently challenged the group to look out for small pockets of time to engage in such micro-practice – while making tea, while consciously sipping water and hydrating, or while commuting to work. Even the busiest of employees can take these micro steps to orientate and ground themselves in the moment. Some might even call this mindfulness! However, it is often crossing the psychological barrier of deciding to self-care that makes the difference, rather than being given yet another thing to do.

Active recovery

Recovery from work and recharging our batteries is really important, but particularly so for neurodivergent coachees who might be living and working in environments that are inherently stressful for them. Recovery does not have thresholds or a binary distinction, where people are either recovered or not recovered, but is best thought of as a dynamic process. Recovery is about regulation of energy levels, which will vary and need to vary across the day and across tasks (Zijlstra et al., 2014). Finnish researchers investigated concrete energy management strategies that are helpful to people (De Bloom et al., 2015). They found that three strategies helped people most:

1. **Focus on the positive**: shifting your focus to things that you like about your job, rather than what you don't like – this is a topic effectively addressed in coaching. We can be prone to a negativity

bias, so noticing more what does work and shifting our attention is something we can all do.

2. **Goal setting**: it is one of the most consistent findings in industrial and organisational psychology that goal setting works. It helps us focus our attention and mobilise our resources. Coaching is a safe space to not only prioritise goals and work towards them, but also check progress.
3. **Pro-active behaviour at work**: it helps our own recovery to offer help to others.

Others have grouped recovery experiences into four categories: psychological detachment, relaxation, mastery and control (Bennett et al., 2018) and investigated challenge as well as hindrance stressors. The higher the challenge demands, the less likely people are to detach, relax and control their recovery, whereas job resources help all of these aspects. Psychological detachment makes people less likely to be fatigued than relaxation or control experiences. This tells us that, in order to recover well, we need to look holistically both at what we do at work (see Chapter 9) and also plan our recovery actively.

Let's look at personal energy management strategies and recovery. Pim is a programme developer who identifies as autistic in a high tech start-up company, which has a young team and everyone works very long hours. Pim has been referred for coaching because they have been off sick a lot. Their company offers one-to-one coaching as wellbeing support. With their coach they looked at their job, their job-related wellbeing and priorities to address in coaching. The first question was about what they liked about their job, to which Pim answered, "that they could go about it as they thought best as long as they delivered", i.e. a high degree of autonomy. They had felt micro-managed in their previous job, which they didn't like, and appreciated the trust in their current company. What they didn't like was that since they were seen as effective and getting the 'job done', they were given more tasks than others and rarely praised for what they did. The coach worked with Pim to identify what could be different and set a goal – this was for the team to become more explicit about sharing successes as well as the actual load and scope of their work. Pim suggested 'show and tell' sessions as part of their team meetings. As they were usually done online, everyone got the option to 'tell' or just type into the chat what they had done last week. Others noticed the speed and quality of Pim's work. Pim shared tips from their experience, as they had an effective way of using charts and flow diagrams to structure their work and helped others to develop something similar. This way the team developed more visibility of what everyone was doing, acknowledging the value of others became more routine and expertise was shared. As a result, people all around become more effective at what they did. Pim then felt empowered to challenge the long working hours. Their team developed a clear process for managing by outputs, not time spent at people's desk. "Good job swiftly done" became their catch phrase.

Pathological Demand Avoidance and radical acceptance

Pathological Demand Avoidance (PDA) is a controversial issue in neurodiversity research but deserves a mention here so that you can formulate your own view over time as to whether it has a potential influence on wellbeing. Newson (2003) described PDA in autistic children as behaviours including using social manipulation to avoid demands, resisting every day demands and requests and being very concerned about control and avoidance as a distinct developmental disorder. The definition has been criticised, including by autistic academics (e.g. Milton, 2013) for pathologising difference, but recent meta-analytic scholarship (Kildahl et al., 2021) documents that there is a subset of children and adolescents who persistently avoid demands. Children and adolescents grow up so we can surmise that such behaviours will persist. Some practitioners suggest that PDA may be present in ADHD and refer to it as a "pervasive desire for autonomy", to make it more neutral than described in current literature and not assume malicious intent – yet working with PDA takes skill.

PDA manifests as an intense response to being asked to do something or follow a rule. It is not known how prevalent PDA is within the neurodivergent community but when you come across it you will know! PDAers need an extra helping of compassion and reservation of judgement – you will need all the skills in this book around clean and open questioning, drama dynamics, management of wellbeing and creating a low demand reflective coaching space. Radical acceptance is the term coined by Kristy Forbes,[4] a PDA specialist in education and family work, as an environment where PDAers are accepted unequivocally. This may be your coaching space and a worthy outcome might simply be that you held space for them long enough to build a relationship.

For PDA coachees, supervision is essential and it should be qualified supervision with someone/a group that understands PDA, therapy and professional boundaries. Understanding PDA presentation as an acute anxiety and wellbeing issue is the first step to a non-judgemental frame, which is the best route to building relationships with this neurotype.

Work–life balance and hybrid working

You will have noticed that it can be hard to address work issues without looking at the person holistically. We turn to work–life balance (WLB) as the last topic in this chapter. In the past, research took rather traditional views of 'families' framing the balancing of different roles as inherently stressful, which causes people to experience work–family conflict (see Greenhaus & Beutell, 1985). People assumed that it was better to keep a clear demarcation between domains in their lives, a bit like shutting a door at the end of the day – a separation perspective. But equally, we can learn and transfer skills across different domains in our lives (Greenhaus & Powell, 2006). This is reflected in an integration perspective – work and life are seen more as an integrated whole, without rigid boundaries between domains. A simple exercise, tried and tested on many cohorts of MSc students, is to get people to indicate on a line with 1 at one end to symbolise total separation and 10 at the other end to symbolise total integration. Where would people rate their balance now? Then repeat this exercise again, this time indicating where they would like to be. If there is a mismatch, between now and the ideal, this is where there is a call for action and reflection. If work and life are more integrated then they'd like to be, how can people start to manage boundaries? If there is more separation then people would like, for example if it is hard to talk about life at work, what shifts could happen? If people rate themselves in the middle, with no strong preference, this is also interesting to explore – are they genuinely sitting on the WLB fence, or does their preferred fit vary a lot between situations and/or over time?

As several of our academic colleagues point out, WLB is not a neutral concept, we know that WLB experiences vary between different demographic groups, such as by characteristics that give us power at work, our gender identity and our age (see e.g., Özbilgin et al., 2011). Indeed, marginalised identities and intersectionality have an influence on how we access and influence resources. Therefore, Almuth has proposed the following definition to capture this (McDowall, 2023):

> Subjective experience of work–life balance comprises individual active engagement with their alignment of different life and work domains, in their present context through active negotiation and communication with others in accordance with their values and current priorities. This experience is contingent on context and likely to be influenced by intersectional marginalisation as well as time and finance.

Neurodivergent coachees might bring a number of work–life balance challenges to coaching. Let's take hybrid and flexible working as an example. Such set-ups are often touted as a 'solution of choice' to facilitate WLB, where part or all of the job tasks are undertaken in a location other than a shared office and put into places as an adjustment for neurodivergent workers. Many organisations have implemented hybrid and flexible working in the wake of the global pandemic as a work set-up for all or many employees and workers. This was a social experiment at scale, as we now know that businesses can and continue to function well with flexible or hybrid set-ups, which dispelled the myth that people need to be present in the office, presumably with a degree of surveillance, to do good work and not be shirking. We also know that flexible work, with choice, is good for everyone's health at work (Shifrin & Michel, 2022). The advantages of flexible working (in this example researched for autistic employees) are the limitation of sensory overload and flexibility, as well as reduction in stressful commutes. But there are also downsides, such as reduced helpful social contacts and reduced WLB – it can be much harder to manage work and life boundaries if there is no 'transition routine' that tells you that the working day has ended. There is some evidence that remote working is deleterious for ADHDers, for example (Das et al., 2021), due to the stationary nature and time blindness. Remote work is not a panacea for neuroinclusion. A personalised, flexible workplace is recommended.

Addressing WLB has challenges in coaching as the coach needs to be clear about boundaries. For example, it may be that the coachee wants to make work decisions that have financial implications, such as taking early retirement or cutting down work hours. Coaches should never solicit any kind of financial advice, as they should also refrain from giving health advice (see above), unless they are professionally qualified to do so. The other challenge is that WLB is about subjective individual perceptions, so what might work for you might not work for someone in a similar situation, but also involves negotiation and communication with others. We tend to avoid the word 'WLB' in coaching as many people then think that there is such a thing as absolute balance, and that coaches have 'cracked it' and have advice to offer. The reality is that everyone needs to work out what works best for them and their fit changes as they move through different life stages.

A good way to look at WLB is to make this explicit and tangible in coaching using a circumplex diagram, which we adapt to suit with some creativity in relevant sessions. The diagram usually starts with a smallish circle, which symbolises the person, and then different parts around this. The coachee labels these – their work, their advocacy role, their children, their partner, their hobbies and so on. Then the next task might be to colour these in – green for what gives the coachee energy and what they are happy with, orange for potential danger zones and red for what currently doesn't work. For example, a coachee found that voluntary advocacy work they were doing gave them a lot of satisfaction, and transferrable skills as they learned how to summarise information into lay people's terms and make this accessible. It also gave them a sense of satisfaction about helping others. But the advocacy work took a lot of time and had a detrimental impact on energy levels. Coaching helped with better boundary management strategies, such as switching off electronic devices and not looking at social media during 'cool off periods', but also using the knowledge gained through advocacy to campaign for more inclusive work set-ups.

Carers, and in particular dual carers who care for both young and elderly dependents, have particular WLB concerns. Unpaid care work remains largely undertaken by women (ONS, 2016). As there is a genetic component to neurodiversity, this means that neurodivergent workers are also relatively likely to care for neurodivergent dependents. An early piece of research found that parents of autistic children had to prioritise family over work, that they thought the quality of their work diminished, that they had to decrease work hours and/or frequently adjust work schedules to meet family demands (Matthews et al, 2011). This quote from the paper illustrates the inner struggle well: "I always feel that I am not giving my best to anything – my kids, my marriage and my work – and even myself. It is very hard to balance" (p. 634).

Their order of priority is telling – first their children, then their partner, then their work and only last themselves. Coaching work might therefore challenge and explore what might happen if the self is put first. Empty batteries and lack of resources don't help anyone – there is much to be gleaned from putting our oxygen mask on first, before attending to others. Almuth gratefully acknowledges Monique Valcour who helped her realise this when she had coaching a few years back – she is certain that without this wise challenge she would have risked burning herself out at the time.

Conclusion

Wellbeing and work–life balance are complex topics but rewarding and essential to address in neurodiversity coaching. Neurodiversity often comes hand-in-hand with health challenges – coaches need to acknowledge this context. We have summarised research and practice literature on mental health and wellbeing, on stress, strain and coping and burnout. We introduced key concepts, but also provide further points of reference for coach and coachee alike about what 'good' looks like. Compassion for the self and self-care are important and can be fostered. Coaching can challenge and address psychologically inflexible beliefs. We have explained PDA as an acute response to neurodivergent anxiety and burnout. It is important to have a holistic approach to work–life balance and recognise potentially common challenges, for example about WLB boundary management and how to ensure that hybrid working 'works' and mitigate unintended negative consequences.

Reflective questions

- Thinking about the workplaces you come across, both regarding where you have worked and where your coachees work, how common are 'enhanced standards' to support mental health at work? Are they more likely in some contexts rather than others?
- To what extent is it helpful to consider the organisational context in coaching? How would you go about this, having read this chapter?

- Think about one issue you find challenging – for example, working with certain coachees whom you find more challenging than others? What are your 'away moves'? Write these down. What are your 'toward moves'? Write these down. How can you action using more toward moves in coaching?
- How would you frame your own work–life balance? Have you noticed issues that contribute to conflict and things that make you feel enriched? How do you negotiate boundaries? What have you observed in your coaches – to what extent do preferences matter, and what are the implications for wellbeing?

Notes

1 These definitions are published by the WHO on their website at www.who.int/data/gho/data/major-themes/health-and-wellbeing
2 www.safeworkaustralia.gov.au/doc/model-code-practice-managing-psychosocial-hazards-work
3 https://mentalhealthcommission.ca/national-standard/
4 www.kristyforbes.com.au/

References

Bellosta-Batalla, M., Ruiz-Robledillo, N., Sariñana-González, P., Capella-Solano, T., Vitoria-Estruch, S., Hidalgo-Moreno, G., Blasco, J. P, Romero-Martinez, A., & Moya-Albiol, L. (2018). Increased salivary IGA response as an indicator of immunocompetence after a mindfulness and self-compassion-based intervention. *Mindfulness, 9*, 905–913.

Bennett, A. A., Bakker, A. B., & Field, J. G. (2018). Recovery from work-related effort: A meta-analysis. *Journal of Organizational Behavior, 39*(3), 262–275. https://doi.org/10.1002/job.2217

Cavanaugh, M. A., Boswell, W. R., Roehling, M. V., & Boudreau, J. W. (2000). An empirical examination of self-reported work stress among U.S. managers. *Journal of Applied Psychology, 85*(1), 65–74. https://doi.org/10.1037/0021-9010.85.1.65

Das, M., Tang, J., Ringland, K. E., & Piper, A. M. (2021). Towards accessible remote work: Understanding work-from-home practices of neurodivergent professionals. *Proceedings of the ACM on Human-Computer Interaction, 5*(CSCW1), 1–30. https://doi.org/10.1145/3449282

Davidson, R. J.,& McEwen, B. S. (2012) Social influences on neuroplasticity: Stress and interventions to promote wellbeing. *Nature Neuroscience, 15*, 689–695.

De Bloom, J., Kinnunen, U., & Korpela, K. (2015). Recovery processes during and after work. *Journal of Occupational and Environmental Medicine*, *57*(7), 732–742.

Doyle, N., McDowall, A., & Waseem, U. (2022). Intersectional stigma for autistic people at work: A compound adverse impact effect on labor force participation and experiences of belonging. *Autism in Adulthood*, *4*(4), 340–356. https://doi.org/10.1089/aut.2021.0082

Greenhaus, J. H., & Beutell, N. J. (1985). Sources of conflict between work and family roles. *Academy of Management Review*, *10*(1), 76–88.

Greenhaus, J. H., & Powell, G. N. (2006). When Work And Family Are Allies: A Theory Of Work-Family Enrichment. *Academy of Management Review*, *31*(1), 72–92. https://doi.org/10.5465/amr.2006.19379625

Healy, S., Nacario, A., Braithwaite, R. E., & Hopper, C. (2018). The effect of physical activity interventions on youth with autism spectrum disorder: A meta-analysis. *Autism Research*, *11*(6), 818–833. https://doi.org/10.1002/aur.1955

Johnson, J. V., Hall, E. M. & Theorell, T. (1989). Combined effects of job strain and social isolation on cardiovascular disease morbidity and mortality in a random sample of the Swedish male working population. *Scandinavian Journal of Work, Environment and Health*, *15*, 271–279.

Karasek Jr, R. A. (1979). Job demands, job decision latitude, and mental strain: Implications for job redesign. *Administrative Science Quarterly*, *24*, 285–308.

Kildahl, A. N., Helverschou, S. B., Rysstad, A. L., Wigaard, E., Hellerud, J. M., Ludvigsen, L. B., & Howlin, P. (2021). Pathological demand avoidance in children and adolescents: A systematic review. *Autism*, *25*(8), 2162–2176. https://doi.org/10.1177/13623613211034382

Kubicek, B., Uhlig, L., Hülsheger, U. R. Korunka, C., & Prem, R. (2022). Are all challenge stressors beneficial for learning? A meta-analytical assessment of differential effects of workload and cognitive demands. *Work & Stress*, *37*, 269–298. https://doi.org/10.1080/02678373.2022.2142986

Lamontagne, A. D., Keegel, T., Louie, A. M., Ostry, A., & Landsbergis, P. A. (2007). A systematic review of the job–stress intervention evaluation literature, 1990–2005. *International Journal of Occupational and Environmental Health*, *13*(3), 268–280.

Lazarus, R. S., & Folkman, S. (1984). *Stress, appraisal, and coping*. Springer.

Lee, E. E., Govind, T., Ramsey, M., Wu, T. C. & Daly, R. (2021). Compassion toward others and self-compassion predict mental and physical wellbeing: A 5-year longitudinal study of 1090 community-dwelling adults across the lifespan. *Translational Psychiatry*, *11*(1), 397. https://doi.org/10.1038/s41398-021-01491-8

Litwiller, B., Snyder, L. A., Taylor, W. D., & Steele, L. M. (2017). The relationship between sleep and work: A meta-analysis. *Journal of Applied Psychology, 102*(4), 682.

McDowall, A. (2023). Work–life balance through a diversity lens: Implications for research and practice. *The Market: International Journal of Business,* Vol 4, 63–77, https://cim.ac.cy/wp-content/uploads/2023/06/MARKET-VOLUME-4-2023-WEB-version.pdf

Mantzalas, J., Richdale, A. L., & Dissanayake, C. (2022). A conceptual model of risk and protective factors for autistic burnout. *Autism Research, 15*(6), 976–987.

Maslach, C., & Schaufeli, W. B. (2018). Historical and conceptual development of burnout. In W. B. Schaufeli (Ed.), *Professional burnout: Recent developments in theory and research* (pp. 1–16). CRC Press.

Matthews, R. A, Booth, S. M., Taylor C. F., & Martin, T. (2011). A qualitative examination of the work–family interface: Parents of children with autism spectrum disorder. *Journal of Vocational Behavior, 79* (3), 625–639, https://doi.org/10.1016/j.jvb.2011.04.010

Milton, D. E. M. (2013). "Natures answer to over-conformity": Deconstructing pathological demand avoidance. *University of Kent Repository.* The University of Kent's Academic Repository KAR. https://kar.kent.ac.uk/62694/

Neff, K. D. (2022). Self-compassion: Theory, method, research, and intervention. *Annual review of psychology.* First published as a Review in Advance on August 12, 2022. https://doi.org/10.1146/annurev-psych-032420-031047

Neff, K. D., Knox M. C., Long P., & Gregory K. (2020). Caring for others without losing yourself: An adaptation of the Mindful Self-Compassion program for healthcare communities. *Journal of Clinical Psychology, 76,* 1543–1562.

Newson, E. (2003). Pathological demand avoidance syndrome: A necessary distinction within the pervasive developmental disorders. *Archives of Disease in Childhood, 88*(7), 595–600. https://doi.org/10.1136/adc.88.7.595

Office of National Statistics (ONS, 2016). Women shoulder the responsibility of 'unapid work'. www.ons.gov.uk/employmentandlabourmarket/peopleinwork/earningsandworkinghours/articles/womenshouldertheresponsibilityofunpaidwork/2016-11-10

Özbilgin, M. F., Beauregard, T. A., Tatli, A., & Bell, M. P. (2011). Work–life, diversity and intersectionality: A critical review and research agenda. *International Journal of Management Reviews, 13*(2), 177–198.

Querstret, D., Morison, L., Dickinson, S., Cropley, M., & John, M. (2020). Mindfulness-based stress reduction and mindfulness-based cognitive therapy for psychological health and wellbeing in nonclinical samples: A systematic review and meta-analysis. *International Journal of Stress Management, 27*(4), 394.

Raymaker, D. (2022). *Understanding autistic burnout*. National Autistic Society.www.autism.org.uk/advice-and-guidance/professional-practice/autistic-burnout

Roman-Urrestarazu, A., van Kessel, R., Allison, C., Matthews, F. E., Brayne, C., & Baron-Cohen, S. (2021). Association of race/ethnicity and social disadvantage with autism prevalence in 7 million school children in England. *JAMA Pediatrics, 175*(6), e210054–e210054.

Shaw, T. A., Juncos, D. G., & Winter, D. (2020). Piloting a new model for treating music performance anxiety: Training a singing teacher to use acceptance and commitment coaching with a student. *Frontiers in Psychology, 11*, 882.

Shifrin, N. V., & Michel, J. S. (2022). Flexible work arrangements and employee health: A meta-analytic review. *Work & Stress, 36*(1), 60–85.

Skews, R., & Palmer, S. (2016). Acceptance and commitment coaching: Making the case for an ACT-based approach to coaching. *Coaching Psychology International, 9*(1), 24–28.

Stevenson, D., & Farmer, P. (2017). *Thriving at work: The Stevenson/Farmer review of mental health and employers*. UK Government. https://assets.publishing.service.gov.uk/government/uploads/system/uploads/attachment_data/file/658145/thriving-at-work-stevenson-farmer-review.pdf

Stiglbauer, B., & Kovacs, C. (2018). The more, the better? Curvilinear effects of job autonomy on wellbeing from vitamin model and PE-fit theory perspectives. *Journal of Occupational Health Psychology, 23*(4), 520–536. https://doi.org/10.1037/ocp0000107

Stutts L.A., Leary M.R., Zeveney A.S., & Hufnagle A.S. (2018). A longitudinal analysis of the relationship between self-compassion and the psychological effects of perceived stress. *Self Identity*, 17(6), 609–626.

Tan, B. W. Z., Pooley, J. A., & Speelman, C. P. (2016). A meta-analytic review of the efficacy of physical exercise interventions on cognition in individuals with autism spectrum disorder and ADHD. *Journal of Autism and Developmental Disorders, 46*, 3126–3143. https://doi.org/10.1007/s10803-016-2854-x

Tujague, N. A., & Ryan, K. L. (2021). Ticking the box of "cultural safety" is not enough: Why trauma-informed practice is critical to Indigenous healing. *Rural and Remote Health*, *21*(3), 1–5.

Vysniauske, R., Verburgh, L., Oosterlaan, J., & Molendijk, M. L. (2020). The effects of physical exercise on functional outcomes in the treatment of ADHD: A meta-analysis. *Journal of Attention Disorders*, *24*(5), 644–654. https://doi.org/10.1177/1087054715627489

Warr, P. (1994). A conceptual framework for the study of work and mental health. *Work & Stress*, *8*(2), 84–97.

Wajszilber, D., Santiseban, J. A., & Gruber, R. (2018). Sleep disorders in patients with ADHD: Impact and management challenges. *Nature and Science of Sleep*, Volume 10, 453–480.

Weinberg, A., & Doyle, N. (2017). *Psychology at work: Improving wellbeing and productivity in the workplace*. The British Psychological Society.

Wissell, S., Karimi, L., Serry, T., Furlong, L., & Hudson, J. (2022). "You don't look dyslexic": Using the job demands—resource model of burnout to explore employment experiences of Australian adults with dyslexia. *International Journal of Environmental Research and Public Health*, *19*(17), 10719.

Whitmore, J. (2010). *Coaching for performance: The principles and practice of coaching and leadership*. Revised 25th Anniversary Edition. Hachette UK.

World Health Organization (n.d.). *Constitution*. www.who.int/about/governance/constitution

Zijlstra, F. R., Cropley, M., & Rydstedt, L. W. (2014). From recovery to regulation: An attempt to reconceptualize "recovery from work". *Stress and Health*, *30*(3), 244–252.

Chapter 11

Contracting

Nancy Doyle and Almuth McDowall

Introduction

We outline the essentials of good contracting as a baseline for professional neurodiversity coaching. While experienced coaching readers will recognise the importance of contracting, this chapter draws attention specifically to elements of neurodivergence such as disability status and how this might impact scope, consent, data protection, safeguarding and more. We emphasise that disability status, which is not a given for neurodivergent people but a possibility, puts all interactions and data into the category of legally 'protected condition' and 'medical grade' confidentiality. We suggest that this chapter is good revision and practice benchmarking for any coach, and essential reading for novice coaches.

Contracting is an essential part of the training for any coach because it sets the tone for the relationship, which is the most important driver of successful coaching (de Haan & Duckworth, 2012; Palmer & McDowall, 2010). "Time spent on good contracting is never wasted, although it can be time consuming" (Newton & Napper, 2010, p. 174). As is standard in all coaching contracting, you will need to establish the logistics and the relationship, and work through the expectations that both sides are bringing to the coaching. For neurodivergent coachees, you may need to be more precise than usual to clarify the logistics. For example, you may need to give more information about the exact location, time, and activities in each coaching. Many neurodivergent coachees have never had coaching before; therefore, they may not know what to expect.

DOI: 10.4324/9781003368274-14

Clarifying that the coaching will be like a conversation and that they might have to do preparation work or follow-up tasks in between might seem obvious to you, but it might not be obvious for a coaching novice. We recommend over- rather than under-explaining as you establish your ways of working with each other.

Regarding coaching that takes place remotely and online, some neurodivergent people find 'cameras on' overwhelming. It will help to build rapport if you make it clear that the camera can be turned off if they need a break and that they can ask you to do so (Doyle, 2023). Other neurodivergent coachees might like to move while they are talking. A walking coaching session could be ideal for this cohort – offer them the opportunity to talk to you on the phone while they are walking or on a treadmill/exercise bike, and offer to meet them for an outdoor coaching session if you are meeting in person. It is always important to make the coaching logistics congruent with how coachees work at their best, and in particular so for this group. Relevant offers can be made in email/phone calls when setting up the coaching, but also as you progress and learn more about how coachees think. Thinking back to Chapter 8 on the psychology of coaching, contracting is where you build your alliance and it starts way before the first session. This is what we call the psychological contract in organisational psychology, which is about a mutual set of expectations. Clarifying mutual expectations is always helpful, whereas not doing so leaves room for interpretation.

With regard to relational aspects, novice coachees may be bringing assumptions that building a conducive relationship is not going to work out. They may expect you to be their saviour (rescuer drama) or they may be thinking that this is just another thing that won't work for them. It can be time well spent to focus on making such expectations explicit and then mutually agree what can be addressed in coaching. Sometimes, how coachees approach negotiating their set-up is indicative of the way they approach many things at work. It can be insightful to reflect back to your coachee what is happening. "I notice that you are interested in having all the details and times of our sessions planned out in advance. Is this the same or different in your day-to-day work?"

In order to contract successfully with neurodivergent coachees, you need to have solid skills in everyday contracting and consent paired with some background knowledge on: (a) disability status and the implications for coaching at work; (b) informed consent when people are vulnerable; (c) data protection and confidentiality; (d) working with employers; and (e) safeguarding. This chapter aims to give you the essentials on these specific aspects.

Disability status

Disability status, establishing it and the extent to which your coaching is part of a reasonable adjustment or accommodation, is not within the remit of your coaching contract. However, we provide some detail on this because it is useful background and could help you unpick this issue with your coachees, where they might try and co-opt you in arguing this case with them/for them. This section is written so as to be in line with the United Nations Convention on the Rights of Persons with Disabilities (sic) ratified in 2007 (UNCRPD, 2006). Most major economies in the world have a national disability rights legislation that is compliant with the UNCRPD, so it is the most universally applicable.

The first question your coachee may need to address is whether or not, as a neurodivergent person, they can qualify for disability status. Most national statutes base this on establishing the impact of a condition on normal, day-to-day activities over a period of at least 12 months. In the UK, for example, normal day-to-day activities are stated to include memory, communication and learning, as well as movement and operating standard machinery (Equality Act, 2010). Memory can be affected by ADHD, the 'four Dys' (dyslexia, dyspraxia, dyscalculia, dysgraphia) and acquired neurodivergence, but is less likely to be affected by autism. Communication can be affected by all neurodivergent conditions when we consider verbal and written forms. Learning can be affected by all conditions. Movement and operating machinery can be affected by dyspraxia, specifically, but movement also includes commuting and travelling, which can be affected by all, due to difficulties in reading timetables, planning connections, finding the experience overwhelms the senses and more. There is plenty of scope for defining neurodivergence as disabling and there is sufficient case law history to affirm this position, but also cases where disability status was not reached by a plaintiff. Do be aware that it is not a given, some coachees may need to manage their expectations. In many US states, for example, neurodivergence is not considered disabling in education unless at least one score in a cognitive ability profile is in the bottom 25% of scores (IDEA, 2006), so a spiky profile that is all average or above may not be considered disabling, even when there are comparative struggles in memory, learning or communication.

Secondly, an employer is obliged to make reasonable adjustments/accommodations for disabled workers. Accommodations for neurominorities are numerous, and typically include the following categories (Doyle, 2019; Khalifa et al., 2020; McDowall et al., 2023):

- Flexibility in location, hours and schedule to accommodate sensory overwhelm and distraction caused by commuting and busy environments.
- Provision of assistive technology to reduce demands of literacy and concentration when writing/reading.
- Provision of a specialist coach (yes that could be you!) to help the individual work out strategies and techniques for playing to their strengths and managing their challenges.

Note that the legislation, worldwide, is clear that accommodations are something that an organisation does to support a person, not a way the person must change to suit the job. We would not expect a wheelchair user to 'work harder' at physiotherapy in order to do a job, neither should we expect a neurodivergent person to just 'try harder' to spell, concentrate or ignore distractions. That said, the business is only obliged to make 'reasonable' adjustments or accommodations. That doesn't mean that they should compromise safety or deliverables; for example, giving extra time might be appropriate for preparation of specific tasks, like a presentation, but it doesn't mean that a neurodivergent person can deliver less work for the same money as their peers on an ongoing basis.

Navigating what is reasonable is highly skilled work, it ultimately comes down to a legal decision. It needs to consider the industry, size and resources of the business as well as the individual need. It is not the job of the coach to advise on what is or is not reasonable, as you do not have exposure to the rest of the team and their needs, the customer experience, the finances of the business etc. We have said this before, and we are going to say it again. It is NOT your job to advise your coachee on what is reasonable or not. We say this repeatedly because in our practice we see coaches getting into this muddle over and over again. You will be invited to discuss what is reasonable with some of your coachees. They will want to talk about it and ask your advice. A few coachees will try hard to get you on side in their argument of what is fair, unfair and what their employer should have done differently. Take a stern warning that this is not a conversation in which to become embroiled. If there is a legal dispute in the future, you need to make sure you have not led your coachee in any direction, or are even suspected of doing so. A court of law is likely to ask you to defend your expertise in making adjustment recommendations. If you do not have formal training in workplace performance and/or disability law, you might find yourself liable. Instead, refer back to the source of your introduction – this might be an HR department or Occupational Health, some sort of trained workplace-needs assessor – more on this below. You can refer on to a mediator or for legal advice, but up front in your contracting and expectations you should make it quite clear that agreeing what is/is not reasonable is out of your remit.

Contracting scope

Disability legislation also affects the scope of the coaching in a workplace context. The following areas are within your remit. You should make sure that you and your coachee have reviewed and agreed this at the very start of the coaching:

- Cognitive skills and strengths, compensation strategies for the following areas:
  - Memory
  - Concentration
  - Time keeping
  - Organisation
  - Planning and prioritising

- Finding directions and orientation
- Learning style and approach
- Creativity
- Visual thinking and planning
- Literacy
- Numeracy

- Emotional resilience and management

  - Handling strong emotions at work, your own and others
  - Boundaries and remits
  - Working with conflict and confusion
  - Relationships and social expectations at work in general

- Behaviours in the workplace

  - Understanding one's own rhythm of work and circadian rhythm
  - Frequency and styles of communication
  - Supporting wellbeing.

Coaches need to be clear about what is not in scope. We have outlined this in previous chapters but return to it now for absolute clarity:

- Advice on health, nutrition or exercise (unless you are also trained in this and have been contracted accordingly with coachee and bill payer).
- Recommendations for therapies or services not provided by the employer or standard health provision.
- Therapeutic work regarding past trauma or distress.
- Advice on how to do the job role itself (unless you are also a specialist in their field and have been contracted accordingly).
- Advice on reasonable adjustments and accommodations (as above).
- Advice on legal matters such as constructive dismissal or discrimination at work – you can signpost to other people, but do not give details as to what to do as you do not have everyone's side of the story.
- Advice on matters outside the workplace such as family, friends, or community.

Contracting should set out the objectives for the coaching. This may take the full first session, as they work with you to define their goals. They may change and evolve, but a clear direction from the start is advisable. Remember that for this coachee group, who think differently and don't always pick up standard social conventions, you may need to be more explicit than with other coachees. You may, for example, need to consider informing them how to contact you between sessions, what to expect from response times and for what types of enquiry. You might need to explain specific cancellation policies in more detail than with previous coachees, such as when they or you cancel, the timescales involved in sacrificing the cost of the session or any costs in rebooking for a later date. Be exact and stick to these rules.

Nancy once had a coachee who would call her three or four times a day to ask advice on their daily work routine. During coaching discussions, it transpired that this was normal behaviour for the coachee and, in fact, she called her manager at work between 8 and 15 times a day. This behaviour caused conflict between them, but the manager had not known quite how to describe it and had just said she was 'needy'. A practical conversation about how many times it is appropriate to call someone, followed by a check-list reminder, worked wonders. The coachee had simply misunderstood a social convention at work, and when invited to reflect adapted with ease. This example illustrates that in neurodiversity coaching, more so than in other contexts, it can be necessary to spell out social conventions as an explicit reference point for conversation and activities. There will be times when such clarity and directness is needed.

Expectations about coaching effectiveness, and what the envisaged purposes and aims are, should also be spelled out explicitly. Many neurodivergent coachees are coming to coaching for the first time and don't really understand the rules of coaching, or what to expect from the process. Nancy once had a coachee express that she wanted the coaching to be like a "magic wand that fixed all her problems". This is clearly an unrealistic expectation. It's important to state what is likely to happen during the coaching process and what results are dependent on – i.e. coachees' own hard work. Coachees need to hear right at the start that, like any change process, their own action, motivation and time will make a huge difference in success. They will need to practise new strategies, perhaps make notes to help them remember key experiences, try new things, even though they may be a little anxious. Try to anchor expectations in concrete, observable behaviours. You can take the magical wand statement and rework it as a 'miracle question' as outlined in Chapter 7 – what would you see or hear if a wand had been waved? What would you be able to do now that you can't currently do? And then make sure these outcomes are well formed. For example, if coachees say they want to "feel less distracted at work and able to finish things", ask them, "what kind of things do you want to feel able to finish? What are some examples? When you are less distracted, what will you be able to do more of?" Use real life activities, tasks and events as anchors so that it is clear for both parties where the coaching needs to focus.

We also recommend asking the coachees scaling questions to score how they are doing now on each of the topics or goals for the coaching. You can check back in on these at the end of every session as a measure of progressive goal attainment, to help navigate progress and make sure that coaching stays on track.

Informed consent

Informed consent can be complex for neurodiverse coachees. Generally, we expect all adults to enter coaching willingly, of their own free will and to be able to make this decision without undue influence. However, some neurodivergent coachees may feel that engaging in coaching is the only way to hold onto their jobs. They might feel coerced by a boss who is not listening, and/or the process might feel intrusive. They may be suspicious of your motives or whether you are reporting back to their employer any details that could be used to exit them from their job role. Therefore, you need to handle consent for coaching in more detail than would be necessary for workplace coaching in general.

It is advisable to discuss, in advance or at the first contracting session, their right to withdraw, their right to see any notes or data that you are holding concerning them and to make it very clear that you are a coach for them, whoever is paying your bill. The service user takes precedence over the bill payer in this instance. We recommend stating these arrangements in writing and to get a signature, or email acceptance, as a record in case you need to rely on this later. Reassurance that you are protecting their rights is a good counterbalance for the exceptional circumstance of having to submit to coaching in order to prevent job loss due to disability.

Once practicalities have been addressed, focus on building and sustaining rapport. As explained in Chapter 8, there is a wealth of evidence in coaching and therapy to suggest that the most important ingredient in a good coaching programme is the strength of relationship between coach and coachee (Gessnitzer & Kauffeld, 2015; O'Broin & Palmer, 2007). This relationship starts with mutual trust and shared understanding of what is being consented to; how to withdraw and what action to take if there is a change or misunderstanding is essential. Many neurodivergent people have experienced professionals as rude or dismissive. Many have been misdiagnosed, underdiagnosed, assumed to be wilfully deviant, rude and lazy. They may have had teachers, doctors or previous employers who shared information about them without their permission. They may have seen reports that describe them in pejorative terms. You need to reassure through high levels of professionalism, for example in obtaining consent and managing this throughout the coaching process. Getting such logistics right can be a healing experience for your coachee and go a long way to restoring trust in helping relationships.

Data protection and confidentiality

Information about a person's neurominority diagnosis is usually considered medical grade data, meaning that you need to understand the laws of the land where you practice and maintain safe data storage systems. Such data will include your coachee's name, contact details, any information about their condition and your coaching notes. If you have hard copy records, it is good practice to store these in a locked, fireproof container. If you have electronic records, you will need password protection and ideally multi-factor authentication. You will need to restrict who has access to your files. You may need to register with an official body as a 'data controller' – this is the case in the EU and UK, for example.

You will need a clear data protection policy to set out: (a) what level of security you take; (b) clear contact details for people wishing to remove or check their data and; (c) a process for handling data breaches. Data breaches must be documented and communicated to those involved with an apology. For example, you might send a coachee another coachee's notes by accident. You might send an email to a group of coachees, perhaps to inform them you are ill or going away, but if you put all their names in the 'To' box rather than the 'BCC' box then they will know that they are all your coachee, and by implication that they might have a neurodivergent diagnosis.

Confidentiality always operates on a need-to-know basis. Confidentiality is also necessary regarding workplace on site visits. Any receptionist does not need to know which company you work for or the exact purpose of your appointment, so be careful what information you share. You do not need to know detailed background information, so don't store it. You don't need to know the names of colleagues with whom the coachee may be interacting with at work, so don't store them. The employer doesn't need to know the details of the conversations had in coaching, so don't share them. Be very transparent about what you are storing and not storing, so that you can avoid risk to the coachee and yourself. Stick to your rules and confess quickly if there is a human error. The occasional mistake is understandable and forgivable, but being caught out pretending is unprofessional.

A coachee or employer can ask for compensation if you have broken confidentiality or committed a data breach, depending on the impact on them personally. It is best to have professional indemnity insurance for this eventuality, which will provide a legal team to handle the fall out of errors. The best response to an error is to apologise transparently and explain what steps you have taken to make sure it doesn't happen again. If you live somewhere where you have to report a data breach, it is important to do this swiftly and with details of corrective and preventative actions. You can be fined in some countries by the regulator, so having insurance is a great safety step.

A word about coaching notes

We have outlined above that some notes are helpful in coaching – you will want to record rudimentary personal information as an aide-memoire and reference point. You are also likely to want to track progress, such as recording stated goals and benchmarking progress with scaling questions. You might also have written exercises or other activities, whether pen and paper or electronic. In addition, you might want to prompt a coachee about activities in between sessions. Whether or not you record additional coaching notes is up to you. Some coaches feel strongly that taking notes during the coaching process hampers active listening and embodied presence. Other coaches find this helps them concentrate. Likewise, some coachees like it when coaches take notes, and others find it a distraction. Taking extensive notes will also mean that you have some tidying up and refining to do once the coaching session has ended; this adds to workload but can provide useful reference points in supervision. How you contract this is a matter of personal preference and individual circumstance and need. You will also need to consider how long to keep notes for. If you are employed as a coach by a third party, there should be a clear policy. If you are working on your own, you need to make length of storage explicit as part of your data storage and protection policy. As a rule of thumb, we would advise no more than one calendar year, but it depends if you have coachees who are likely to come back in a few years or need to call on your notes in future mediation with their employer.

Working with employers

Employers are critical to the success of workplace coaching in general – this is known as the 'Coaching Triad' in coaching psychology literature (O'Broin & Palmer, 2007). The coaching triad represents the role the employer plays as a key stakeholder for a successful outcome, particularly in contexts where they have commissioned the coaching. They frequently have good insight into the performance of your coachee as well as company resources that can be shared. For neurodivergent people there is the additional element of reasonable adjustments – employers need to officially support strategies and personal accommodations. It is good practice to build a relationship with managers and/or Human Resources where coaching has been contracted through an organisation. We advise inviting them to the first session and getting their input on coaching goals and objectives. You could also ask them to rate the coachee's performance on their target areas before the coaching starts, and after – confidentially if their prefer. We conducted some research on this in 2015 and found that coachees consistently rated their performance as lower at the start compared to their managers (Doyle & McDowall, 2015). This could be because coachees are down on themselves, or it could be because managers do not see how hard someone is working to stay ahead. However, at the end of the coaching, managers and coachees tend to rate their performance at about equal, with a good gain from both parties. This is a great way to evaluate your coaching practice. It can give you helpful statistics to share with nervous coachees and help you win more work.

Even when they pay the bill, employers do not need to know what happened in the coaching – conversations are confidential. The British Psychology Society, which guides Nancy and Almuth's practice, determine that the end user, the coachee, is the person whose rights must take precedent, not the fee-paying client. However, employers may need to know which strategies come out of the coaching. Those strategies might be construed as disability adjustments or accommodations themselves. For example, if a coachee with difficulty concentrating in meetings comes up with a mind-mapping strategy that involves using a large drawing pad to capture notes during meetings, it would be useful for the employer to know about that, so that they can support it as an activity. This is where you can use brief coaching notes, or short emails to joint parties to summarise activities that a coachee will be developing as a strategy. Or perhaps, you can do a report for the employer at the end, summarising all the strategies that you and your coachee have devised to help them at work. This, of course, needs permission from your coachee before sharing and depends on what you have been contracted to do, and are getting remunerated for. Transparency and clarity for all involved is key from the outset.

Reaching out to managers can be critical in getting the right goals for the coaching, if issues of contracting, consent and sharing of information have all been agreed transparently. In Chapter 6 on transactional analysis, we described a mismatch in performance ratings between Audrey and Estelle. This had come to light at the contracting stage, when Audrey had given permission for Estelle, as her manager, to come into the coaching and discuss goals. Estelle took Nancy to one side afterwards. She said, "I'm sure you're very lovely, but I really don't see how this is going to help?" After some explorative questions, it transpired that the goals for the coaching were not addressing the core issue. Audrey perceived herself to be very good at her job but in need of help with planning and prioritising. However, Estelle informed Nancy that the problem was that her literacy was exceptionally poor and, as an administrator for senior professionals in health care, not up to the job. The coachee needed assistive technology and training in how to use it; three coaching sessions were not going to be adequate for resolving a lifetime of dyslexic spelling and grammar issues. There appeared to be unresolved contextual issues that needed addressing. So Nancy went back to the workplace needs assessor who had recommended the coaching. It transpired that they had conducted the workplace needs assessment on a day when Estelle was absent and the HR representative deputising had no idea how much Estelle had been rescuing Audrey. Nancy fed this new information back to the workplace needs assessor, from an external company, who contacted Estelle directly, made a further recommendation of Assistive Technology and amended their original report. Audrey still had coaching, but she now also had Assistive Technology and several training sessions to help her learn how to embed this in her daily tasks. This **is** within remit and is a great way to handle mismatches in adjustment need and provision.

The example of Audrey and Estelle illustrates that it is possible to influence any adjustments/accommodations that your coachees have been offered without making them directly yourself. However, this involves going back a step in the contracting process and being clear on how and when others need to be involved. You need to be transparent about any change in contracting and gain consent from all parties to ensure that you don't find yourself in legal jeopardy, making recommendations that you are not qualified/contracted to make or passing data/confidential details that you do not have permission to share.

Safeguarding

For complex reasons, which to explain fully is outside the scope of this book, neurodivergent coachees are more vulnerable to experience of mental distress, traumatic pasts and exploitation from abusive relationships. You need a protocol for handling disclosures that fall outside of the remit of the coaching but that need action. Issues could include suicidal ideation, abuse, self-harm or more. We advise taking contact details of a next of kin during contracting so that you have an agreed point of contact if you are worried about a coachee's immediate health or welfare. You need to mention calmly but firmly that this is part of your contracting procedure for all coachees in the case of eventuality. For example, if a coachee had been reporting experiences of a mental health issue and you referred them for medical treatment, but they then failed to show at their next appointment, you might want to check with their next of kin that they were okay.

We will talk more about supervision in the final chapter but signpost here that having a structure and process for considering any safeguarding is very helpful. You need a colleague, or a circle of colleagues, with whom you could anonymously debate whether a disclosure needs to be revisited, signposted elsewhere or reported. Often these are not straightforward decisions. Having other professionals to support you is essential for safe practice and your own wellbeing. Of course, you need to be up front about all of this, letting the coachee know in advance what your process is and when you might activate it. This is best practice. It is wise to take a safeguarding course separately to your coach training for working with this coachee group.

Protecting yourself

You also have to safeguard yourself. At its most extreme, this includes your life. In the UK, there was a famous case of an estate agent, called Suzy Lamplugh, who went missing and was never found after attending a meeting with a client to view a property. One of the learnings from this sad case was that people working alone should always have someone know where they are, and with whom they are meeting. If you are a sole practitioner, perhaps join up with other practitioners to form a circle of support for in-person meetings on private property. While most neurodiversity coaching takes place online or in workplaces, occasionally people who work from home request their coaching there. You need to make an informed choice whether to agree or not. If you decide to visit a coachee at their home office, tell someone where you are going and have them call you in the first 15 minutes with a code question to which you give a code answer, for example, "where are the car keys", followed by "the kitchen table" or "the hallway", one of those answers indicating all is well and the other indicating that you do not feel safe. The unsafe code, or a failure to answer the call should result in a call to the police. Police are aware that lone workers conduct these sorts of protocols, approve of them and will provide immediate support – you shouldn't feel embarrassed about it.

Regarding how you treat and respect each other, you do not need to accept rude, illegal or unsafe communication from your coachees. Coachees may not understand that their behaviour is inappropriate and you need to use your professional judgement whether a simple instruction to desist is okay before proceeding, or whether to end the coaching relationship and explain why. It is okay to stop if someone is making you feel unsafe. You can refer them on even if you feel it is a 'you thing' and not a 'them thing'.

You will also need to protect your boundaries and energy from excessive demands. A small proportion of neurodivergent coachees may become dependent on your support and encourage you to act outside your remit. Good, upfront contracting is the best pre-emptive measure and having the skills to enforce it. This can be difficult to navigate and necessitates firm, but gentle conversations. You need to ensure that your coachee is working towards independence, not transferring their dependence to you. Such activities are not healthy for the coachee or for you. A good colleague of ours, Whitney Iles, who works with complex trauma, has a lovely phrase, "I hold the space for my clients to hear their difficulties, I don't hold their difficulties for them". She also (wise woman) says that, for those who work in social justice and equality, it is vital to "protect your peace". As tempting as it may be to just do something extra for a coachee or have a call on the weekend to help them, these one-offs can quickly become expectations and you have to choose where you will hold the line. It can be harder to walk a line back than to never let it be crossed in the first place.

We are aware that many neurodiversity coaches are neurodivergent themselves, and may have their own difficulties in interpreting social communication or coming to terms with personal experiences of exploitation, discrimination or abuse. It is not your job, as a coach, to heal trauma or help someone who doesn't behave safely learn how to behave safely. The moment they select you as the object of an obsession or hyperfocus, you are no longer able to provide coaching. It is not safe for them or you.

Conclusion

The genuine purpose of this chapter was to give you pause for thought. Coaching practice based solely on lived experience without thought to professional confidentiality, boundaries and safeguarding is potentially risky. The main aim of this chapter, for us, was to clearly explain the guardrails needed for professional practice in this field. They are more stringent than standard workplace coaching because of the additional needs of the coachee group. If you are already a practising workplace coach, or related professional, it shouldn't be too hard to make these additions. Consider this chapter a good practice audit. However, if you are approaching neurodiversity coaching without prior professional training, we hope this chapter encourages you to take that step. There are plenty of organisations who provide relatively cheap and accessible coach training, where you can learn more about the basics of contracting, consenting, confidentiality and safeguarding.

Reflective questions

Ask yourself the following questions to benchmark your contracting arrangements and take some time to jot down the answers. These are useful questions to return to in order to continually audit your practice:

- Have you prepared: (a) a confidentiality policy; (b) a data protection plan and; (c) a safeguarding policy that you can share with coachees?
- Do you have a coaching contract that is written down to which your coachees can sign up? Can employers be added if they become involved in co-coaching?
- Do you have a method of obtaining informed consent?
- Do you have a process for when people want to withdraw consent? Where is it stored? Do coachees get a copy?

- Do you have some good starting questions to prepare the coachee for coaching and can you use them to capture some self-rating scores, against which you can track progress?
- Do you have a system for keeping records of coaching outcomes, for example strategies that are working?
- Do you have anyone to escalate a concern to, or with whom to anonymously discuss an issue?
- Do you have lived experience of being manipulated or exploited? Have you done personal work on these issues in a professional forum? Can you bring these issues to supervision if they are triggered by your coaching practice?
- Under what circumstances would you exit a coachee from your services? Do you have a confidential space in which to discuss this? Are unsafe behaviours clearly described in your coaching contract?

References

de Haan, E., & Duckworth, A. (2012). Coaching outcome research. *International Coaching Psychology Review, 8*(1), 6–19.

Doyle, N. (2019). Reasonable adjustments for dyslexia. *Occupational Health at Work, 16*(2), 28–31.

Doyle, N. (2023). Digital coaching with neurodivergent people. In *The digital coaches handbook*. Routledge.

Doyle, N., & McDowall, A. (2015). Is coaching an effective adjustment for dyslexic adults? *Coaching: An International Journal of Theory and Practice Coaching, 8*(2), 154–168. https://doi.org/10.1080/17521882.2015.1065894

Equality Act, (2010). United Kingdom Parliament, London. www.legislation.gov.uk/ukpga/2010/15/introduction

Gessnitzer, S., & Kauffeld, S. (2015). The working alliance in coaching. *Journal of Applied Behavioral Science, 51*(2), 177–197. https://doi.org/10.1177/0021886315576407

IDEA. (2006). Individuals with Disabilities Education Act. U.S. Department of Education's Office of Special Education and Rehabilitative Services (OSERS). https://sites.ed.gov/idea/statuteregulations/

Khalifa, G., Sharif, Z., Sultan, M., & De Rezze, B. (2020). Workplace accommodations for adults with autism spectrum disorder: A scoping review. *Disability and Rehabilitation, 42*(9), 1315–1331. https://doi.org/10.1080/09638288.2018.1527952

McDowall, A., Doyle, N., & Kisleva, M. (2023). *Neurodiversity at work 2023: Demand, supply and gap analysis.* Neurodiversity in Business. 1–60.

Newton, T., & Napper, R. (2010). Transactional analysis and coaching. In E. Cox, D. Clutterbuck & T. Bachkirova (Eds.), *The complete handbook of coaching* (1st ed., pp. 172–186). Sage.

O'Broin, A., & Palmer, S. (2007). Re-appraising the coach-client relationship: The unassuming change agent in coaching. In S. Palmer & A. Whybrow (Eds.), *Handbook of coaching psychology* (pp. 295–324). Routledge.

Palmer, S., & McDowall, A. (2010). The coaching relationship: putting people first. An introduction. In S. Palmer & A. McDowall (Eds.), *The coaching relationship* (pp. 1–8). Routledge.

United Nations Convention on the Rights of Persons with Disabilities (UNCRPD) (2006). United Nations, Geneva. https://social.desa.un.org/issues/disability/crpd/convention-on-the-rights-of-persons-with-disabilities-crpd

Chapter 12

Reflective practice

Almuth McDowall and Nancy Doyle

Introduction

Bringing it all together, this last chapter outlines the professional context for neurodiversity coaching, centred around the idea of reflective practice. Broadly, this means that you reflect on your own skill as a coach, then you challenge yourself to walk the talk and seek feedback and supervision to learn more. We stress the need for an overarching framework in which we can hold ourselves to account. We introduce our INVESTS model, which outlines a set of principles as a reference point for professional coaching practice in this field. It stresses the need to validate intersectional neurodivergent experience while recognising, and where necessary addressing, any coach biases. This leads us to consider timings and endings before turning to the need for informed professional supervision and calibration practice. Neurodiversity coaching is incredibly rewarding, yet potentially demanding on the coach's energy and resources. Our self-care is crucial. We emphasise the need for continuous professional development as an essential part of reflective practice. We close by offering a vision for the future of neurodiversity coaching.

The INVESTS model for neurodiversity coaching

There are many cross-cutting themes in this book that inform our professional practice and approach to coaching. These themes coalesce as the INVESTS model of neurodiversity coaching.

I stands for **intersectionality** – it is likely that neurodiverse coachees present with additional marginalising identities. Even

DOI: 10.4324/9781003368274-15

where coaching does not explicitly focus on strengthening personal or professional identity, coaches working in this context nevertheless need to have heightened awareness.

N stands for **neurodiversity** – embracing human functioning in all its differences.

V stands for **validation** – we corroborate the core of our coachees' experience together, leaving aside our own preconceptions. We acknowledge that prior experience may well have involved a degree of trauma. Coaching provides a space for moving on.

E stands for **exploration** – through clean questioning we explore, share and reframe real life stories. We might put more resources in a caravan. We might facilitate coachees to step over a dam for the first time. We remain curious, the goal being to develop and elicit more knowledge and metacognition of patterns in order to gain understanding and control.

S stands for **strategies** – cognitive and other strategies are a 'baseline' for many neurodiverse coachees – helping coachees to help better self-organise, memorise, navigate emotions and relationships is a necessary baseline to success.

T stands for **time bound** – time is an important aspect of other coaching models and goal-setting frameworks. Time is also a limited resource and is precious in neurodiversity coaching – often coachees have been referred for a select few sessions. It is up to coach, coachee and client to harness these opportunities.

S stands for (specialist) **supervision** – no coaching should be done without supervision and coaches need to turn to people with the right domain knowledge to support and reflectively question their practice.

We summarise our model, and exemplar guiding questions for reflective practice in Table 12.1. In time, we expect you would want to collate your own questions. Some coaches may prefer to work with particular coachee groups and specialise, and/or work with distinct

Table 12.1 The INVESTS model of neurodiversity coaching

Principle	Working definition	Exemplar reflective questions to guide practice
Intersectionality	Active acknowledgement that coachees may have more than one marginalising identity	When and how do I acknowledge and inquire about marginalising identities in coaching? How do I rate my knowledge on intersectionality research and evidence?
Neurodiversity	Variations in cognitive profiles, so how we think, feel and act, are natural and to be expected	How do I relate to concepts such as neurodiversity, neurodivergence, neurotypicality? How have I considered issues about language and framing? What is my approach to keeping up to date with relevant research to inform my coaching?
Validation	We validate our coachees' experience and leave aside our own preconceptions and interpretations	How do I validate coachees' experience over time? To what extent have I noticed the influence of previous trauma? How do I navigate any boundaries between coaching and therapy? What biases and preconceptions have I noticed in myself, and how do I bring these to supervision?
Exploration	Through clean questioning we explore, tell, and reframe real life stories	Which stories have I noticed in coaching? What kinds of techniques and prompts help coachees reframe?
Strategies	Development of skilful strategies to harness strengths in cognitive functioning and deal with potential weaknesses in areas such as memory and concentration as a 'baseline' for neurodiverse coachees	How do I facilitate coachees to expand and utilise their strategy toolkit? What is my knowledge about such strategies, and what can I do to upskill my knowledge?
Time-bound	Time is a valuable resource in coaching – and needs to be used wisely in neurodiversity coaching, which is often tightly time-framed	How do I plan and execute tightly timebound coaching series? How do I signpost and negotiate endings? How do I refocus coaching when time is of the essence (e.g. coachees detour, stop making progress, lose interest)?
Specialist Supervision	Engaging in regular and specific supervision	What are my hopes, expectations, and fears about specialist supervision? What other means of support and review are available to me – for example peer reference groups?

coaching foci such as career coaching, or executive coaching. Some reflective questions might apply regardless of context, whereas others need to be more specific.

Four of these principles we have discussed extensively as the history of neurodiversity, intersectionality, exploration and strategies have extensive sections in Chapters 2 through to 7. We now elaborate on validation, time-bound coaching with focus on endings, and supervision in turn, to complete the INVESTS model knowledge base. The supervision section is vital reading to help manage our boundaries, using exemplars to outline some of the conundrums you may face that require careful self-reflection and supervision.

Validation and our own preconceptions

Our chapters on the challenges, opportunities and Clean Language in neurodiversity coaching outlined how important it is to stay close to the coachee's lived experience. Many coachees have experienced prior trauma and a history of feeling like a failure, of not being good enough, being singled out or even laughed at and ridiculed. Clean Language-based interviewing and active listening are key to enquiring, understanding and validating individual experience. There are issues that require skilful navigation. Chapter 2 alluded to the fact that our evidence base is far stronger for some conditions than others – but not necessarily correlated with condition prevalence rates. For example, right now research and public awareness is focused on autism (see Doyle & McDowall, 2021). Hence there are autism at work programmes, for example, in various geographical locations. Two decades ago, attention was focused on dyslexia, yet right now the 'four Dys' are under-researched (see Chapters 3 and 4). Chapter 10 on wellbeing outlined that stigma and prejudice prevail around mental health and where that intersects with neurodivergence (PDA).

We emphasise that any lack of public awareness or insufficient research does not mean that individual experience is not legitimate – quite the contrary. To validate others without judgement, we need to be aware of our own preconceptions. Almuth remembers that some years ago she intermittently undertook work–life balance development, training and coaching. This was her main research and practice area at the time. During one particular coaching session Almuth recognised how she was judging the coachee – they only had one child, they were a stay-at-home mother, whereas Almuth had three children and a full-time job. Surely, their experience could not have been that bad – did it even merit coaching? Almuth recognised straight away how her own way of thinking and living was influencing her views. She reflected that there was a good deal of post hoc rationalisation – Almuth had chosen her busy life as a full-time working mother and therefore it became her frame. But in this example, the rationalisation led to judgement about her coachee. Almuth asked herself circular questions, about her own experience and what the coachee might be thinking and brought these to supervision. She reflected that the coachee had come to her from a position of trust, wanting to explore how to better manage work–life balance when returning to a part-time role. Behind this overt goal Almuth sensed a yearning for deeper meaning and validation in life – the coachee had talked about being at home as a limiting factor. Once Almuth had noticed the vulnerability of the coachee's position, she was able to validate the coachee's experience for what it was and leave aside her prior judgement.

Neurodiversity coaching will require careful negotiation of the balance between validation and advocacy. As Chapter 2 showed us, the advocacy movement is a powerful change agent in the neurodiversity landscape. It is likely that coaches will need to negotiate boundaries at some points. It all depends on what they have been contracted to do, and what our skill sets are. In Chapter 9 about good work and Chapter 11 about contracting, we made the point that it is usually NOT your role to advocate work design or environment changes directly with the organisation where the coachee works. However, if the client has contracted coaching and you have a tri-lateral agreement to share broad outcomes from a series of coaching sessions, while keeping the process confidential, it may be warranted to have a three-way meeting with the coachee's line manager. This conversation could centre around what has worked well in coaching and how relevant strategies and ways of working could be implemented in their current work environment.

Timings and endings

Neurodiversity coaching is often tightly time framed – the UK Access to Work[1] scheme to support workers with a disability or health condition will only fund a handful of sessions for example. A tight time frame is both a challenge and an opportunity. A challenge, because a fast pace may not suit some neurodivergent coachees who need time to build trust and think. If that's the case, it can be fruitful to concentrate on a few key priorities rather than endeavour to cover too much ground. A tight time frame is also an opportunity as it necessitates a focus on solutions rather than going over what hasn't worked. Miracle questions, as explored in Chapter 7 (De Shazer et al., 1986) signpost clearly that there is a definitive end to coaching and contract this right from the start. Using this technique, coachees are asked to imagine that a miracle has occurred and a problem has gone away. The coachee is then facilitated to describe in detail what has changed, what the solution looks, feels and sounds like, and how they know that they are doing things differently and that change has occurred. In neurodiversity coaching, coaches might need to frame the question tighter to focus on how the coachee will have implemented new strategies for working differently with others – rather than expecting change in others as a catalyst for change.

Dr Elaine Cox (2010) outlines some principles in her chapter on ending well, making the point that good endings are pre-planned from the contracting stage and transparently executed to allow closure for the coachee and coach. When coaching does not end, or not end well, this can be due to a number of reasons (ibid.). It could be that the coachee has become overly dependent on the coach or presents with issues that are more suited to counselling, therapy or other helping relationships. It could be that the coach is reluctant to end the engagement because they feel that they have not done enough for the coachee or want to make things better for the coachee. The third issue is dealing with resistance and push back. Coaching is hard graft and can unearth strong and sudden reactions. Some coaches might perceive resistance as a prompt to end a coaching relationship or refer on. All three issues are well addressed in supervision. Coaching fizzling out without a clear end is not likely to be a conducive process. Ending this way is not psychologically safe, as there has been no mutually agreed space to review, learn and consolidate. Sudden endings can be brutal and traumatic, particularly where the coachee has begun to make changes that at first feel uncomfortable and is then left feeling unsupported. Over-dependency is also not healthy or conducive.

Supervision

Supervision is essential for all coaching work. We like the words "reflective container", which Hawkins and Schwenk (2010, p. 210) used to describe supervision – it's a "safe thinking space" to develop and hone our graft as coaches. Supervision has three functions (Hawkins and Schwenk, 2010, in Hawkins & Schwenk, 2010):

1. **Qualitative**: supporting coaches to deliver the best professional service to clients and coachees.
2. **Developmental**: supporting professional and personal development through action learning and reflection.
3. **Resourcing**: supporting coaches to resource and support themselves.

A well-known model of supervision is the seven-eyed model, which has been used across different professions (Hawkins & Schwenk, 2010). We would call the seven different modes lenses (rather than modes) for supervision and practice reviews as they offer different perspectives:

Lens one: the coachee's system. Focus is on what happened in actual sessions – how coachees presented, react, beginnings and endings of sessions. The idea is to get to what actually happened rather than what the coach thought happened.

Lens two: the coach's interventions. Supervision through this lens focuses on processes in the session and what activities or interventions the coach suggested and initiated, including exploration of possible alternatives.

Lens three: the coaching relationship. The focal lens here is the relationship that has been created together, and how this might reflect (or not) other relationships the coach has formed.

Lens four: the coach. Supervision through this lens focuses on what the coaching experience stimulates; for example, which feelings, or which memories it invokes.

Lens five: the supervisory relationship. This perspective focuses on overt and covert dynamics in the coach–supervisor relationship, and to what extent these might reflect other interpersonal experiences.

Lens six: the supervisor self-reflection. This lens focuses on how the supervisor has attended to dynamics and also their own reactions, sharing them with the coach to stimulate reflection.

Lens seven: the wider context. This is the broadest lens, which is about the overall work, societal, cultural, contractual and ethical context.

Skilful supervision will move through the lenses fluidly, and encourage noticing of shifts and real time practice. While not every supervision session will address all seven lenses in one session, we observe that it is often useful in neurodiversity coaching to adopt lens seven to commence supervision. This is because neurodiversity is context-bound, and intersectional experience matters so much, as depicted in the INVESTS model. Supervision can harness lens seven as a meta-lens to consider lens one to bring the coachee into focus. Lens four focuses on the coach, including their feelings and any blocks; we highlight there are instances when neurodiversity coaching is likely to be emotionally demanding, and how important re-spooning is for the coach. We turn to the value of group restorative supervision in the next section.

Restorative supervision

Derived from clinical practice, restorative supervision practice is designed to support professionals who experience significant emotional demand (Wallbank, 2007; 2013). Restorative supervision uses groups to focus on working through professional experiences that have been emotionally challenging. The focus is on personal interactions, reflecting on the impact, for example, of how individuals deal with conflict, exploring alternative courses of action and the impact these may have. This model of supervision deliberately draws on the joint social and intellectual capital in the group in an environment of psychological safety where professionals can try out and practice solutions without fear of judgement or getting it wrong. While the seven-eyed model focuses on illuminating and reflecting on past experience, restorative supervision has an experiential (group) element as well as a reflective (individual supervision) element to practice alternative strategies and encourage and support critical thinking. Restorative supervision was developed because clinical supervision was historically focused on safety and fitness to practise through a checking, challenge and audit process. These aspects can then 'crowd out' the reflective, restorative and learning aspects of supervision. Neurodiversity coaching is not health care or clinical practice but remember that you will be working with coachees who might come with complex health and medical histories and a prior history of trauma. Restorative supervision was developed for individuals who deliver complex care and puts the health and wellbeing of the individuals delivering the care centre stage. This is because strong emotions impair our capacity to work well and think clearly. We summarise the key insights from the restorative supervision model adapted from Wallbank and Wonnacott (2015), which complement the seven-eye model as a framework:

- Creating a supportive yet challenging supervision environment.
- Focus on the capacity of the professional to be resilient and recognise personal challenges.
- Enhance social capital by building relationships with other professionals.
- Focus on issues that the professional can control and change and refer on or escalate where this is not the case.

Evidence for restorative supervision is convincing as engaging in supervision prevents burnout and helps to maintain compassion satisfaction. The opposite of satisfaction, compassion fatigue, has deserved much attention in health-care professions such as nursing (e.g. Sabo, 2006; Sinclair et al., 2017). Recent evidence tells us that compassion fatigue is ill defined, therefore hard to measure and an umbrella term for a whole range of stress responses experienced by people in caring professions. But regardless of whether this concept exists or not, it is clear that working closely with others, particularly when emotionally demanding interactions are involved, is tough. Remember the analogy about putting on your oxygen mask first? Self-care is crucial in neurodiversity coaching, and restorative supervision is one way of taking positive steps towards this. Obviously, this requires a supervisor trained in such methods.

You might find supervision a useful mechanism for expanding your understanding of different lived experiences. For example, in the coaching supervision book, *Voices from the Americas* (Campone et al., 2022), the authors advocate a multidimensional approach to coaching supervision, which expands the supervisee's cultural sensitivity. Coaches may seek a supervision model more aligned to their own cultural and spiritual background than those provided by Western institutions. The 'Good Road of Life' coaching supervision model (Kelley & Small, 2020) draws on the theme that 'healers need healing too' and contextualises coaching from the perspective of the global majority. Equally, those of you with lived experience of neurodiversity, LGBTQ+, other coexisting disability, feminists, may seek supervision in a context that allows you to be both your authentic selves and be challenged to understand multiple perspectives.

Ethics and professional boundaries in neurodiversity coaching

As registered practitioner psychologists, we abide by the British Psychological Society's Code of Ethics and Conduct (2021), which has four overarching principles:

1. **Respect**: the underpinning values are dignity and worth of all people to comprise issues such as consent, privacy and confidentiality, power, and our regard for and attitudes towards others.

2. **Competence**: underpinning values are continuous professional development and standards (and limits) of competence to comprise issues such as practical and technical skills, advances in the evidence base and limits of our competence.
3. **Responsibility**: underpinning values are our responsibilities to people, the public and to our profession, to comprise issues such as professional accountability, responsible use of our expertise and respect for the welfare of others.
4. **Integrity**: underpinning values are honesty and integrity to comprise issues such as fairness and openness, addressing misconduct and maintaining professional boundaries.

Specified as a summary set of ethical principles for neurodiversity coaching, we summarise that we:

- Should do no harm and enable coachees to make informed choices and take responsibility for their welfare and performance.
- Respect difference and act fairly.
- Base our practice on best available evidence and ensure that we have domain-specific knowledge, skills and attitudes to validate neurodiversity.
- Act in the best interest of coachees and clients with transparent and accountable ways of working.

Ethical challenges

There will invariably be ethical challenges in neurodiversity coaching with unique nuances. We summarise common issues as:

- Working with coachees who appear to present as neurodivergent, but do not have a diagnosis, or discussing self-identifying as neurodivergent.
- Managing boundaries: coachees who contact coaches outside of contracted sessions for advice, or want advice on issues that the coaching is not contracted for.
- Emotionally challenging coaching encounters.

- Navigating the boundary between coaching and therapy or giving health advice.
- Coaches who are neurodivergent working with neurodivergent coachees who have different preferences and ways of working.

Key to navigating all of these issues is transparent contracting – for example, if you have not been contracted to deliver health coaching, then don't. We must not practise outside our area of competence either. When Almuth first got interested in coaching and coaching research, several of her professional acquaintances were both trained clinicians or therapist and coaching psychologists. Their boundary was to either see coachees as a clinical practitioner or as a coach, because the roles have different purposes and contracting, but not in both roles. This was a good example of how to set clear boundaries from the start. Emotionally challenging coaching sessions can be tough, on coach and coachee, as strong feelings can surface. Coaches need to remember that they are the party with appropriate expertise and training and that the person in the room with the fewest resources and spoons needs the most support. But coaches are not there to deliver therapy. Where issues that surface in coaching need referral, it is important to raise these issues early and transparently and point coachees to a range of other resources and referral options. We've discussed in previous chapters about being contacted outside sessions, coachees taking tangents, requiring you to 'rescue' them, these all need to filter into what you can ethically deliver as a coach. Sometimes the relationship isn't right and the coaching needs to stop. That is okay. Just as we wouldn't enjoy going for a coffee with everyone we meet, sometimes we cannot build enough rapport for the coaching relationship to form. Being able to acknowledge this and transparently referring someone on is a matter of ethical principle.

Protect your peace

Some people are controlling; some coachees meet this profile whether they are neurodivergent or neurotypical. Some seek to manipulate from the victim position, which can be very domineering but confusing because they are simultaneously expressing sadness. Coercive control is, however, an entirely separate matter to neurodivergence and requires therapeutic support. Narcissism and other personality traits that result from trauma are part of neurodiversity – affecting neurotypicals and neurodivergents across the world. However, being diagnosed with a neurodivergent condition does not justify unhealthy, coercive or abusive behaviour and you do not need to accept this from your coachees. Effective coaches learn to recognise when they are being coerced into rescuing or acting beyond their remit. There may be overlaps with trauma, but again, this is not within the remit of coaching. These are the reasons we have been so insistent on supervision and safeguarding your own practice.

The first rule of trauma-informed work is to maintain your own boundaries and not subject yourself to abuse in order to contain another person's hurt. Remember our colleague Whitney Iles' advice – protect your peace and hold the space, do not get engaged in holding the trauma for your coachees. Rescuing can contribute to long-term damage as it encourages dependence. Remember Almuth's colleague the NLP coach from Chapter 8. Don't set up a relationship imbalance that you can't sustain.

As we were writing this book, we asked coaching colleagues who work in the neurodiversity context what they were currently struggling with and on which issues they sought supervision, as shown in their responses to our question below.

"Coachees seem to be getting more complex and funding reduced, it's a tricky balance."
"Often coaching is framed as being given to fix the employee, whereas it turns into helping an employee get out of a drama triangle to challenge their managers and employers to understand their part in assisting them."

"The only way I experience a challenge of balancing coachee's needs and what I've been contracted to deliver is in having to write a report."

"We are sometimes used as an HR tool rather than a genuine support tool."

"A challenge that can be difficult is when the coachee might only have a small number of sessions. It takes time to build a trusting relationship and then the sessions come to an end."

"I sometimes wonder whether assuming coaching is an appropriate intervention at the time I am asked to provide it, is correct. I wonder if this because of the extent to which coachees do their 'homework' (implement strategies, further directed reflection), which is pretty mixed; and a sense that some are really not ready to make a change and so are perhaps not committed to the work."

"Emotional outbursts are challenging: in my coaching this is coachees crying. I infer from this they feel safe in the session, are able to release their emotions and feel better and relieved afterwards. The bullying I hear about I find hard to hear."

"Being aware of the expectations of the organisation and the manager and knowing that is not what the coachee would prefer to focus on in the sessions is a challenge."

"I think some of these issues listed can be reduced if the coach manages boundaries and contracting well."

"Sometimes coachees are miserable in their role, and their employer is miserable with them in the role. The best feedback I have had is from coachees who decide to move on and find something better for themselves."

"It is sometimes impossible to identify all the facts from different perspectives. This really weighs on my energy and stays after hours. Not having clear structures around what my role is in handling boundaries is difficult."

"It's not without its challenges, sometimes coachees can struggle to engage, and sometimes our flavours of neurodivergence can create clashes – for example I like to have pace and humour but a coachee might be slow and dry in their communication – and I need to adapt to them, rather than expect them to adapt to me."

"Sometimes feeling like the coachee is in the wrong role – being able to see the bigger picture and how the role they're in is a very round hole to their square peg – this causes me a dilemma because it's not for me to identify this as a coach."

"I've noticed an increasing depth and breadth of mental health issues amongst coachees post-pandemic. Maybe people are more aware or maybe MH issues have increased or maybe both."

"Some coachees start off reluctant to have coaching. They have been told they have to have it. I can usually help them to get something from each session but there can be many 'yes buts' that challenges my coaching. I like a challenge."

"A few years ago, many coachees seemed to be on performance measures and coaching was really hard because they were in such high levels of stress, there was high levels of drama between colleagues/managers and the coachees and there were often high levels of absence during the programme due to stress-related illnesses."

"I think since about 2018–19 and the emergence of more awareness and acceptance of mental health/disability issues, the coaching has taken a different turn. I now rarely have coachees on performance measures. While there are still elevated levels of stress and sometimes drama with management, most managers/organisations seem a lot more aware and proactive in trying to support their ND talent. The ND coachees also seem more aware of their 'right' to coexist with neurotypicals, be accepted and embraced. A lot of the stress still comes from comparing themselves to neurotypicals and from setting themselves really high standards or having a loud internal critic. But there seems to be a marked reduction in stress purely due to organisational attitudes and expectations. This makes coaching much more enjoyable and I feel much more productive, because the coachee can be at cause for more of their stress reactions and it's therefore easier to find coping strategies when you're not trying to help people to thrive in a systemically broken environment."

"I always guard against over dependence and catch it before it becomes an issue."

"A more therapeutic approach is sometimes part of coaching – as long as you progress to something more directional."

"Coachees who are in the worst job for them, but who appear to have little choice due to financial constraints and/or partnership commitments."

"Sometimes a coachee's 'office' or 'organisational' culture can be so overbearing for them, that many session can turn into a 'rant' valve. This is fine as there can often be nuggets of info a coach can tap into and turn around to an insight. The most frustrating thing is when these types of sessions just seem to repeat themselves with just one or two coachees, even with firm contracting and agreement in place. No matter how good your training (as a coach) this can still be draining!"

Peer practice groups, managing boundaries and case reviews

There are other methods of calibrating practice and encouraging reflection. Peer support circles and case reviews are another means of doing so. The British Psychological Society's Division of Coaching Psychology recommends peer practice groups (PPGs).[2] These are communities of practice for peer supervision, promoting of ethical and professional standards and opportunity for input on experiences of challenge or interest. In order to join, coaches have to become members of the society and the division. Organisations such as the International Society of Coaching Psychology provide more open access to peer support, as does the Clean Language community. There are also coaching bodies who provide lists of qualified coaching supervisors. Do some research and find what works best for you. Remember to prioritise the alliance! Nancy's colleague once had a coaching supervisor tell him that she "didn't believe in dyslexia" and that he should stop projecting his anxieties on to her and expecting her to compromise! Needless to say, he abandoned this relationship.

Continuous professional development

Continuous professional development (CPD) as coaches is crucial to our practice, and our professional bodies and/or regulators may audit our regular engagement. Nancy, for example, seeks supervision and peer mentoring from multiple sources and does not over-rely on one group of people. She keeps a log of her supervision and continuing professional development, including the hours invested in each event, which can be reviewed annually to identify any gaps or oversights. While getting into a regular habit of logging to prepare for audits might seem quite stark, it is also necessary. Professional standards and the evidence underpinning our practice change as new knowledge is gleaned and the context in which we work evolves. We recommend that coaches regularly set aside time to read, learn and reflect. This is a vital means for re-spooning and charging our batteries. This way, we learn new insights that can inform the tools and techniques we use in coaching and keep our practice fresh. Neurodiversity coaching is by its nature integrative. We need to know about coaching psychology and about neurodiversity, which requires a varied toolkit. This is because while neurodivergent strengths converge, neurodivergent challenges diverge and can be condition specific – this means that we have to adapt our practice to suit the coachee and their context.

In essence, CPD requires breadth as well as depth. Based on our own professional experience, we recommend the following mechanisms for CPD:

- **Coaching psychology conferences and neurodiversity conferences**: to keep up to date with research and practice and network. Ask around in your network which conferences are worth the investment – some more commercially orientated conferences can be pricy yet offer only high-level insights. Some academic conferences offer insight into contemporary research and thinking, yet can be overwhelming. It can be difficult to know which talks are worth going to and so a range is recommended.

- **Peer practice groups and restorative supervision**: to exchange, network and learn from each other. These are invaluable for ongoing practice, but less useful for starting out. You will need a baseline of knowledge on which to stand before you can get the most out of these groups – you shouldn't expect them to educate you for free. You need to do your own due diligence to your craft.
- **Academic literature**: we recommend triangulation of literature on intersectionality, on neurodiversity and disability, on coaching, but also on good work and leadership. Reading meta-analysis and systematic reviews will give you good overviews of current knowledge, whereas in-depth studies on specific samples offer better insight into current experience. Our note of caution is the pathologising and othering frame in which much academic literature is still couched. Critical disability studies and, interestingly, workplace psychology take a more neurodiversity-affirming stance, but much of the clinical and educational literature remains in the medical model.
- **Books**: as a one-stop shop to upskill in depth on certain topics. This might be controversial to some community members, but we value books written from an academic context to inform coaching more than lived experience encounters. You need help to understand the breadth of experience, even when your own depth of experience brings insight and empathy. This is the critical transition from amateur to professional coaching.
- **Social media**: can we be honest? Proceed with caution. Advocacy communities are vocal, and information can be overwhelming as well as partially inaccurate, so you need rigorous self-reflexivity. One influencer was advising followers that all adjustments must be reasonable – this is simply not the case, legally – whereas others are spot on. You need to cross-reference advice with

multiple sources rather than take any single influencer's recommendations as complete. Social media is a helpful means of keeping abreast with changes in language and contemporary concerns, however.

- **Your education**: have you thought about undertaking a professional coaching course, postgraduate certificate, doctorate, or further education in this field? If not, then perhaps our book has given you some food for thought. Some universities will accept applications for Master's degrees on the basis of professional achievement – you don't necessarily need to start from scratch. One of our colleagues has completed a Master's at Kings in Mental Health and Neuroscience without even a GCSE to her name.

The future of neurodiversity coaching: what next?

We conclude our book with reflections for the future. We asked ourselves the miracle question – what would have to have happened to ensure that neurodivergent coachees no longer faced misunderstanding and prejudice? Almuth said that organisations would need to sign up to and implement neuroinclusion, allowing people to thrive in a variety of roles and manage by outputs, while recognising that inputs (so how people work) can be different. Nancy said that schools would practise inclusive education, including acknowledging that some children are not better off at school and might learn better on their own, so that fewer neurodivergent people arrive in adulthood with trauma scars and experiences of bullying by teachers. Inclusive education would produce adults who are used to making adjustments and allow those with different needs to learn according to their preference. They would arrive in the workplace with disability and inclusion literacy and, most importantly, a great attitude. This alone would shift the creative potential for their neurodivergent colleagues to achieve.

However, we both agree that the major change would be for neurodiversity coaching to be like any other coaching. We're aware that we've spent a lot of time in this book dealing with negativity – cognitive difficulties, relationship imbalances and power dynamics, emotional overwhelm, sensory sensitivity. It is currently almost impossible to address neurodiversity in the current context without acknowledging trauma, exclusion and difficulty. In organisational psychology we call this the boundary conditions, that is, the context in which we currently live and work. As we transition to a more personalised system and universal design as a baseline for education and work we will be able to fulfil everyone's hopes and ambitions through harnessing the power of flexibility. Having our systems and standards designed for best average fit excludes too many people – our medicines are becoming personalised, so too shall our work appraisals and career goals. Neurodiversity can lead the way in figuring out the 'how' and 'what' of the future of work, because when neurodivergent people point out what needs to change, we create a more conducive environment for all. Of course, there is a fine balance to be struck between helping everyone to live their best working lives while ensuring a healthy compromise. We have emphasised the word community throughout the book. True change will only happen if we work with each other from a position of respect and valuing of authenticity.

We remind our readers of our INVESTS model – good neurodiversity coaching starts with an appreciation of intersectionality. In time, we hope that marginalisation because of who we are and what group we belong to also becomes less and less prominent. What does this mean for coaching? We hope that coaches and coachees together can spend more time on harnessing talent and making the most of strengths and that less time is spent on addressing unhappiness and what has not worked well. We look forward to a near future where coaching neurodivergent people is weighted 70/30 to career highlights, objectives, reaching potential, rather than the current focus on dealing with the psychological impact of exclusion.

We are passionate about the value of human interaction and expect this to continue, even as electronic coaches become part of the coaching landscape. Artificial intelligence-based 'coaching-bot' work is unregulated, and we don't have longitudinal data on safety and, right now, we need a note of caution. Neurodivergent people are outliers which necessitates a tailored approach to coaching to allow coachees to be heard and validated. This requires empathy, feeling and connection. There is a lot to research in the neurodiversity coaching arena to maintain progress and ethical practice. We hope we have inspired some research projects and maybe the odd piece of doctoral research. And, speaking of authentic human connection, we'd like to end on a high note. We also asked our colleagues in coaching what their greatest joys are in working with neurodivergent people; the box below outlines their thoughts.

"Supporting coachees to find their way to undo a lifetime of negative messages."

"I gain inspiration from many ND coachees, from their approach to having coaching support and to be open with curiosity about what coaching can bring in terms of insights."

"I just love it so much when it seems to click. The aha! moments."

"The joy of knowing that your coachee's days are better because you were there for them, listening with insight, and responding with strategies that work."

"Coaching has a huge role to play in helping people be the best they can be. The side effect of doing this is businesses growth and helping the economy, not a bad side effect!"

"What brings me joy is witnessing the unfolding that happens throughout the coaching journey. It is great when a coachee begins to trust and accept who they are and what they need and can take confident action to get their needs met."

"I knew little about the nature and impact of neurodiversity on people who had discovered they had a particular difference, until I started coaching in this field. Pretty much everything I've learned has come from my coachees and it has been a great pleasure and privilege to have played a part in their coming to accept themselves more deeply and to find their way towards achieving more agency in their working lives."

"The wonderful diversity, refreshing honesty, emotional journey we travel together, the celebration of increasing resilience."

"Supporting coachees in recognising and then communicating their strengths as well as their support needs, more effectively to those around them (including to their manager)."

"Essentially coachees want to be seen and heard, to understand and to feel understood."

"I would add as an important one: helping coachees to find 'fit', particularly with regard to relationships at work. ND coachees can find it difficult to disentangle emotions. And often they can say what they don't like, but not what they do like. So, finding the fit, a job that suits your talents and where you have the interaction you are comfortable with challenging hidden bias."

"So much of the work I do is about self-acceptance and self-affirmation. When coachees learn what their friction points are, they can learn how to regulate themselves and then get organised."

"It's an absolute pleasure to coach others, particularly those who have grown up in a neurotypical world and haven't yet been shown what's outside the box!"

"It's a rich and rewarding role. I often feel privileged at how honest and raw the coaching can be and how from that truth new strengths can emerge. I find that many of the concepts that help neuro different coachees are also lightbulbs for neurotypicals too when they are invited to question the norm and start to identify their own individual preferences that may not quite fit the 'everyday' or 'expected' way of operating."

"I am grateful for and delighted by the experience of working with different thinking styles and the levels of creativity and empowerment that can be felt as people step into owning their own approaches to finding success in the corporate world."

"The release that comes with the acceptance of what cannot be changed, the realisation of how much is within their control and the huge amount of influence each person has on changing the way forward for them and those who follow."

"What brings me joy is when coachees start to question their own assumptions, they regain a sense of control over their lives and their mental wellbeing improves. They realise that they are creative and resourceful and can design their own strategies, both during the coaching programme and afterwards. A coachee described the impact of our coaching as life changing. I have also felt joy when coaching junior doctors and I can see that the coaching has a positive impact on them, and also on their patients. This is the joy I find in all coaching; not just when coaching neurominorities. There is a special joy in seeing people's confidence grow, particularly when they start coaching with low self-confidence."

A community with coaching psychology at its heart

Our intention with this book was to inspire you to work with neurodivergence in your coaching and to galvanise you to pay due diligence to your own professional practice. We need accomplished coaches engaging with neurodivergent topics, needs, ambitions and careers. We equally need to raise the professional standards of coaching practice for vulnerable groups. We hope we have shown you the road map of how to provide a safe, respectful and productive space for our beautiful, diverse community. In some communities there is already an inclusive balance of professional expertise and lived experience, such as mental health, substance misuse and other, more mature advocacy movements such as racial justice, feminism and LGBTQ+ rights from which we can learn to build our own sense of best practice. We aspire to support the neurodiversity community to pair a rich dialectic exchange with psychological safety, which requires an organising framework for process, ethics and outcomes. Unlike the recovery community models favoured by mental health and substance misuse, the stance does not assume illness or deficit. We propose that coaching psychology meets this brief.

Coaching is an accessible professional forum in which to develop professional standards and safeguards, it is open and welcoming to those with lived experience and remains committed to strong ethics commensurate with psychological training. Coaching can be learned at different professional levels, reflecting the diversity of academic ability in the community. A coaching psychology framework can hold peer-to-peer relationships, groups and professionals to the same ideals. Though we have focused on the workplace, coaching psychology can accommodate education, health, family and community. Reflective practice, a core coaching psychology component, can keep us all safe, learning and invested in our own self development. Coaching psychology is, we argue, a vehicle for social change and community cohesion. It is an approach for universal rules of engagement that hold us safely while the science catches up with the experience, and the experience becomes better included in the science. Coaching psychology as a discipline sits at the intersection of neuroscience, sociology, multiple stakeholder engagement, ethics, professional training, personal development and communication – all relevant skill areas required for the neurodiversity movement to come of age.

To ensure that this wonderful potential is realised, we need to take care of several things. Neuroinclusion is about knowledge and being informed about what we do, holding back our personal judgement and building on reliable evidence. That's the science bit. Neuroinclusion is also multilayered, complex and full of wonderful surprises. That's the art. You are likely to need many different sized paint brushes to paint neurodiverse technicolour rainbows with your coachees. You will need an element of intuition and plenty of tact to navigate sensitivities and pre-empt any misunderstandings. Remember the plant and water analogy? You need to know when and how to water, so that the plants can thrive and how to spot any vexed conversation loops masking as 'white mould'. Perhaps most of all, we need unconditional positive regard – seeing the best in each other and assuming benevolence. True neuroinclusion is about genuine commitment to making a difference and embracing people for what and who they are. Coaching is a pathway to self-discovery and achieving potential, for both the coach and coachee. We have poured our hearts and minds into this book. Our hope is that many coaching journeys can be made smoother and more fruitful by sharing the collective wisdom accumulated over decades of coaching. We hope you find your neurodiversity coaching journey as cathartic and life-affirming as we have found ours.

Reflective questions

- Can you name the different aspects of the INVESTS model of neurodiversity coaching? Which one is important to you right now?
- How do you engage in supervision? When supervision works well for you, it's like what . . .?
- What is your approach to reflecting on and, where appropriate and necessary, discussing and solving ethical dilemmas?
- Having read this book, what steps will you commit to for future professional development?
- What are you looking forward to in developing a neurodiversity affirming coaching practice?

Notes

1 www.gov.uk/access-to-work
2 www.bps.org.uk/peer-practice-groups

References

British Psychological Society (2021). *Code of Ethics and Conduct*. www.bps.org.uk/guideline/code-ethics-and-conduct
Campone, F., Digirolamo, J. A., Goldvarg, D., & Seto, L. (2022). *Coaching supervision: Voices from the Americas*. Routledge.
Cox, E. (2010). Last things first: Ending well in the coaching relationship. In S. Palmer & A. McDowall (Eds.), *The coaching relationship* (pp. 177–199). Routledge.
De Shazer, S., Berg, I. K., Lipchik, E. V. E., Nunnally, E., Molnar, A., Gingerich, W., & Weiner-Davis, M. (1986). Brief therapy: Focused solution

development. *Family Process, 25*(2), 207–221. https://doi.org/10.1111/j.1545-5300.1986.00207.x

Doyle, N., & McDowall, A. (2021). Diamond in the rough? An "empty review" of research into "neurodiversity" and a road map for developing the inclusion agenda. *Equality, Diversity and Inclusion: An International Journal, 41*(3), 352–382. https://doi.org/10.1108/EDI-06-2020-0172

Hawkins, P., & Schwenk, G. (2010). The interpersonal relationship in the training and supervision of coaches. In S. Palmer & A. McDowall (Eds.), *The coaching relationship* (pp. 221–239). Routledge.

Kelley, A., & Small, C. (2020). Healers need healing too: Results from the Good Road of Life training. *American Indian and Alaska Native Mental Health Research, 27*(2), 60–75. https://doi.org/10.5820/aian.2702.2020.60

Sabo, B. M. (2006). Compassion fatigue and nursing work: Can we accurately capture the consequences of caring work?. *International journal of nursing practice, 12*(3), 136–142.

Sinclair, S., Raffin-Bouchal, S., Venturato, L., Mijovic-Kondejewski, J., & Smith-MacDonald, L. (2017). Compassion fatigue: A meta-narrative review of the healthcare literature. *International Journal of Nursing Studies, 69*, 9–24. https://doi.org/10.1016/j.ijnurstu.2017.01.003

Wallbank, S. (2007) Restorative supervision manual. *Restorative Clinical Supervision Programme.* www.restorativesupervision.org.uk

Wallbank, S. (2013). Maintaining professional resilience through group restorative supervision. *Community Practitioner, 86*(8), 26–28.

Wallbank, S., & Wonnacott, J. (2015). The integrated model of restorative supervision for use within safeguarding. *Community Practitioner, 88*(5), 41–45.

Appendix
Glossary

Our glossary includes most of the words and terms that are important for reading this book. You might want to print this list out on coloured paper and laminate it to have to hand when reading the book.

Term	The definitions we use in this book
ACTA (applied cognitive task analysis)	In-depth interviewing technique, which asks people in depth about their expertise
ACT (Acceptance and Commitment Therapy)	Form of therapy and/or coaching, which encourages people to think about their values and to notice negative thoughts and emotions without becoming overly involved in them
ADHD (attention deficit hyperactivity disorder)	Neurological and developmental (neurodevelopmental, meaning that it develops naturally in the brain rather than caused by external forces such as trauma or injury) condition marked by impulsivity, hyperactivity and inattention. There is also a subtype called ADD without the signs of hyperactivity, which is considered more unusual.
AI (appreciative enquiry)	Organisational development and coaching activity that focuses on what is already working in organisations, teams and communities.
Autism	Neurodevelopmental condition which affects how people think, interact, communicate and behave.
Biopsychosocial (model)	People are (dis-)abled dependent on the extent of their neurological differences, history, demographics and social context, meaning that neurodivergence can be simultaneously enabling and disabling.
Burnout	State of physical and emotional exhaustion.
Capitalisation	We use Capitalisation to denote a formal identity – for example, the Deaf community. We have not capitalised a term where we refer to the science of a neurotype.

Term	The definitions we use in this book
Clean Language	Approach to interviewing and coaching that is about asking value- and assumption-free questions that stay very close to the participant experiences.
Client	Representative of the organisation who is commissioning the coaching. Also used in private therapy to refer to the person who is receiving the therapy.
Client group	A group of clients with a similar characteristic, such as unemployed people, neurodivergent people, an 'older client group'.
Coach	The person doing the coaching – in this book we mainly refer to people who do this in a work context.
Coachee	The person who is being coached, an alternative to client to indicate that there may be a difference between the person being coached and the bill-paying client.
Coaching alliance	The relationship between coach and coachee; can also be a triad which also involves the commissioning client.
Comorbidity	The simultaneous presence of two or more conditions in a person, many communities prefer 'co-occurrence', because this does not assume deficit or ill health.
Condition	A more neutral term for the term 'disorder'.
Co-occurrence	More neutral term for comorbidity that is preferred by people with lived experience.
Diagnosis	The identification of a condition by examination of the symptoms. Depending on the type of condition, this is undertaken by different specialists, such as a psychiatrist or psychologist.
Discrimination	The unfair treatment of others based on (protected) characteristics such as race, gender, age or sexual orientation. This can be direct or indirect and overt or covert.
Disorder	Many health conditions are referred to as disorders by medical professionals, the diagnostic manuals that professionals use also prefer this term. Many advocates prefer 'condition' or 'neurotype'.
Dyscalculia	Neurodevelopmental condition marked by difficulty processing, learning with and working with numbers, size and speed ('numerosity').
Dysgraphia	Neurodevelopmental condition marked by difficulty with writing, for example letter formation and legibility, spacing, spelling and so on.
Dyslexia	Neurodevelopmental learning condition assessed by looking at reading and writing abilities, language development, vocabulary range, memory, processing speed and organisational skills.

(Continued)

(Continued)

Term	The definitions we use in this book
Dyspraxia	Neurodevelopmental condition marked by difficulty with movement, for example with balance and coordination of movement.
4 Dys	Refers to dyscalculia, dyslexia, dysgraphia and dyspraxia, all of which refer to difficulties with a limited, specific acquired skill.
Executive functions	Brain processes that regulate cognitive control of behaviours, such as selecting and monitoring successful strategies, self-regulation including emotion regulation, planning and goal setting and so on.
Feedback	Communication of information to people about their performance, this information can come from various sources including others, the task, the self.
Feedforward interview	Interview and coaching process that focuses on what works well for people, and clarifying the conditions for positive experiences.
Identity first language	Terms where the specific word takes precedence as an identity rather than a separate condition, for example autistic person, or transgender person.
Job crafting	A proactive process where people adjust their job by thinking differently (cognitive), adjust relationships and any tasks.
Job design	How jobs are set up, including the duties and responsibilities, but also the psychological and psychosocial aspects, including how much control and autonomy people have built into the design.
Medical model of disability	This model says that disability is an individual-level impairment that causes dysfunction in life.
Mental health	The World Health Organisation (WHO) states that mental health is a state of wellbeing and human right to enable people to cope with stresses, fulfil potential and play an active role in their community.
Neurocognitive	How humans experience thinking based on our neurology.
Neurodevelopmental (condition)	Conditions that are affected by how the brain develops in humans, which are lifelong and commonly appear in childhood. They may be a result of genetic or environmental factors or a combination.
Neurodifference	How human neurocognitive functions differ from each other.
Neurodivergence/ neurodivergent	Terminology indicating that some neurotypes deviate from a neurotypical norm. This term is seen by some as 'othering' with 'neurodistinct' or 'neurodiverse' preferred.
Neurodistinct	Alternative term to neurodivergent.

Term	The definitions we use in this book
Neurofabulous	An alternative to neurodivergent, though some people may experience as toxic positivity. It's not a term we have used consistently in this book.
Neurodiversity	Human experience and functioning as a spectrum of difference, akin to biodiversity.
Neurominority	Population with a 'spiky profile' that indicates distinct strengths and weaknesses, for example ADHD or Touretters.
Neurotypical/ neurotypicality	People who have not been diagnosed with a neurodevelopmental condition and who do not have a spiky profile; such profiles are less common than typical profiles, hence 'minority'.
Neurotype	More neutral term than 'condition' or 'neurominority' or 'neurotypicality' that references that there are different typologies of behaving and human experience.
Neurodevelopmental differences	This term describes a range of conditions that develop over the lifespan.
Person first language	This is commonly used in disability studies, for example 'persons or people with disability/ies'. Note this term is still preferred by those with learning/intellectual disabilities.
Positive psychology	The scientific study of what is going well and people's strengths and using insights to help people thrive.
Prejudice	An attitude (usually negative) that is not based on actual experience and rather judges a person based on their membership of a social group (here, the neurodiverse community).
Self-efficacy	People's belief in their ability to succeed at something and/or in a particular situation.
Social model of disability	Holds that people are prevented from functioning because of barriers in the environment, not because of how they differ from the norm. Barriers can be physical or due to social norms and beliefs.
(Spectrum disorder)	We bracket the term 'spectrum disorder' which many people use for conditions such as autism because it signposts medical model thinking, to which we do not ascribe.
Spoon theory	This is a metaphor, not a testable theory, that describes that people have a limited amount of spoonfuls of energy each day.
Stress	Our reaction when pressures at work, or from other sources, become excessive.

(Continued)

(Continued)

Term	The definitions we use in this book
Stigma	When people view others in a negative way because they have a characteristic that is thought to be a physical, psychological or social deficiency. Stigma can lead to exclusion and discrimination.
Tic disorder	Neurodevelopmental disorder defined in the DSM (*Diagnostic and Statistical Manual of Mental Disorders*) based on the type (motor or vocal) and duration of tics, which are sudden and rapid movements.
Transactional analysis	A method to understand relationships based on psychodynamics that considers ego states (parent versus child), how we think that we are okay, and the drama triangle or diamond roles.
Tourette syndrome	Neurodevelopmental disorder marked by the presence of movement tics (sudden movements) and at least one vocal tic.
Wellbeing	A state where people thrive in different aspects of their lives including their health, relationships at work and in the community.
Universal design	Set of design principles premised on fairness, flexibility and accessibility for all, which has been used in education, design and more recently at work.

Index